THE BIGGER PICTURE

My Blockbuster Life
& Lessons Learned
Along the Way

JON LANDAU

HYPERION AVENUE
LOS ANGELES NEW YORK

First Edition, November 2025
1 3 5 7 9 10 8 6 4 2
FAC-004510-25233
Printed in the United States of America

Designed by Amy C. King

Library of Congress Control Number: 2025934916
ISBN 978-1-368-11609-1
Reinforced binding

The authorized representative in the EU for product safety and compliance is Disney Trading B.V., Asterweg 15S, 1031 HL, Amsterdam, The Netherlands
email: DCP.DL-EU.bookscontact@disney.com

www.HyperionAvenueBooks.com

Logo Applies to Text Stock Only

For Julie, Jamie, and Jodie,
who are my world

CONTENTS

FOREWORD BY JAMES CAMERON   1

PROLOGUE   9

Chapter 1   23

Chapter 2   45

Chapter 3   87

Chapter 4   101

Chapter 5   129

Chapter 6   163

Chapter 7   169

Chapter 8   177

Chapter 9   215

Chapter 10   221

Chapter 11   233

Chapter 12   249

AFTERWORD BY KATHY LANDAU   259

JON'S FINAL MESSAGE TO US ALL   263

FOREWORD

James Cameron

A s I write this, I have just come from our very first preview screening of *Avatar: Fire and Ash,* a milestone moment in the life cycle of any movie. This preview, eight months before the film's release in December 2025, is a valuable source of data that allows us to fine-tune the movie. From the filled-out audience "cards" and from interviewing a focus group afterward, we learned among other things that the film is too long (not at all surprising). But when the moderator asked for a show of hands of who would want to see the movie again *every single hand shot up without hesitation.* Touchdown!

It left me thinking how much Jon Landau would have loved that moment: the first true validation of a film that has taken us years to make. Sadly, it is Jon's final film. He left this world on July 5 of last year, after his epic and heroic battle with cancer. The Avatar team had lost their leader. We stumbled on for a few months, in a bit of a daze. It was, of course, impossible to replace Jon, but by sharing his duties across a number of people who had surrounded him, we were able to function again, and effectively. At this moment we're confidently on course to complete the film on time. We all feel the pressure to "make Jon proud," to make this film a worthy capstone to his already incredible legacy.

THIS BOOK IS the story not only of his life, factually, but of his inner process and philosophy of life and work, in his own words. I found it both moving and illuminating; Jon and I worked together almost daily for thirty-one years, yet I discovered so much about him that I never knew. We were always creatures of the moment, solving problems as they came at us like some kind of crazed first-person shooter game, so I never learned much about his upbringing or his early years in the business, and I never much pried into his interior thoughts. The sharing of his life in this book contained many revelations for me, though I knew Jon the producer better than anyone.

His inner drive, and how he navigated the treacherous waters of Hollywood, is revealed clearly and with many supporting anecdotes. Anyone who has ever wondered about the world of the producer, and certainly anyone setting out on the path to actually making movies, will find this book not only fascinating, but required reading. Though the task of producing is complex, his message in this book is very simple: To make films that touch people around the world, they must have heart. And to do that, you must have heart yourself, and live not only with single-minded purpose, but with respect and love for those around you.

Jon was a consummate producer, one of the best in the history of the business. His accomplishments speak for themselves. He was running all of physical production for a major studio, 20th Century Fox, at the age of twenty-eight. He went on to produce three of the four highest-grossing films in history: *Titanic, Avatar*, and *Avatar: The Way of Water*. Pause for a second to consider that. What diabolical force of will and Machiavellian maneuvering must it have taken to accomplish such a thing in the cutthroat world of Hollywood? If you're looking for *that* story you won't find it here.

Because that's not how Jon rolled. There are many stories of powerful figures (mostly men) who dominated this business throughout its history and left their stamps on the business and art of cinema. Very few of them (can you think of any?) are known for their kindness. Most lived tumultuous lives, fraught with upsets, scandals, and theatrics of power on par with Italian court politics of the Renaissance era. That was *not* Jon.

Jon accomplished all he did not by wielding power but by spreading warmth. He was always able to make people feel a part of something big and fun. Somehow, he made everyone across our entire crew, down to every grip and digital artist (whom he knew by name) feel valued, maybe even indispensable.

Jon loved the magic of film with all his heart and soul. He had this joy at the process of cinema, and it was infectious. And he practiced the art of producing with his own unique style. The loud Hawaiian shirts and the pants of many-colored patches. The zany sight gags, the practical jokes. The cringey one-liners. Jon was never afraid to play the court jester, ever willing to make a fool of himself . . . by design. To put people at ease. So they'd feel his humanity, and his desire to be part of the team with them, by erasing the hierarchy of power. To bond them together into a team. And what a formidable team they became. Jon made it somehow fun to be doing the hardest work you'd ever done.

He produced with kindness, with an enormous heart, and with a goofy humor that often hid the brilliance of his razor-sharp mind.

Producing is all about making it happen, and Jon made it happen. He was never afraid of the challenge. He always believed that with the right team, any obstacle could be overcome. Impossible dreams, insane solutions, doing things nobody had ever done before. Or as Jon called it, Tuesday.

I was side by side with him in the trenches for over three decades. He was the other half of my brain, and we complemented each other perfectly. He did the parts I couldn't do, and I did the parts he couldn't do. We'd divide impossible tasks and make them doable. And we'd meet in the middle with total trust and total respect. We'd talk twenty times a day. We depended on each other, and we'd share the burden together. We'd fight, we'd laugh, we'd figure it out. Like an old married couple. It's safe to say that we saw each other more than we saw our actual wives and kids. And we became the closest of friends.

But saying we were friends doesn't capture it. We were a trapeze act. In this kind of partnership, you've got to be perfectly synchronized, and you have to be there to make the catch. Every time. You have to have absolute trust and be absolutely trusted. And trust is earned. Over the years, I came to rely on him, not just as the best producer I'd ever worked with, but as a true creative partner.

By example: Jon reviewed every single visual-effects shot on *The Way of Water* before it got to me. That's 3,500 shots. Thousands of hours of reviews. And I trusted him to speak for me. He was the one I trusted most when the movie wasn't working, throughout the editing process, when you're really wrestling with it. Getting the time out, making every scene the best it can be. So here's how it worked: I'd show Jon a scene I'd been working on in the cutting room. He might love it, but very likely he'd have some misgivings. And I'd tell him in detail exactly how full of shit he was. Then I'd sit with it for a day, and it would nag at my sense of perfect brilliance. Then I'd recut the scene, and I'd fix whatever he'd pointed out.

Jon believed utterly in the films that we made together, sometimes more than I did. In the darkest days of *Titanic* and *Avatar*, he never lost faith in the movies. He was like a beacon in the storm. He always believed that it was going to work out, that it was going to be a success, even when that just seemed impossible to me.

As a filmmaker, you show up. That's a theme of your life in this business. You show up every day. You have to make it happen. And Jon had the strength of will to make it happen, every minute of every day for months, for years.

That's what it took, and that's what he brought. Under that goofy demeanor was a supercomputer and an indomitable will. The man never slept. He was a machine. He was up at three a.m. dealing with people all over the world, while I was snoring away, and he was the last one to leave every night.

Those films that we made, those massive, impossible projects, would not have happened without him.

When the *Titanic* didn't sink fast enough, Jon got it to sink faster. This really happened. The first time we tried to sink the set with four hundred extras on it, it was like watching paint dry. We were totally screwed. So Jon mobilized an army of workers, who were cutting and welding and taking out solid floors and replacing them with mesh floors all weekend. By the start of shooting on Monday, that sucker sank. Boy, did it sink. It scared the crap out of us.

Somehow throughout the entire two-year process of making that film, with its massive cost and schedule over-runs, he kept the studio heads calm. Well, I don't know how calm they really were, but at least he kept them away from me. He kept reminding them that no movie was ever a hit because it was done on time and on budget. He somehow kept the wheels on for 152 shooting days, and he carried that massive film on his back.

Cut to later, when we were just starting up on *Avatar*. He made it seem perfectly reasonable to 20th Century Fox that we were going to make a multi-hundred-million-dollar movie where the main characters are all pixels, and there *wouldn't even be a camera*. No camera, no lights, no sets, but it was all going to somehow look 100 percent real. Using technology we hadn't developed yet.

By that time, he'd already done so many outlandish things and pulled them off successfully that they believed him. And then he pulled it off again, and delivered *Avatar* as promised. And it became (and is to this day) the highest-grossing film ever.

That was a production that had no user manual, because we hadn't written it yet. He basically jumped out of the airplane and sewed the parachute on the way down. And then he pulled it off again with *Avatar 2*. All that water . . . above the water, under the water. There was almost no actual photographic water in that entire film. It was mostly all just ones and zeros. What they call *computational fluid dynamic sims*. It was new physics. A whole new way to make a movie—one giant glitchy prototype. But Jon stayed the course. He willed that movie into existence and guided it to success. In the immediate aftermath of the covid-19 pandemic, when ticket sales industry-wide were down 35 percent, *The Way of Water* made $2.3 billion.

Jon gave his all to these films, but he never lost sight of life's true priorities, because he gave his all to his family. I know—that's two *alls*. But as I've said, Jon did the impossible before breakfast.

He lived for those around him, never selfish, always giving. We talk a lot about the Avatar family, and we, who are blessed to be members . . . we feel it. We enjoy each other. We feel alive and appreciated working together. We solve hard problems that other people can't, so we have pride in ourselves and in the people we work with. We have faith in our team. This is the community, the family, that Jon built.

JON COULD SOLVE any problem on the most complex projects the world has ever seen, but he couldn't solve the fragility of life itself, as none of us can. He fought so hard to stay in the game, and his wife, Julie, fought side by side with him.

Even up to a couple of weeks before his death, Jon showed up on the set, with his walker and his IV drip. He loved the process so much that he hated to miss out on it. He gave his all, even when his body was failing him, because he believed in the magic of cinema. It was his dream to make movies the world would enjoy, and he lived that dream every day.

The Na'vi say "all energy is only borrowed, and someday you have to give it back." So now Jon exists in the hearts of his Avatar and Lightstorm family, and in the hearts and the memories of many others beyond.

I personally believe every person we love is a light, and when they go, that light exists only in us who remain, and we become the bearers of that light. We pass it on to others in a ripple that expands throughout the world and through time. Jon leaves behind his family, his Avatar family, and his Lightstorm family, all of whom strive to honor his legacy.

I like to think that as *Avatar: Fire and Ash*, his final film, makes people cheer and cry in all cultures around the world, those of us who finished the film in his honor will have our greatest satisfaction knowing that Jon would have been proud.

—*May 2025*

Evening of the 70th Annual Academy Awards, 1998

I opened the gold statue–embossed envelope that had been hand delivered to my office and stared at the four tickets inside. It was at that moment that it finally sank in that I—Jonny the Jock, the average student (at best), the practical joker—was actually going to the Oscars as a nominee for Best Picture.

It was a long three days before we got into the limousine to make the forty-five-minute drive to the Shrine Auditorium for the big event. With me were my wife, Julie, our son Jamie (age nine), and my mother, Edie; we felt our other son, Jodie (age five), was too young to attend. The fact that I was about to share the evening with three generations of Landaus was very special and meaningful to me. It suggested a certain continuity. I had learned so much from my parents, personally and professionally—some lessons intentionally taught, some learned by the examples they set, all of which I hoped to impart to and model for my sons.

The red carpet was a blur, and we quickly found ourselves at our seats, right up front in row C of the center section. We arrived so early the section was empty. I felt so out of place. But then a few minutes later, Arnold Schwarzenegger came over to wish me good luck before taking his seat in the row right in front of us. There was Jack Nicholson, whom I had met when working on *Dick Tracy*, giving me a pleasant nod as he took his seat in the front row. I thought Cameron Diaz even looked my way and waved... but then I realized she was waving to Matt Damon, who was a few feet away. I was brought back to reality.

The year 1998 was one of the strongest for Best Picture nominees: Curtis Hanson's masterpiece *L.A. Confidential*, three-time Oscar winner James L. Brooks's *As Good as It Gets*, Matt Damon and Ben Affleck's breakout film *Good Will Hunting*, and the acclaimed crowd-pleasing comedy *The Full Monty*. *Titanic* was in extraordinary company.

Billy Crystal opened the show by being lowered to the stage on the bow of the *Titanic* and launched into one of his classic musical opening numbers in which he riffed on the movies nominated for Best Picture. The lyrics compared *Titanic* to the television classic *Gilligan's Island* (oh well) and moved on to suggest "*L.A. Confidential*, you could be the iceberg tonight." I couldn't help but wonder if it would be.

The first award of the evening, Best Supporting Actress, included Gloria Stuart—who played our older, present-day heroine, Rose—among a strong group of nominees. Born on July 4, 1910, Gloria had been one of the founding members of the Screen Actors Guild. Having left acting in 1945 to focus on her career as a fine artist, Gloria's return to the silver screen made her somewhat of a darling of the acting community. With the actors' branch of the Academy consisting of more voting members than any other branch, I thought this first award might serve as a good litmus test for how the evening was going to play out.

Cuba Gooding Jr., who had won Best Supporting Actor the year before for his role in *Jerry Maguire,* presented the award.

"And the Oscar goes to . . . Kim Basinger, *L.A. Confidential.*"

This could be a long night!

But as the ceremony progressed, things got better. Several from our team, whose shoulders I stand upon, were recognized with Oscars for their incredible work: Deborah Scott for Best Costume Design; Russell Carpenter for Best Cinematography; James Horner for Best Original Dramatic Score and Best Original Song; Rob Legato, Mark Lasoff, Tom Fisher, and Michael Kanfer for Best Visual Effects; Peter Lamont and Michael Ford for Best Art Direction; Richard A. Harris, Conrad Buff, and James Cameron for Best Editing; and then Jim won his second Oscar of the evening for Best Director.

It was finally time for the Best Picture award. The indomitable Sean Connery walked onstage to present the award. Yes, the same Sean Connery I would race to see whenever a new James Bond movie came out when I was a kid. The audience hushed as Sean began to speak.

"The nominees are . . . *As Good as It Gets.* James L. Brooks, Bridget Johnson, and Kristi Zea, producers."

I was holding Julie's hand as the audience gave a round of applause. Was it too big a round?

". . . *The Full Monty.* Uberto Pasolini, producer."

The reaction from the Academy members was a little less effusive.

". . . *Good Will Hunting.* Lawrence Bender, producer."

There was an even greater response from the crowd than they had given to *As Good as It Gets.*

"...*L.A. Confidential.* Arnon Milchan, Curtis Hanson, and Michael Nathanson, producers."

It was the biggest, most vocal reaction yet, just as it had been when Cuba Gooding Jr. read the names of the Supporting Actress nominees, the award Gloria Stuart lost.

"... *Titanic.* James Cameron and Jon Landau, producers."

Yes, there was applause, but nowhere near the same level of support that the other films had received. Was I just imagining it? No, I later confirmed this when I watched a tape of the show.

Sitting there, waiting for James Bond to open the envelope, I couldn't help but think back to the night in 1971 when my parents, Edie and Ely Landau, accompanied by Coretta Scott King (Dr. Martin Luther King Jr.'s widow), attended the Academy Awards as nominees for *King: A Filmed Record ... Montgomery to Memphis,* a documentary they had produced. This monumental film, directed by Sidney Lumet and Joseph L. Mankiewicz, chronicles the life of Dr. King from 1955 to 1968 and his rise from regional activist to world-renowned leader of the Civil Rights Movement.

In the days leading up to those Academy Awards, every one of the other nominees for Best Documentary, and even some executives from rival studio Warner Bros., told Coretta and my parents that they were a lock for the Oscar. My dad insisted that Coretta be the one to accept the award. The night of the ceremony, my sisters and I stayed up late in New York glued to our TV as presenters Richard Benjamin and Paula Prentiss opened the envelope.

"And the winner is ... *Woodstock.*"

I snapped back to the present just as Connery fumbled to open the envelope. Looking at the card inside, he did a double take and paused for a brief moment before announcing: "And the Oscar goes to ...

"Titanic."

In that moment, the pressure that had weighed down my shoulders and soul for the three years I'd been producing *Titanic* finally lifted. Only four months earlier, *Time* magazine had published a very negative story on the movie with a bold headline: "Down, Down to a Watery Grave."

With "And the Oscar goes to *Titanic*" echoing in my head, I swept Julie up in a huge hug before embracing Rae Sanchini, our executive producer. Had it not been for Rae, I wouldn't have been hired on the film.

I met Jim in the aisle. We threw our arms around each other's shoulders as we made our way to the stage. Immediately before ascending the steps, I saw both Kate Winslet and Gloria in the front row. I stopped briefly to give them each a slight bow. Without their extraordinary performances, none of this would have been possible.

Onstage, Sean handed me my Oscar, and I made my way to the microphone. After all, if Jim was the first to speak, the music would come up after, and I wouldn't get the chance to say anything. Before acknowledging what I have been told were fifty-three people by name, I shared with a global television audience that "I can't act, and I can't compose, and I can't do visual effects, so I guess that's why I'm producing."

FROM THE HIGHEST of highs, to the lowest of lows.

Proximity to death sharpens vision. The unessential things, the arguments and distractions, fall away. You come to see your life as a story, how everything that happened, bad and good, was essential, a part of the equation that got you here. If you are someone who's had a happy life full of friendship, strong family, and success, the struggles will seem perhaps more memorable than the accomplishments. Looking back with this new perspective, however, you see that your life has a meaning that becomes clear only at the end of the day.

I'm a producer who's been lucky enough to have produced three of the four top-grossing movies of all time. Maybe that's because I can sense the potential for an epic and understand the importance of a third act epiphany. And perhaps that's why I see such narrative possibilities in my own stroke of bad luck.

MARCH 2023. It was twenty-five years after Jim and I stood onstage accepting the Oscar for Best Picture, and I was returning to the Academy Awards as a Best Picture nominee again. While walking the red carpet, I tried to put on a happy face, but my mind was on something other than the ceremony. For several weeks leading up to the award show, I had been having trouble swallowing. It felt like there was a lump in my throat, like I'd swallowed a pill that wouldn't go down. It was the kind of thing you don't notice until you do, then you can't stop noticing.

The Academy Awards are currently held at the Dolby Theatre in LA. Our movie, the second Avatar film, *Avatar: The Way of Water*, had been nominated in four categories. As it turned out, we won only for Best Visual Effects, but I was just happy to be there and particularly happy for the members of the Avatar family who had been nominated. The fact that three of my films—*Titanic, Avatar,* and *Avatar: The Way of Water*—had brought me to the Oscars and gotten me into a tuxedo never stops being astonishing. (During the daylight hours, I tend to be a Hawaiian shirt and cargo pants sort of guy. Wearing a tuxedo is foreign territory.)

Sitting in the Dolby Theatre, I could not stop thinking about my throat. I can almost see my worry in the pictures taken that night. There I am, with my wife, Julie, and our sons, Jamie and Jodie, or with our Avatar team, and I have a kind of double vision in some of the shots. I am celebrating the team's accomplishments but also catching a glimpse of an unfathomable something on the horizon.

Following the Oscars, I flew back to New Zealand, where much of the work on the Avatar sequels is done. At the time, we were heading into the final stretches of the third movie of what we envision to be a five-film cycle. Julie and I had just purchased an apartment in Wellington, New Zealand. The country had become our home. I hoped this problem with my throat was maybe just allergies and would fade, as had so many other health scares and irritations over the years. Work is always the answer. Work until you forget about it. Work until you don't even realize the problem is gone.

Jim Cameron, my producing and business partner of almost thirty years, now calls New Zealand home, too, and when working spends most of his time at our soundstages and offices at Stone Street Studios in Wellington.

Jim is the visionary who dreamt up beautiful and exotic Pandora, home of the Na'vi, the heroes of the Avatar films. In many ways, it's my responsibility as a producer to help bring Jim's dream to life. In order to do that I need to be a problem-solver and a team builder. To me, each new movie is like a start-up business. It's the producer's job to deliver a product that at least meets, but hopefully exceeds, the public's expectations.

If I believed my throat would improve on its own, I was wrong. It only got worse. When it reached the point where I could hardly eat, I dragged myself to my Wellington doctor, who, not liking what he saw, sent me to a specialist to have an endoscopy. When the endoscopy was over, but while I was still groggy from the anesthesia, the doctor told me why it felt like something was stuck in my throat. Because something was. A tumor. The biopsy results came back. *Malignant—* the worst word in the English language. I had esophageal cancer.

My wife, Julie, was at a wedding in Washington, DC, when I got the news. It was noon in New Zealand, eight p.m. on the East Coast in the US. She was sitting down for the dinner when I called. She happened to be seated at the same table as my friend and doctor, Ron Sue. He's been my doctor forever. I told her the news, the word *malignant* exploding between us. A few minutes later, she told Ron, who asked to see the test results. I sent them over. He examined them on Julie's cell phone, then spoke the words that marked the end of my old life and the start of my current misadventure: "Tell Jon to get back to LA as fast as he can."

I booked a flight, went home to our Wellington apartment, and waited for morning. It was probably best that I was alone. Before I would be able to comfort someone or talk this through with anyone else, I first had to deal with it myself. A wave of sadness came over me. Not about the possibility of dying, but rather because of all the things I would never get to experience with Julie and my boys. If I had gotten this kind of news decades ago when the boys were much younger, I might have panicked. I might have googled the disease, fixated on the numbers, paced the floor, and cursed. But what softened the blow was the fact that, even though I'm not old—sixty-three as of this writing—I feel like I have lived a great life, experiencing days of love and success, and, most importantly, I know that my family will be okay after I'm gone. No matter what happens, my wife and boys will be okay. Through their lives, my life will continue. Rather than cry and moan, I spent that long night remembering some of the great moments we had together: the excitement I felt when I first fell in love with Julie during the making of a movie called *Beat Street* over forty years ago; how I asked her to marry me every Wednesday for eight months until she finally said yes; the birth of our sons; traveling the world; the family holidays; the night Jim and I stood side by side to accept the Oscar for *Titanic*. I suppose I was steeling myself for the battle to come.

I WENT TO see doctors at Weill Cornell Medical Center in New York and at Cedars-Sinai in LA. In the end, I chose to receive treatment in LA, because, for almost fifty years, it had been my home. Thirty of those years were spent in a wonderful house in Sherman Oaks. It's where we started our family and raised our boys. Where we survived the Northridge earthquake. And LA is a place where Julie has wonderful friends who could support her on the road ahead.

Julie kept a record of every symptom, side effect, procedure, and medicine I was prescribed. Some operations were planned. Others addressed emergencies that resulted from the progress of the disease or unanticipated side effects of the treatment itself. Taken together, the list reads like something from the book of Job. I do not need to catalog all of the hiccups I have experienced this last year. You get the idea.

As my mother used to say: "Man plans, God laughs."

So, what am I doing?

Trying to enjoy the laughter.

That's what we get; that's all we have instead of certainty, instead of an endless stretch of tomorrows. And you *can* enjoy it, too, and should. Laughter is the best thing in the world. In such a situation, some people pledge to focus all their energy on beating the disease. But I am focused less on not dying than on living every day to its fullest. And so, I never forget to find and create joy.

Much of that joy is my work, so I keep making movies. I have meetings, visit the sets, solve problems, balance budgets, help build the franchise program, approve marketing plans, smooth hurt feelings, and put out fires. When I am scheduled for treatments, I go to the hospital, where they do what they have to do. Then I go back to work and live my life.

Everyone gets knocked down. Getting back up, that's the thing. Whatever else happens is not in your power to control. If you set sail for happiness, you will never reach it. Happiness is something that happens along the way. And, despite everything, I keep experiencing it.

An illness like mine lends a person a new perspective. Certain things become clear. When I worked with Warren Beatty on *Dick Tracy*, I remember him saying I was a good producer because "you dream about the movie every night." And that's true. I did, and do. But I see things more plainly now. It's not that the movies are my life, but that my life is a movie, with every scene and character supporting or advancing the plot.

People often ask me what makes a great film. A great film is one that stays with you, I tell them, one you think about long after you've left the theater. They often think this is because of the wattage of the stars, the stunts, the special effects, the music, the scenery, or the twists and turns, which is why so many writers, producers, and directors become obsessed with plot. But what actually makes a movie great are the themes that bring out emotion. The plot is what you leave at the theater. The theme is the emotion you take away when you go home.

This is true for life as well. It's the emotional connections I feel, and not facts, that tie my life and work together.

When I first read the script for *Titanic*, I thought of it as a "three-hankie movie." Some people remember the plot or setting: the beauty of the ship, the stratification of the classes, the iceberg, the cold, dark water. But it's the themes that linger with the majority of the audience. The themes of love and sacrifice, the goodness of some, the badness of others, the stubbornness of time. Without the themes, the plot would have no meaning. It's the same with *Avatar*. The plot is wild. Intergalactic travel, invasion, war. But it's the themes—freedom versus colonialism, dignity versus exploitation, the sanctity of nature, and the love that binds a family—that pull at your heartstrings and make it more than just another sci-fi movie.

It's been the same with my life—that's what I've come to realize. The story has been grand: a childhood in the Bronx and LA, the early start in film, the great mentors, close family, partners and projects, the surprising success. But it's the emotional ties that have made me something more than an interesting page on IMDb. It's the love of my parents and siblings, the close friendships, the obstacles, and the lessons that have made my life so memorable.

Before my mother died in 2022, we filmed an interview in which she told her entire life story. She wanted to preserve it for her grand-kids. She wanted to see to it that nothing was lost. I remembered those recordings when I got my diagnosis, and the solace they'd given my mother and, in turn, all of us. So I sat down to write these pages. As I worked, I realized this undertaking was not just for the next generation but also for myself. By writing, I hoped to take stock of my life. The result is the story of a producer, the movies, anecdotes, stars, inside scoops, and simple truths. It's also a primer for anyone who wants to make a mark in any business and a text for those who wish to understand the machinery of entertainment. I have put down the lessons I've learned in the course of my career, the dos and don'ts, the secret ingredients of the sometimes-magical formula. From the early years to *Titanic* and *Avatar*, these are fables from a career in the trade.

THE BIGGER PICTURE

Chapter 1

If you were plotting this story in a writers' room, you'd say the main character (that would be me) has a sweet backstory.

I was my mother's firstborn, and only son, prized from the beginning. My mother, Edie, had had a miscarriage before I was born, and she feared she could never have children. When I did arrive, I was sickly at birth. I came into the world on July 23, 1960, with a fifty-fifty shot at survival.

What was wrong with me?

Everything.

Undersized. Weak. Bad heart. Bad lungs. My first weeks were spent in the NICU of the Mount Sinai Hospital in New York. My mother sat vigil at the hospital. One afternoon, shortly after I was born, my father showed up with a jewelry box. He'd purchased a gold chain with a pendant: a pair of tiny, solid gold boxing gloves. He looked at Edie and said, "This kid is a fighter. He will make it." You get hit, you hit back.

I am not telling you that I remember this, of course. The story was told to me, and told to me, and told to me, until the image of those tiny golden gloves burned into my mind. At Cedars in 2023, as I was going into or coming out of surgery, my wife Julie hung a replica of those golden gloves from my bed. The originals were lost, but the message remained. You get hit, you hit back.

My parents were living in Westchester County, New York, when I was born. They were finally able to bring me home in August 1960. Then we moved into a Manhattan apartment they'd purchased from the *Candid Camera* host Allen Funt. It was a big place at the Beresford, a Gothic castle of an apartment building across from Central Park on Eighty-First Street. It was all towers, setbacks, and hidden wings, just perfect for a kid, the sort of place in which the devil took up residence in *Rosemary's Baby*. The Beresford was filled with fascinating people. We lived down the hall from the violinist Isaac Stern. The sound of his rehearsals, scales and tunings, and storms of notes is the soundtrack of my earliest years.

We moved to Riverdale—specifically the Fieldston neighborhood— in the Bronx when I was old enough to start school. People think of burned-out buildings and graffiti-covered subways when they think of the Bronx in the 1960s, but Fieldston was a paradise, a small town within the city, a world of lovely homes, magical backyards, and mom-and-pop stores on two main streets that hummed with life. There were views of the Hudson River everywhere. We lived in a wonderful house perched high on a hill on Fieldston Road.

We made great friends in Riverdale. (The Abramowitzes, whom my parents met through the PTA, are still like family.) We had a swimming pool, a library, a screening room, a built-in ice-cream parlor, a gymnasium, and bedrooms for every one of my siblings—my sisters,

Kathy and Tina, and my half brothers, Les and Neil. Kathy and Tina went on to very successful careers of their own, Kathy in the nonprofit world and Tina as a playwright and theater director. My half brother Les became a television director of shows such as *Star Trek*. Then there was my half brother Neil, who took me to my first rock concert: Three Dog Night at Gaelic Park. Sadly, Neil got mixed up with gambling and drugs, stole from my parents, and died young.

Growing up, we were very privileged. We had a nanny named Kay and a cook named Thelma. A tutor came to teach us French (unsuccessfully—I still don't know any language but English). Willie, our driver, drove us to visit our parents at work and took us to school when the weather was bad. On nice days, we walked. I spent those first years at a private school called Ethical Culture Fieldston School. To get there, we walked to the end of the driveway and turned left. To get to Riverdale Country School, where I transferred in ninth grade, you took a right instead of a left. To me, the Bronx was as small and cozy as a movie-set village.

Back then, you'd have never guessed I'd follow my parents into movies. My sisters were the artists. I was the athlete, and sports was my first love. If there was a ball, a puck, or a racket involved, I played it. They called me Jonny the Jock. Football was my passion. I was not big, but I played hard and tough. At Riverdale, which was a football power-house at the time, I made varsity as a sophomore. That same year, I also played varsity basketball. The heights of the starting lineup went something like this: six foot ten, six foot six, six foot six, six foot two, and five foot eight. Yup, that last one's me. In the spring, I was in the starting lineup on the varsity baseball team, too.

I loved being on all the teams, but the coach who left the biggest impression was the head football coach, Frank Bertino. He was a legendary Bronx character. He taught me about leadership, how to get more out of people than they think they can give—not by threats or punishing drills, which was the typical coaching style of the time, but with inspiration. You show the players a vision and get them to accept and believe in it, and they'll work to make it real.

As we came down the steps for my first varsity game, Coach Bertino pulled me aside and asked, "Are you nervous?"

How are you supposed to answer a question like that? Is it wrong to be nervous?

I finally did what I always do in such situations: When you don't know what's expected or what you're supposed to say, just tell the truth.

I said, "Yes, Coach. I am nervous."

He said, "Good. Because, when you stop being nervous, you stop caring."

I have lived by that mantra ever since. Nervous is good. It means you're still invested, still growing. When people tell me about *their* nerves now, I repeat the coach's wisdom, with a caveat: "It's good to be nervous, it means you still care, but you shouldn't be worried."

If you are prepared and do your best, you never have to be worried.

THE YEARS OF my childhood were a dream era for the New York sports fan. I was nine when the Mets won the World Series in 1969. I was ten when the Knicks won the NBA championship in 1970. I was at Madison Square Garden for game seven of the series when Willis Reed, the injured team veteran who we'd been told was too hurt to dress, limped out for the pregame warm-ups, sending the crowd into delirium. Reed hardly played that night, but it didn't matter. His entrance, the image of the revered athlete playing through pain, was enough to inspire his teammates—Walt Frazier and Bill Bradley among them—on to victory. That moment showed a future movie producer everything he'd ever need to know about drama. And resilience.

My mother's brother, Mendy Rudolph, was an NBA referee. Now and then, when I went to a game, Uncle Mendy would be officiating. One night, I watched a crowd of thousands boo one of Mendy's calls. "Mendy is a bum! Mendy is a bum!" rang out throughout the arena. It was an object lesson: How do you react when the entire world turns against you? I would have lost it, but my uncle didn't even respond. He acted as if nothing unusual had happened and simply continued his work.

Once, Mendy took me to the locker room to meet the great Kareem Abdul-Jabbar. For a kid, shaking hands with the seven-foot-two-inch Kareem was like shaking hands with Zeus. I recounted this memorable moment when I met Kareem again not long ago. Half a century had elapsed.

I said, "Meeting you after a game when I was twelve was one of the great thrills of my life."

He said, "That means we're both really old."

As a kid, the only thing that captivated me as much as sports was movies. Do what you love—that's something I've always believed. And I have always loved movies. My mother's father, Harry—"Poppa Harry"—worked as a projectionist in a theater on the Upper West Side of Manhattan. There was nothing like slipping in the back door to see Poppa Harry on a hot summer afternoon, then sitting in the projection booth or going down to the front row and watching the beam of light from the projector illuminate the dust motes on its way to the screen, where it transformed into images that were a gateway to another world.

Both of my parents were in the movie business. My father, Ely, had had a tough childhood. Because his own father died when he was young, Ely had to work like a dog to support his family. He was driving a truck at sixteen, before going into the army during World War II, then came out looking for work. Believing television was the wave of the future, he started in a low-level TV advertising position. He eventually ended up running National Telefilm Associates, which acquired a handful of television stations, including Channel 13 in New York before it became a PBS affiliate. When Ely started in television, it truly was a "vast wasteland," and he was always looking for quality content to fill all the staticky hours. Along with *The Mike Wallace Interview* and *Open End*, hosted by David Susskind, Ely created a Peabody Award–winning series called *Play of the Week*.

As a man of the New Deal Left, a fighter of the good fight, Ely used what power he had to rehabilitate the reputations of some of the great actors, directors, and writers who'd fallen victim to the Hollywood blacklist. He cast blacklisted actors like Lee Grant, Jack Gilford, Morris Carnovsky, and Zero Mostel in a *Play of the Week* version of *The World of Sholom Aleichem*. But this was not just his politics at play; it was also a reflection of his commitment to great artistry. As a producer, Ely knew a talent like Mostel was too precious to be wasted, and he continued to find special vehicles for him, including a television production of *Waiting for Godot*. Ely actually looked enough like Zero Mostel that people would sometimes mistake him for the actor and ask for an autograph.

My father liked to claim he "made a career out of overestimating the American public," and it was his interest in the plays of Eugene O'Neill that helped him transition from television to motion pictures. In 1960, he convinced Eugene O'Neill's widow to give him the rights to *The Iceman Cometh* for a *Play of the Week* production, and he hired veteran television director Sidney Lumet to direct a cast including Jason Robards and a young Robert Redford. The O'Neill family was so impressed with the production, they offered him any of O'Neill's plays to adapt for film. He picked *Long Day's Journey into Night*, then went out and got Katharine Hepburn to star in it. That's how Ely got into the movie business.

Ely had a terrific nose for talent. If he wasn't spotlighting an established star, he was discovering someone new. Ely helped to launch Sidney Lumet's filmmaking career by hiring him to direct both *Long Day's Journey* and *The Pawnbroker*, which starred Rod Steiger and was one of the first American pictures to deal with the Holocaust. *The Pawnbroker* also gave Quincy Jones his first opportunity to compose an American movie score.

Ely had married young, but that early attempt at matrimony did not last. He and his first wife had two sons, Les and Neil. My father met my mother, Edie Rudolph, when she applied for a job at his production company in 1953. He made her an offer, but it was for less than what she knew she deserved. She turned the job down and made her reason clear. And so he upped his offer, and upped it, until she said yes.

Over the course of time, my parents fell in love. They made it official in 1959 when, headed to LA for business, they stopped in Las Vegas to get married at the neon-lit Little Chapel Around the Corner, a kind of holy site in Landau lore ever since.

My father knew what he was getting in Edie: a razor-sharp, strong-willed woman driven by a never-failing moral compass. It kept her facing North. She intuitively knew right from wrong and never stopped fighting for what she believed in. Edie was a frequent letter writer. If a business or a corporation had not kept a promise, had been indecent or unfair, they were going to hear about it.

As I write this, I am looking at an article that ran in *The New York Times* on January 25, 1958, under the headline "Woman Executive Protests Exclusion from 'Executive Flight' for Men Only." In those troglodyte days, United Airlines had a weekday afternoon flight from Chicago to New York that was meant exclusively for men; women and children were verboten. Steak and martinis were served in the air. The all-female flight attendants were young by design, attractive, and seemingly available. (To maintain the illusion, pregnant flight attendants had to switch to another flight.) United's advertising tagline went something like: *Men, leave your troubles behind.* Edie would never have known about this flight had she not been in a hurry to get home on a Friday afternoon after a day of meetings at their Chicago TV station. When she was not allowed to purchase a ticket, she protested, "But I *am* an executive!" and then began a letter-writing campaign and filed an official complaint with the Civil Aeronautics Board that contributed to the end of the executive flight.

Edie and Ely (yes, we called our parents by their first names) worked together on dozens of films. They were independent producers, working outside the Hollywood system. It was moviemaking at its purest: They found a book or play they wanted to adapt, raised the money, hired the writer, hired the director and actors, oversaw the shoot and edit, then made a deal with a distributor. They produced documentaries and features. Their movie *The Madwoman of Chaillot* (1969) starred Katharine Hepburn and Charles Boyer and featured Danny Kaye and Yul Brynner, among other great talents. Perhaps their most ambitious and innovative offering was a series of plays adapted to film called the American Film Theatre, where they arranged with over five hundred local movie theaters to offer subscriptions to two seasons of movies, just as subscribers might buy tickets to a season of stage plays at a local playhouse. On selected Monday nights, audiences would travel to their local movie house, read a "cinebill" describing the movie, and see great actors tackle great works, like Harold Pinter's *The Homecoming* (1973) or Sir Laurence Olivier's production of Chekhov's *Three Sisters* (1970). They cast Zero Mostel, Gene Wilder, and Karen Black in Eugène Ionesco's *Rhinoceros* (1974) and wooed Katharine Hepburn to accept a $25,000 salary to appear in a filmed adaptation of Edward Albee's *A Delicate Balance* (1973).

Their crowning achievement was probably *King: A Filmed Record . . . Montgomery to Memphis* (1969), which, as I said, was nominated for an Oscar but ultimately lost to *Woodstock*. The documentary, directed by Sidney Lumet and Joseph L. Mankiewicz, featured readings by Harry Belafonte, Paul Newman, Ruby Dee, and James Earl Jones, among many others, speaking the words of the late great civil rights leader. To make the movie, which was to be released for one night only as a nationwide benefit event for the Martin Luther King Jr. Center for Nonviolent Social Change, they worked closely with King's inner circle, including Andrew Young, who would go on to be mayor of Atlanta, a congressman from Georgia, and later US ambassador to the United Nations. One day, they set up a screening for Young of archival footage they had uncovered of some of the atrocities that had occurred in the South. Suddenly, Young got up and bolted out of the screening room. He explained later that the footage they'd been watching showed a traumatic event that he'd repressed from his teenage years. It was of Young being brutally beaten by police.

During the making of the film, we became close with the King family. My most memorable Thanksgiving was the one we spent at Coretta

Scott King's house in Atlanta. During that same period, maybe 1969, two of the King children joined our family for a getaway in Montauk on Long Island. The big event my parents planned for the weekend was horseback riding, which my sisters and I had enjoyed doing a few times previously. When we arrived with the King kids for our scheduled rides, the manager looked at us, then turned to Ely and said, "There are no horses available." After a bit of back-and-forth—"We booked this time, I see the horses right there," and so on—Ely lost it. My father was not a person whom I ever saw lose his temper or composure, but he was furious. I can only imagine what was going through his mind: Martin Luther King Jr. had dedicated his life to the dream that his— as he said in his famous "I Have a Dream" speech—"four little children will one day live in a nation where they will not be judged by the color of their skin but by the content of their character." Here we were, with the children of the slain hero, and we were unable to protect them from the kind of ignorance, hatred, and discrimination he had been fighting against. It was an unforgettable moment for me.

Andrew Young said that the King documentary taught him about the power of movies to change lives. A person can tell you what's right and what's wrong, but, in the end, those are just words. Through the combination of words *and* images, a movie acts like a dream. It can get into your subconscious and become a lens through which truth is revealed.

MY SIBLINGS AND I were raised around movies the way George Steinbrenner's kids were raised around baseball. Although we didn't know it at the time, the terminology of the industry, the ins and outs, were embedded in our minds. *Budget overrun* and *shot list, jump cut, dolly shot, mise-en-scène, storyboard*—we absorbed them all. Producing movies is always a challenge, and all the more so for Ely and Edie, independents working outside the studio system. But they always kept their eye on the ultimate goal: getting the picture made. They never let the drudgery of the process obscure the magic waiting at the end, the way only a great movie can make you feel.

At the start of every summer, with this magic in mind, my parents used their industry access to get prints of a dozen or so movies to host a private film festival at our house in Riverdale. They called it the Annual Landau Movie Orgy (ALMO). Each year they'd type up a schedule and send it out to friends. Screenings ran all weekend, from eight a.m. to midnight. Food was laid out in the dining room throughout the entire time, so friends could stay all day or come and go as they liked, depending on the films that intrigued them. Some of the movies were new, some were classics, and each year was built around a theme. I first saw John Ford's *The Grapes of Wrath* at ALMO. I loved the 1970s blockbusters most of all: *Butch Cassidy and the Sundance Kid, The Sting*, the James Bond flicks. But if I had to name the one movie that impacted me most, it'd be *Mary Poppins* (1964). Julie Andrews singing and Dick Van Dyke drawing on a sidewalk with chalk captivated me. I was especially taken by the scene in which Dick Van Dyke's character, Bert, tells the Banks children that they can jump right into one of his chalk drawings, and then they do! I probably couldn't put it into words at the time, but now I realize that, for me, going to the movies is like jumping into one of Bert's drawings. It thrilled me in the way I want every kid who sits down for an Avatar movie to be thrilled.

For my parents, there was no real division between home life and work life. They brought everything home, and took us to their office or a film set whenever possible. To me, it seemed like a winning formula.

And so simple: If what you do for work is also what you do for fun, you'll be happy.

I got to witness my parents navigating every aspect of the business. It's how I first learned the tasks of a producer, who, depending on the kind, can be a cog in a machine or a dream maker.

I have always considered myself to be a key player on the team. Maybe that comes from Coach Bertino at Riverdale. I'm a problem-solver and a bridge builder, the one person on the project who understands and can champion both sides of the coin: the director, whose needs are artistic; the studio, whose needs are financial. I'm there to help the director achieve their vision within the limits set by the studio. I'm also there to push those limits when necessary, to remind the bosses that it's sometimes better business to spend more money.

There's a famous scene in James Cameron's 1994 movie *True Lies*, the first project Jim and I worked on together. I was the executive vice president of feature film production for Fox at the time. Arnold Schwarzenegger, playing undercover agent Harry Tasker and dressed in a tuxedo, blasts his way out of an enemy trap, races across a field, then, in one quick move, bounds over a high stone wall. While on location with Jim, I was also working on a three-year business plan for my department to present at an upcoming corporate retreat. One day, as filming wrapped, I asked Jim if he would do an additional take. This time it was not going to be Arnold going gracefully over the wall—it was going to be me, tuxedo and all, struggling awkwardly to get over the wall. That shot went into our presentation with a statement: "This is what you'll get if you don't want to spend." The execs in the room laughed their heads off, and we got our money.

Imagine a producer grappling with the vision Jim presented in that first *Avatar* script: spaceships and weaponry, the dream of planet

Pandora, floating mountains and flying creatures called ikran, the blue ten-foot-tall Na'vi characters, all of which needed to hold your attention and earn your love. Helping create new worlds, bringing stories to cinematic life—that's the job of a producer. In and of itself, it takes some artistry, which I began to learn as a child on the set with my parents in the 1970s.

In 1980, while Edie and Ely were filming *The Chosen* in New York, I was hired to be a production assistant on the film, as well as an extra. I ultimately went on to be the assistant to the executive producer. My first task was teaching actor Barry Miller how to play softball. The movie, based on Chaim Potok's bestselling novel, is about a friendship between a Hasidic kid and a secular Jew in Brooklyn in the 1940s. They first meet and confront each other at a softball game. Barry, who'd just come off the movie *Fame*, played the secular kid, and Robby Benson, the slight, soft-spoken, blue-eyed star of the basketball movie *One on One*, played the Hasidic kid.

If you watch the movie, you can see me at around minute fifteen, in a hat, side curls, and a long black coat. For me, this was the first in what would be a career of cameos. If you have time, and like to check out old movies, you can play a kind of cinematic version of Where's Waldo? Only it's Where's Jon? You will find me in films from *Campus Man* to *Titanic*. Mostly I did it for fun, to keep everyone on the set loose and laughing, but also because it left a cinematic record of my journey, a celluloid trail of my adventures.

I was in college when I worked on *The Chosen*, with no idea of what I wanted to do with my life. Even so, that small job was the start of my career. You are performing two tasks when you work on a set. You're helping with the shoot, and you're also auditioning for your next job, even if you don't realize it.

The world of film production is small. The cinematographers, production designers, "money men" and executives, directors, editors, actors, caterers (you need to feed a lot of people on set), and teamsters—you meet the same people again and again. If you are a hothead or can't get along, word will spread, and it'll be hard to find work. If, on the other hand, you do your job well and lend a hand whenever and wherever needed, you will find work and rise through the ranks.

I FELL IN love with Los Angeles the same way as many Americans—on vacation. Our parents first took us out there when I was seven or eight years old. We stayed at the Beverly Wilshire Hotel and hit all the spots: Disneyland in Anaheim and Muscle Beach in Venice, the Griffith Observatory, where James Dean had a knife fight in *Rebel Without a Cause*, and the carousel on the Santa Monica pier.

Was this paradise?

It sure seemed like it.

My parents took us to see some of the Hollywood studios, and we got to walk around the old sets. The big Southern mansion from *Gone with the Wind*. A replica of lower Manhattan right in the middle of sunny LA! At the Fox lot, we played on the train tracks used in the Yonkers scene in *Hello, Dolly!*, a movie directed by Gene Kelly that had big stars: Barbra Streisand. Walter Matthau. Louis Armstrong. Playing on the set was like stepping through the screen into that world.

We visited the set of the TV show *Maverick*, which starred James Garner. My sisters and I were standing in one of the fake saloons when we heard footsteps and the click of a gun behind us. "All right, hands up!" It was Garner with a prop pistol. It was a joke, but it scared the hell out of us.

However, for me the highlight of our trip was Grauman's Chinese Theatre, where the stars leave their handprints and footprints in the cement. I remember putting my hands inside the handprints of Dick Van Dyke, whom I'd loved in *Mary Poppins*. My hands were so small! I never could have dreamed that five decades later my own handprints and footprints would be in cement outside Grauman's Chinese.

I was turning sixteen when Ely and Edie decided to move the family to LA. Their work demanded it. For me, the issue was football. It was still the biggest thing in my life, and I was still young enough to dream of college gridiron glory. Moving west would mean missing my junior and senior seasons with Coach Bertino at Riverdale. And it wasn't just football; I had a life in the Bronx. When I voiced these concerns, I was given the option of staying behind to finish school at Riverdale, to live with family friends, then move to LA after graduation. I entertained this idea, but rejected it. I didn't want to be away from my family. Football was not important enough to do that. Deep down, I knew my future lay elsewhere.

WE MOVED INTO a house on Canon Drive in Beverly Hills that had once belonged to Kirk Douglas. This was a new world to us. Homes were not filled with doctors, lawyers, or Wall Street businessmen in Beverly Hills. It was all movie people—producers, directors, actors. In my memory, the sun never stopped shining during those first California days. It was always seventy-two degrees, no humidity. Beating against one another in the Santa Ana winds, the palm fronds sounded like applause. Nature itself was cheering.

I enrolled at the Brentwood School, a private school, for my last two years of high school. For the first time in my life, I began to feel Jewish. I had always known I was Jewish as my parents were Jewish, but we were not observant and didn't practice other than in a cursory way. For us, it was less about what you practiced than what you did and believed. Where we lived in the Bronx was very Jewish—especially Fieldston. It didn't seem to be something noteworthy. The Jewish thing was hard to ignore at Brentwood. When I went to the first football practice, one of my teammates looked at me and said, "You're Jewish and you play football?!" Later, when the miniseries *Holocaust* was the biggest thing on TV, I learned that the father of one of my new friends was actually a Holocaust denier. And it wasn't just Jews that some of my more ignorant classmates had an issue with. When Halloween rolled around our first year in LA, I threw a party for my Brentwood friends. Two kids showed up in blackface. Edie was enraged. She gave them a choice: Scrub it off, or leave. Edie's outrage exemplified the moral compass she hoped to instill in her children. Follow that compass, and you'd never get lost.

It was at Brentwood that I first felt the sting of stereotype. I worked myself dizzy on a senior thesis only to be accused of plagiarism. The evidence against me? My work was too good! It couldn't have been written by Jonny the Jock. I worked harder clearing my name than I had on the thesis itself, but I took away a lesson I've benefited from ever since: Don't limit others by your expectations.

Meanwhile, I picked up on the football field at Brentwood where I'd left off at Riverdale. In my senior year, I received recruitment letters from a handful of small colleges. If I was known for anything in the sports program at Brentwood, it was my work ethic. Football, baseball, basketball—I played harder than anyone. If you're not the most gifted, you can close a lot of the gap with hustle. That's what I've always believed. Hard work doesn't just augment a talent. It is a talent. Some have it, some don't. The school created an award in my name after I graduated. Given to the basketball team's hardest worker, it was called the Jon Landau 110% Award. I am proud of that to this day.

I realized I had no interest in going to some out-of-the-way college just to squeeze a few more years of football out of my body. By that time, my attention had already shifted to movies, so in the fall of 1978 I enrolled in USC's undergraduate film program (I'd never get in today). They assigned me to an apartment with a student in the graduate film program, which meant our TV was monopolized by the work of obscure European auteurs. He was into "films," but I was into movies, the blockbusters rolling into the theaters at what seemed like a rate of two a weekend in those days. *Alien. Raiders of the Lost Ark. E.T.*

At the time, the cinema school was mostly in a refurbished barn. There were screening rooms on campus, but nothing matched watching a movie in a crowded theater—the way you feel when you step out of a movie like *Star Wars* in the early evening, amid a throng of people, like you've returned from another world. That amazement is what we want people to experience when they take off their 3D glasses after an Avatar film. It's why I don't worry about the challenge TV poses to movies. No matter how good the technology becomes, home is still home and a theater can still be a gateway to another universe. Give people an experience they can only get at the cinema—that's magic.

I'd never really thought about joining a fraternity until an old Brentwood friend asked me to join his frat at USC. I decided to check it out and discovered that one of the things fraternities offered was a competitive interfraternity sports program. And so I rushed my friend's fraternity. He and I were both confident I would get accepted. But I wasn't. Why? My friend told me it was because I was Jewish. I was angry, and, in that moment of anger, rushed and joined the Jewish fraternity Sigma Alpha Mu, commonly known as Sammy. My interest in frat life started with sports, but I ended up enjoying the overall experience so much I became president. It was a strange role for me, especially because much of fraternity life revolves around alcohol, and I don't drink. Not at all. Never have, never will. (The fact that I've never had so much as a single drink has not precluded me from amassing, for Julie, for my friends, and for fun, a first-class wine collection.)

My abstinence started with a vow made in high school. As the youngest kid on the Riverdale football team, I found myself at parties with juniors and seniors who got stupid drunk on whiskey and beer after games. The sight of these normally good people changing personalities under the influence, becoming aggressive, careless, and even mean, really bothered me. Right then, I told myself I'd never give up self-control like that. I'd never drink. It's a vow I've never broken.

I have a handful of other personal trademarks as well. First, there is my dress, which, unless I'm forced to wear formal attire, tends to be extremely casual; Hawaiian shirts and cargo pants are my standard. Second: the beard. It's not as famous as that of Santa Claus or Abe Lincoln, but people know me for it. They usually assume it dates to the 1970s, when everything was footloose, but that's not the case. The beard actually came as a result of an early job.

When I went looking to earn a little extra money during college, the best offer came from my high school, Brentwood. They needed someone to coach the JV football team. As it turned out, there's no greater preparation for a movie producer than a few seasons leading a team from the sideline. It's better than film school. You learn how to inspire, bring people together, set a goal, and create a strategy to meet it; how to spot and develop talent, deal with rebels and stars, weather setbacks, and placate higher-ups; and how to handle a win, which can be an even bigger challenge than handling a loss. Because I took that job a year out of high school, some of the kids thought I was still their classmate. Since students were not allowed to have facial hair at Brentwood, I decided to grow a beard to make my position of authority clear. I've worn it ever since.

When I finished college and my coaching career ended, I didn't know if I'd had the kind of impact on any of my players that Coach Bertino had on me. But many years later, shortly after I had won the Oscar for *Titanic*, I received an early morning call from one of those players, Doug Johns. He called to say, with surprise and delight, "Coach Landau, I saw you win the Oscar!" Close to twenty years after Doug had been one of my players, he was still calling me "Coach." That answered my question about the impact of my coaching. And made me proud. It doesn't matter when you find the teachers that affect your life. It might be in grade school or on a movie set at age fifty-five. But you must find them. They are your lodestars. Being this for others, passing on what you've been given, might be your entire purpose.

LIFE SEEMED EASY and happy, but life changes, and, when it changes, it changes fast.

In 1983, my parents were in London prepping for a movie called *The Holcroft Covenant*. They were flying home to LA and asked me to pick them up at LAX. I waited for them at the gate. And waited. The entire plane emptied, but they hadn't come out. I went to the gate agent, who asked my name, then told me that my father had suffered a stroke over the Atlantic. They'd taken him off the plane on the tarmac and rushed him to the hospital by ambulance. My mother had left a message for me saying to meet her at Daniel Freeman Memorial Hospital in Inglewood. My father was in the ICU. He spent months there. He had to learn how to do everything—talk, write, eat—all over again, and he was confined to a wheelchair the rest of his life. He left for London as one kind of person, and returned as another.

Many people lose control of their emotions after a stroke. Some laugh all the time. My father became a crier. You'd walk in and say "Hi, Ely," and he'd start weeping. He was finished as a movie producer, which meant the company that he and Edie had run side by side for more than thirty years was in jeopardy. Ely was sixty-three. Edie was fifty-seven. As independents, they'd never made blockbuster money. They'd continually reinvested everything in their next project, believing there would always be a next project. They'd never saved for a rainy day, and now the storm had come. Everyone had to help. Edie completed *The Holcroft Covenant*, then went on to produce a few small movies for HBO, including *The Christmas Wife* with Jason Robards and Julie Harris and *Mr. Halpern and Mr. Johnson* starring Jackie Gleason and Sir Laurence Olivier.

Ultimately, Edie got out of the business and took over a friend's nanny placement agency. That became her new career. She ran it successfully and happily for the next thirty years. One of the funny things my mother would say about the nanny business was that the studio executives who would never return her call when she was an independent film producer called back immediately when looking for a nanny.

My sister Tina was a rising senior at Yale when my father got sick. She helped as much as she could, but the burden fell hardest on our little sister, Kathy. Part of it was her personality. Kathy is always the first to step up, to run into the burning building. She had just finished her freshman year at Brown but dropped out when Ely had the stroke, and stayed in LA to help Edie take care of Ely and their business. She went back to Brown later, but her life was upended.

I knew it was time for me to step up, too, as Ely had done for his family when he was young and crisis hit. I didn't graduate from college, and I never would. It was time for me to start contributing. And so began my own Hollywood journey. It has been quite a life—I have gotten to travel the world, provide for my family, and be part of successes and failures, and I have fought with and found common ground with moguls, geniuses, aspiring stars, and legends. Through it all, I have had an amazing amount of fun. And in the process, I have learned lessons and strategies that only a lifetime can teach.

Chapter 2

I began looking for a job. I was twenty-three, and the world seemed wide open to me. That should be your state of mind when you start out: wide open.

There are some lives you live without ever having actually lived them—because you've imagined them. Because you've experienced them in your mind. That's how it was for me and movies. I'd been privy to that life, watched my parents live it, and now I wanted to experience it for myself. My task was to go out and get it.

The first opportunity came from a friend, someone in the network I'd started building with my very first job. His name was Jonathan Bernstein. He had been an executive producer on *The Chosen*. I do not remember exactly when we first met. Maybe it was when I was in that scene costumed as a Hasid, or maybe it was when I was teaching Barry Miller how to swing a bat—with a slight incline, as if you want to send the ball soaring. Maybe it was when Robby Benson was teaching me how to eat sushi. (I'll always be grateful for that introduction.)

Jonathan believed in me enough—he knew I'd give it my all—to hire me for his next picture, a small TV movie that was called *Max and Sam* before the title was changed to *Found Money*. Perfect name. It was like found money to me, a piece of good luck, a door that would open into the rest of my life.

Found Money was filmed in and around New York. I stayed at the apartment my parents still had in the city, which made the whole thing possible. You couldn't have purchased a bowl of matzo ball soup with what they were paying me. Jonathan was the line producer, the on-the-ground person in charge of handling day-to-day tasks, logistics, budget, scheduling, problems, and the like. He hired me with no particular job in mind, just figuring, well, Landau is good and we can always use good people.

The best thing about the movie was the cast. Sid Caesar and Dick Van Dyke—these were my heroes. The plot of the movie was muddled: Two guys, sick and tired of the meanness of the world, establish a fake company and set about doing good. But, of course, doing good is never that simple.

The director, Bill Persky, who had worked on the old *Dick Van Dyke Show*, had no use for me. I was not one of his guys. That's how a lot of things work, not just in showbiz: Are you one of the inside guys, or are you on the outside? Since Jonathan had hired me, not Persky, I was on the outside. Can you find a way to contribute, to learn and make yourself known, even when you're not wanted? That was my challenge.

Most of the movie was shot on the campus of IBM in Armonk, New York, a suburban town in Westchester County. When I turned up, Persky just stared at me. He had nothing for me to do. He had to think before he finally came up with a job he believed I could handle: walkie-talkie guy. The director, the grips, the producer—they all communicate via walkie-talkie, and I was the walkie-talkie guy, which looked at one way is busy work, but looked at another is a crucial task. My job was to hand out the walkie-talkies each morning, collect them each afternoon, and recharge them each night.

IBM was about an hour north of Manhattan. As the walkie-talkie guy, I had to be on set early. I had befriended the movie's second AD, Chris Griffin. The second AD—the second assistant director—puts together the schedule of scenes and the shot list for each day, retrieves actors from their trailers, gets them in and out of makeup, and so on, which means they (Chris, in this case) have to arrive just as early as the walkie-talkie guy. Every morning, an early bus took the crew up to Armonk. I would sit next to Chris on that bus and pepper him with questions. The fact that Chris—who was in his mid-thirties, while I was in my early twenties—was a good, patient person, willing to explain everything, turned out to be a lucky break for me. That's the backstory of any successful career—a million lucky breaks, almost all of which will be forgotten.

In the course of perhaps two dozen early mornings—the sun sitting low on the East River, the airplanes circling above LaGuardia, the rush hour traffic flowing into the city—I asked everything I could think to ask about the movie business, things so routine they seemed invisible, small things too unimportant for my parents to have mentioned or for me to have observed. I asked about the Screen Actors Guild and its rules. I asked about the extras. I asked about food services and budgets, trailer rentals and boom operators, production designers, stunt coordinators, Steadicams, set dressers, grips. I asked about call sheets, and I asked about production reports. By the time we entered the third week of production, I'd probably learned enough to get a master's degree in film production.

Some of the tasks Persky asked me to do, especially when we were filming in the city, felt like hazing. (Remember, I was a fraternity president; I know hazing.) One night, we were shooting at Rockefeller Center, and Persky sent me to the top of an office building, where I spent the night relaying messages from an assistant director to a follow spot operator: *Aim it a little more to the left; a little more to the right.* Busy work, essentially—menial and meaningless—and we all knew it. I stayed up there till morning. They say the days of a life are long, the years short. That was one of the long days. Everyone has had a few of those. Maybe they provide a lesson about the people in your life you choose and the ones you don't. I know that seemingly pointless night was a lesson for me. I had found my people. They were Jonathan Bernstein and Chris Griffin.

At the end of the shoot, Jonathan pulled me aside as the cast and crew were saying goodbye. The end of a shoot is a moment that marks the line between active production and postproduction. When the actors go home, the editors and directors get down to business—that's postproduction. Jonathan asked if I wanted to stick around and help. Though I had no idea what would be expected of me, I said yes anyway. Why not? When opportunity presents itself, "yes" will almost always lead somewhere more interesting than "no."

Postproduction work did not seem especially rewarding at first. Jonathan had described it as "accounting," and I never did like accounting. I was good with numbers, but not excited to be a bean counter. But you never know where the important information will come from. My job was to compile all the contracts—for the actors, crew, everyone—and organize and file them. These were still the early days of the personal computer. I'd been goofing around with some of the machines, even writing some of my own code and creating my own programs. I did it for fun. The most popular commercial program at the time was called Multiplan. Nobody will remember, but Multiplan was a precursor to Microsoft Excel. That's what I used for the contracts. They loved it upstairs. If you even knew how to turn a computer on in the early 1980s, you were considered a whiz kid.

For me, it was not the computer that mattered but the contracts—the documents and what was in them. I read every clause, rider, exemption. It was the best education in the movie business a person could get. I was learning how production actually works. I was learning about salaries, budgets, hierarchies. I was learning about exemptions, best- and worst-case scenarios, the rights that mattered and those the studios were willing to give away. I had been through film school at USC. I had watched my parents produce movies. But I learned more about the behind-the-scenes workings in those few weeks of computer inputting than I have learned anywhere else.

The lesson?

Never consider yourself too good for a job, even those jobs that might at first seem uninteresting or unappealing. You never know where, in what pile of grunt work, you will find the piece that completes the puzzle, that will help you understand the true nature of the game.

WHEN POSTPRODUCTION WRAPPED, I went home to LA, and *boom*: Just like that, I got another job. A movie director named Ron Maxwell—he directed *Little Darlings* with Kristy McNichol and Tatum O'Neal—hired me to be his assistant. Not an assistant director, that's a whole different thing. I was to be the director's assistant. This was for *The Pope of Greenwich Village*, a movie that had a stellar young cast in place: Mickey Rourke, Eric Roberts, Daryl Hannah. It was based on a

Vincent Patrick novel. Director Michael Cimino, who won the Oscar for *The Deer Hunter*, had already been hired and fired. If I had been older, and knew more, I would have taken that as a warning. It meant the production was in flux, the pieces still floating. But what you don't know, you learn.

I signed on at $200 a week. It cost me $700 just to get to New York for the job. The math didn't add up, but I wanted to keep working. I showed up on the set, got ensconced, and went at it as hard as I could from the moment I arrived until the moment, two weeks later, when Ron Maxwell was fired. Why? It's the movie business. There doesn't need to be a reason. He was replaced by Stuart Rosenberg, who you couldn't call a bad choice. Stuart Rosenberg had directed *Cool Hand Luke*. Most of the cast and crew stayed. If I'd been the assistant director, I might have stayed, too. But I was not. I was the director's assistant. That made me Ron's guy. He went, I went. It was the first time I'd ever been fired, and needless to say, I did not like it.

I had paid for my own flight to New York, so I asked the production team to reimburse me. They refused. I asked if they could at least get me a ticket back to LA. Nope. I was off the picture and on my own. I had worked for two weeks and came away with less than I had when I started. I try to remember how this felt whenever someone on one of my productions needs help. Years later, while filming *Honey, I Shrunk the Kids* in Mexico City, a crew member came to me desperate for the money to get back to Los Angeles for personal reasons.

He asked us to pay his airfare, even though we were not obligated to. I said, "Let's flip for it."

I showed him a quarter, then asked him to choose heads or tails.

He thought I was serious, but of course I was going to buy him a ticket in any case. It was the right thing to do. It's how I wish I'd been treated on *The Pope of Greenwich Village*. But this way, when he left with his ticket, instead of feeling unlucky—because of whatever family emergency had taken him off the job—he would feel lucky because he'd won the coin toss. (Yes, I knew how to ensure that.)

I DID NOT go back to Los Angeles right away. I didn't have money for a ticket. I hung around New York, living in my parents' apartment until the check I was due for my work in *Found Money* came in the mail. Meanwhile, I made phone calls and sent out résumés. As I like to do everything a little bit differently, with a slant—it's often not experience or credentials but that slant that gets you noticed—I designed my résumé as a movie-set clapboard, the sort an assistant director holds up to the camera before each take: "*Found Money*, scene three, take five." *Clap!* It had my name instead of the name of the production on it, along with my experience, which was slim, and my phone number. I sent copies to every studio and production company in LA. The response was silence.

I flew back to LA, where I was still living with my parents, as soon as I could pay for a ticket. I arrived late and went straight to bed. The phone ringing woke me what seemed like ten minutes later. I answered in a daze. It took a moment to remember where I was. Not New York. Los Angeles. It was a line producer named Mel Howard calling.

Mel asked if I could meet with him in his office in Manhattan that morning. He was prepping for a movie that would be filmed in and around New York, and he was looking for an assistant. It took me a minute to realize why he thought I was in New York City: I'd forwarded the calls from my New York number to my phone in LA. He'd dialed a number with a 212 area code. If he'd known I was in LA, he never would have considered me for the job.

"Come in today," he said, "and I'll tell you about the movie and the job."

I looked at the clock. It was six a.m. Pacific Standard Time, so nine o'clock in New York.

"Can we make it tomorrow?" I asked.

He sighed and said, "Okay. Sure. But let's do it early."

I didn't even need to pack. I'd never taken my clothes out of my bag. I got the first available flight back to New York and was in Mel's office at eight a.m. the next morning.

The movie, *Beat Street*, was being directed by Stan Lathan. It told the story of hip-hop culture, the musical art being pioneered on the playgrounds and in the clubrooms of the Bronx. Boom boxes and breakdancing—that was the backdrop. *Beat Street* captured New York City in a moment of decay, the late imperial days, the city of Mayor Koch, graffiti-covered subways, boarded-up apartments, and vacant lots.

Beat Street was a quality production. The script was based on a story by Steven Hager, one of the first journalists to cover the scene, and the screenplay was filled with authenticity and insider knowledge. The soundtrack is a landmark, a collection of performers who were or became the first great generation of hip-hop and rap stars. There are songs and appearances by Grandmaster Melle Mel and the Furious Five, Doug E. Fresh, and the Treacherous Three. Rae Dawn Chong, the It girl of the moment, was the star, along with Tonya Pinkins and a slew of newcomers.

That this youth movie should have been of such high-quality production was no surprise. *Beat Street* was produced by two of the greats: David Picker, who'd been largely responsible for *A Hard Day's Night* with the Beatles and the James Bond series; and Harry Belafonte, the great actor, singer, and civil rights leader. Belafonte, who had marched with Martin Luther King Jr., brought calypso music to North America. It might have been Belafonte who recommended me for the job. He knew Ely and Edie from the Civil Rights Movement. They'd worked together on my parents' MLK documentary, and they were politically aligned. When Richard Nixon ran against George McGovern in 1972, Ely took out an ad in papers across the country that said, "Are you really going to sit there and let Nixon get reelected?"

As assistant line producer, it was my job to shadow Mel, know everything he had in mind, and help him do it.

Beat Street was the turning point in my career and life. Thanks to Mel, I had my own areas of real responsibility. That's where I learned film production and the challenges of shooting on location, especially when working in a city like New York with its politics, traffic, and weather. But most importantly, that's where I met Julie.

ABOUT A MONTH into production, Mel had to leave. Both his parents were ill. The fact that he drew this line—by his exit, he let us know family takes precedence—was the last thing he taught me on *Beat Street*, but probably the most important. Whenever I feel a twinge of guilt about exiting a meeting or screening early because of a personal matter, I think of Mel Howard and *Beat Street*. He was a good role model.

The studio hired Peter McIntosh to replace Mel. But since the production was already up and running, and it would have been impossible to get Peter up to speed without slowing everything down, they elevated my role, promoting me to production supervisor. Because I'd been shadowing Mel and had made it my business to know everything he had planned, it was an easy move for me to make.

The outdoor shoots were tricky but also exciting. One of the lasting impressions of that movie can be found in the scenes we filmed in the streets, which capture early 1980s New York in an authentic way, almost in the vein of a documentary. The avenues, the rundown tenements, the subways limping between stations—it's all preserved. We shot in the Bronx, Manhattan, Brooklyn, and Queens. We shot at the Hoyt–Schermerhorn station in Brooklyn, at the Fifty-Seventh and Sixth station in Manhattan, and at Fresh Pond Road, one of the original stations of the old BMT, in Queens. We shot at City College and at The Roxy nightclub on Eighteenth Street in Chelsea when Chelsea was Chelsea.

A typical movie takes something like six to twelve weeks to shoot. We finished *Beat Street* before the deadline and under budget. It cost $9.5 million, modest even for the time. As the cast members left for other jobs—it's like the parting of a family that will never meet again—the producer, the director, and a handful of crew members settled into an office on the West Side of Manhattan for postproduction. Once again, I was asked to stay on. At the last minute, Kerry Orent, who was supposed to be our postproduction supervisor, had to leave to work on *The Cotton Club*. The producers needed to find a replacement fast. David Picker asked me if I wanted to stay on and supervise postproduction.

I knew very little about postproduction, but I did not tell him that. I just said yes.

It might seem like my career advanced by a series of seemingly random circumstances. If Mel Howard had not left the movie... If Kerry Orent hadn't unexpectedly been needed on *The Cotton Club*... But here's the truth: Someone is always stepping away, moving on, or leaving early. There's always movement, and it always means opportunity. Recognizing and making good use of it—that's the key. That's why you have to learn to say yes. We're often given chances in life, but sometimes we're afraid to take them because we don't think we know how to do what needs doing, that we don't have the answers. Here's what I say to that: You don't need to know the answers to take the opportunity; you can learn the answers along the way, but only if you embrace that opportunity.

SOMETIMES, LYING IN bed at night, I try to remember the name of every movie I've ever worked on. I do this instead of counting sheep. Listed in chronological order, it's the story of my entire career and so many of the people in my life. If I get from *The Chosen* all the way to *Avatar: Fire and Ash* and I am still awake, I try to think of at least one key lesson—or counter lesson—I learned on each picture. Every movie, no matter the budget or box office, was important. On *Beat Street*, one particular conversation shaped the way I have approached every picture that followed.

I was twenty-three years old and still figuring out what it means to have responsibility. David Picker had given us a hard deadline. We had to have the movie locked and ready to go in time for the Cannes Film Festival. About ten days out, the supervising music editor, Tom Drescher, came in to see me. He said, "Jon, we've got a problem. There's no way we're going to clear the rights to all the songs in time for Cannes."

I thought I knew exactly what to do. Be up-front and honest, right? Tell everyone everything as soon as you know. So I said, "Okay. Let's go tell David Picker."

I marched with Tom into David's office and said, "Tom tells me we're not going to make the release date."

David did not get upset. He just looked at us and said, "I pay the two of you to tell me how it can get done, not that it can't get done." Then he stood up and left.

Forget the details. Here's the kicker: We cleared the rights and made the deadline. We got it done. I can't count how many times I've thought about what David said that day. I thought of it on *Titanic* when we were building an entire studio in Mexico. Everyone on the crew was muttering: "No way. Can't do it. Can't do it." I went to a bookstore and ordered dozens of copies of *The Little Engine That Could* and gifted a copy to each department head with the inscription: "I know we can, I know we can."

And guess what?

We did.

Years later, when we were working on the first Avatar, we hit a similar impasse. This time, I was the one experiencing doubt, overcome by the seeming impossibility of the task. A crew member who'd been on *Titanic* handed me his old copy of *The Little Engine That Could*, with my inscription: "I know we can, I know we can." He said, "Hey, Jon. You're the guy who told me we can do anything." On every movie, there comes that moment of doubt. Here's what I say: Don't bitch. Don't complain. Don't kick your problem upstairs. Just do the work. Get it done. If you think you can accomplish a task, you're almost always right. After all, moviemaking is the art of the impossible.

MOST OF THE *Beat Street* crew had gone on to other projects. Just a few people remained in the postproduction offices on the West Side, including David Picker, a handful of editors and assistants, and a cute blond accountant from Long Island named Julie.

What did I like about Julie?

Everything. She was funny, personable, and warm. She was smart as a whip. And brave. An actress, she had even dabbled in stunts. Even if you don't think you've ever seen her, you probably have—falling out of a bus, driving backward over the 59th Street Bridge at high speeds. That's Julie in *Titanic* hanging from the bow as the ship goes down.

The life of an actor or stuntperson is filled with downtime. You're between jobs but still need to make money. Some wait tables, some become carpenters, some write novels. Because she was good with numbers, Julie bridged the gaps by working as a movie industry accountant. Eventually, she left acting altogether and built a career behind the scenes. On a production, managing the finances and understanding and controlling the numbers is just as important as acting or directing.

Without quite meaning to, I found myself lingering by Julie's desk in the *Beat Street* production office. I'd had a lot of platonic relationships in my life, but never a girlfriend. I don't think I even understood at the time that's what I wanted from Julie. I was so inexperienced. I wouldn't have known how to go about it even if I did understand. So I goofed around with her instead, making her laugh. Seeing her smile.

The office was in an old warehouse. There were almost no windows, and the crew complained all the time. I hung a huge poster of a window that looked out on a New York street up in the main room and said, "Here's a window." Julie got a kick out of that. She began hanging out in my office. Without realizing it, I'd managed to commit the classic romantic error. I'd turned Julie into my buddy. I was trapped in "the friend zone."

I am ashamed to say I actually dropped her off at and picked her up from a date once, then engaged in a postmortem like a best girlfriend.

We'd talk all the way back to her apartment in Queens. Those rides were the best part of my day.

Once, Julie asked why I never went on any dates. This led to a discussion of my own tastes, what sort of women I liked, what sort of relationship I was looking for. Julie secretly decided to set me up. She brought her friend Cindy along to the circus one night, thinking maybe we'd hit it off. She tried again with her friend Tina on a day spent at City Island. At the time, I didn't realize Julie's intentions, that these were supposed to be fix-ups.

In the office, I was doing a lot of my work on computers, which, as I've said, were still a relative novelty in production offices in the early 1980s. People were fascinated. One day, Julie inquired about the budget spreadsheet I'd programmed and asked if she could see how it worked. I said yes, and she surprised me by sitting on my lap. It surprised me in the best way.

I then invited Julie and David Picker's assistant, Vicki Stein, to meet for dinner at Benihana, the Japanese steakhouse, on Fifty-Sixth Street in Manhattan. I was still too shy to ask her out on a date, and I figured Vicki would be a nice buffer. Conveniently, Vicki, noticing sparks had been flying, said she had other plans. And so, Julie and I had a wonderful meal alone. We'd gone out before, but only as friends. This felt different.

We went back to my apartment after dinner and played Scrabble. Julie lost, then, when I moved closer to console her, she kissed me. It was one of the greatest nights of my life.

I had to catch a flight early the next morning to carry the final print of *Beat Street* to Cannes. My head was spinning. What had happened? What did it mean? Julie had had other partners. But I hadn't. I knew what she meant to me, but didn't know what I meant to her.

I called her as soon as I arrived in France.

"Were you drunk last night?" I asked.

"Unfortunately not," she said with a laugh.

That joke marked the beginning of our lifelong love affair and decades of shared laughter. May 18, 1983—it was the beginning of everything.

When I got back to New York, it was like returning to a new city. The streets were golden all summer, shot through with light. We went everywhere, did everything. Julie was the foreground. Everything else was background. I had fallen in love.

Okay, I am going to get a little personal. Julie and I became a couple right after I got back from Cannes. We spent all our time together. Then one night it happened. We made love. I had told her many things about myself, but not everything. So, she turned to me after and said, "Now you are going to tell me you were a virgin."

I smiled and said, "Correct. Past tense. I *was* a virgin."

"If that's the case," said Julie, "you don't really know how good I am. You need some basis of comparison."

But that was something I never wanted. Julie is, in fact, the only woman I've ever been with. I will forever refer to Julie lovingly as "my one and only."

Julie gave up her apartment and moved in with me on Fifty-Fifth Street. From that moment, I knew I wanted to marry her. I knew this was for keeps. There were signs. For example, Julie and I both had the same couches in our apartments. And it wasn't just that they were from the same store or manufacturer; they were the same exact pieces, in the same gray fabric. When she moved in, we simply added her sofa to mine, and we had a perfect sectional. It was a metaphor and a message—from the start, we fit as if designed for the purpose.

We were both just starting out in our careers. Young, unencumbered, in love. I started working on a new movie, *Key Exchange*, while Julie was working on *Desperately Seeking Susan*. She did her job, I did mine, then we came back together at the end of the day. We had the best dates and turned everything into an anniversary. Every May, we celebrate the anniversary of our first date at Benihana.

I loved finding ways to surprise her. I still do. There was a French restaurant next door to our apartment on Fifty-Fifth Street. Literally next door. We'd been dying to go, but it was out of our price range. I saved up on the sly, then, one night, said to Julie, "I found a great place I want to take you to for dinner, but I want it to be a surprise." I didn't have a car, so I put her in the passenger seat of her car in a blindfold, then proceeded to drive around for twenty-five minutes before parking right back where we started. I led her into the restaurant that was, in fact, next door to our apartment, then took off the blindfold. She looked around, confused. I took her outside to see where we were. It took a moment to register. Then we both just laughed.

I played practical jokes on Julie from the start. This is one of my hobbies. I practice the long joke. You must plan carefully, weeks or even months in advance of the payoff. You might not even be present to watch it go off, but that's okay. Knowing and imagining is enough. For the prankster, the goal is to add a little bit of joy and wonder into an often mundane world.

One year on her birthday, Julie woke to find me wrapping a giant box in our living room. She was meant to see this; it was part of my plan. I was building anticipation. I listened to her guess what was inside. A bike? A washer/dryer? She was still guessing when she left for work.

I had a production assistant bring her a single rose every hour until three that afternoon, even when she went to the hairdresser (an appointment I had booked for her). When she got back to the office—she was working at Orion Pictures on Fifth Avenue—the box was there. Julie and her coworkers stood around eagerly guessing the contents. When she finally tore off the wrapping paper, here's what she found inside: me! I stepped out wearing a tuxedo and gave her a pair of diamond earrings, put them on her ears, then took her by horse-drawn carriage to the Rainbow Room for dinner.

If Julie could stand all that—mystery, embarrassment, excess—I figured we had a real chance to make it as a couple.

Why do we get along so well?

Because we can laugh with each other, at each other, and at ourselves. That's the key. We both do stupid things sometimes, but we don't hide them. We don't harbor or lie. We don't let the anger, which everyone experiences, stay with us. We fess up, and we move on. When the bad times come, as they inevitably do, we face them, then leave them in the past. And we do it all together.

Julie has learned to live with my exuberance and outsize personality. That's been crucial. An easily embarrassed person could probably not stand life with me. We did fight about it once. It was our first blowup. We drove to Cape Cod for the weekend, then stopped at a little restaurant in the middle of nowhere on the way back. As we were eating, I started talking to the server and asking her lots of questions. I then said, "Hey, what other restaurants would you recommend in this town?"

It really annoyed Julie. "Why ask a server if there is another restaurant better than her own? What's the point? We're not staying here, and we're probably never coming back."

"It's just talk," I told Julie. "I like to make conversation."

We bickered about it all the way back to the city. It actually made me realize something about myself, and Julie ultimately understood it, too. I am a person who reaches out to strangers. If I'm sitting next to someone in a restaurant and that person is alone, I'm going to say, "Hey, do you live around here?" I'm going to start a conversation. Meeting new people—that's how you learn about the world. It's also a way of reaching out, showing recognition, creating a shared moment. This idea is embedded in the Na'vi greeting "Oel ngati kameie," which means "I see you." We all want to be acknowledged. We all want to be seen.

Even now, in the course of my many hospital stays, I have made it my business to know something about every nurse, doctor, and patient I encounter. "What brought you here?" I ask. "How are you doing? Do you have kids? Tell me about them." One day, a nurse came in to sit with me just because she wanted to talk. I thought that was so great.

I remembered that Cape Cod fight recently. Julie and I were eating at True Food Kitchen in Century City, and a woman was sitting alone two tables away. Julie leaned over and asked, "Hey, do you live around here?" And I thought to myself, *See! See!* They ended up exchanging numbers and even went out to dinner together. That's what can happen when you reach across a seeming distance.

While I wanted to get married as soon as we moved in together, Julie wasn't ready. I would ask her every Wednesday: "Julie, will you marry me?" She'd laugh me off and change the subject. Then, after eight months of weekly proposals, I asked again, and nonchalantly Julie said yes. I quickly sat up and said, "Did you just say *yes*?" I was at first surprised, then beyond elated. We immediately started planning our wedding.

A few days later Julie flew to London, while Kathy was there with my mother, Edie, working on *The Holcroft Covenant*. Julie broke the news of our engagement to Edie and Kathy, who were so excited they took her shopping the next day for a wedding gown. Success—they found the gown that very day. My sisters, Kathy and Tina, took Julie in as another member of the Landau family.

JULIE'S PARENTS WERE middle-class people from Lindenhurst, New York. Her father, Marshall, was an electrician. Her mother, Kathryn, kept the home and managed the finances for Marshall's business. We drove out to tell them the news of our engagement. They were thrilled. I'd been close to them, but became much closer after the announcement.

I grew up Jewish, Julie Christian. We asked a minister and a rabbi known to perform interfaith ceremonies together to lead our ceremony. They agreed, but first each asked to meet with us. We started with the minister. He lived in a beautiful house near the water on Long Island. We were like, "Wow, God is a good business!" We talked to him, and the conversation went well. When we asked about the fee, he said, "I've recently learned that I've been charging less than the rabbi. So, let's say you can pay me whatever you pay him." In geopolitics and the entertainment business, they call this "most-favored-nation status." It made us laugh.

Next up, the rabbi. We were on the Long Island Expressway, heading out to meet him, when I started to feel funny. My stomach was doing somersaults. I didn't know why. Maybe I'd had a bad piece of fish for lunch. Whether it was food poisoning or an ill-timed stomach bug, I had to stop at a little restaurant and run to the bathroom. While in there, I suddenly leaned over and vomited in the sink, which then clogged. I spent what felt like an hour trying to unclog it. But the rabbi was waiting, so back in the car I went.

I was dripping sweat when we finally made it to the rabbi's. We knocked on the door. He opened it, then stepped back when he saw me. He said, "Oh my, are you okay?"

I asked if I could use his bathroom, then made a run for it. My stomach finally settled down enough to speak with the rabbi, but I kept having to race to the bathroom. I even had to ask for more toilet paper. How humiliating! How awful! I had clogged multiple sinks and toilets that day. Then, to top it off, I puked in the rabbi's garbage can. Cleaning up, I put the garbage can into the bathtub under the spigot to wash it out, turned on the water, and the shower came on instead—I ended up getting soaked.

"What happened?" asked the rabbi.

"Everything is okay," I said, "but do you have a plunger?"

While it was not my best day, the next time we were with the rabbi was—September 1, 1985, the day I married Julie.

THE CEREMONY AND reception were held at the Water Club on the East Side of Manhattan. There was no bride's or groom's side of the aisle. The day before the wedding we rented a bus, and all of our friends from LA got to meet Julie's friends from Long Island and from drama school. We hired a tintype photographer and all got dressed in vintage wear to have our pictures taken with a cardboard cutout of Babe Ruth. We had the best time. So by the wedding day, everyone knew everyone. Family, movie friends, childhood friends—we were all together. My sister Tina wrote a song for the occasion called "The Marriage of Julie and Jon." It was performed by Laurie Abramowitz, an old Riverdale friend, and Jerry Pavlon, a newer family friend, and it captured our lives perfectly. Tina had written it from the heart.

After the reception, a big group of us went back to our hotel suite and sang songs around the grand piano until dawn, when Julie and I had to leave for the airport. We were going to Tahiti for our honeymoon but were spending a couple of days in LA beforehand. On arriving in LA, and still in the afterglow of the wedding, I turned to Julie and said, "Forget this, we have thirty-six hours till our flight. Let's go to Vegas."

We didn't go to gamble, but just to run around to shows. We spent most of our time at Circus Circus, a casino—everything in Vegas is a casino—that bills itself as the world's largest permanent circus. There's a midway, a trapeze, and an indoor amusement park called the Adventuredome. At one point—maybe while waving my arms around on the roller coaster—I noticed that my left hand was bare. I'd been married less than forty-eight hours, and my wedding ring was gone.

I retraced my footsteps like a detective. This brought us back to an attraction on the midway we knew only as "the clown's mouth." You grabbed balls out of bins and tried to throw them into the mouth of an automated clown as it opened and closed. We took out all the balls and searched the bin. No ring. We walked around the clown, looking at the floor. Nothing. Where could it be? To lose your wedding ring so early in a marriage and in such a ridiculous place seemed like a bad omen. I was on the edge of panic when I had a realization: *It's not on the floor or in the bin. It's inside the clown's mouth!*

The kind manager shut down the attraction, and presto—we found the ring inside. It must have come off my finger as I threw one of those balls. Bull's-eye! What can I say? Not a bad omen at all.

✧ ✧ ✧ ✧

THE FIRST YEARS of marriage were incredibly fun. We were still living in my parents' old apartment on Fifty-Fifth Street. We still had the same furniture. We didn't buy anything new, saving our money for a boat instead. We had agreed that in lieu of buying an engagement ring, we'd buy a boat. We loved the water, loved being out on the bay. We found our boat at the New York Boat Show at the old Coliseum in Manhattan. Seeing a boat in a building in the middle of the city, going on board and ducking into the sleeping cabin—it was magic.

It was a twenty-eight-foot Bayliner aft cabin meant to be our summer getaway. We named it *JOLIE*. J-O for Jon. L-I-E for Julie. Jolie also happens to mean "pretty" in French, and to us that boat was as pretty as could be. We docked it near Julie's parents' house in Lindenhurst on a canal in the Great South Bay. Heading through those little islands and out into the Atlantic Ocean was thrilling.

We were on the water almost every weekend that summer. We hosted friends, explored, and pioneered. Learning how to navigate by getting into and out of mishaps was a phenomenal adventure. We'd meet people in coves on the bay, tie our boat to theirs, go deck to deck, and visit. It was a great way to entertain and to meet people. Sometimes we'd even sleep on the boat. It was the perfect way to escape the noise and chaos of the city. It was another world.

I think I started to understand a little more about marriage in those first years. Do you make each other better? That's an important question. I know Julie makes me better. I think that I make her better, too. That's the key ingredient to long-term success. You can get away with anything short term, but if you want to go the distance, you need complementary qualities. You also have to learn how to forgive, forget, and move on. Don't dwell. If you have a disagreement, fight it out, find your way back to each other, and don't think about it again.

Most of our arguments were about raising the kids: how to reward, reprimand, and teach them. I was much more lenient than Julie—maybe that's a reflection of how we were each raised—but Julie tolerated my idiosyncrasies. The real secret to all this is humor. Those who laugh, last.

DURING OUR COURTSHIP, engagement, and early years of marriage, I worked on several movies.

For me, the film after *Beat Street* was *Key Exchange*. Paul Kurta, a veteran television producer, hired me. Based on a play, *Key Exchange* was a romantic comedy about the trials and tribulations of dating in New York. It was a passion project for Paul, and it wasn't hard to see why. A little like Mamet, a little like *Seinfeld*; it was terrific. Paul tapped Barnet Kellman—he now teaches at USC—to direct. For the leads he secured Brooke Adams, Danny Aiello, Daniel Stern, and Ben Masters. Paul split his own job into two parts—he gave me charge of everything on set while he stuck to the big picture, which meant dealing with the studio, the actors, the writers, things of that sort. Still just twenty-three, I found myself working as a production supervisor in New York City. It was my first big real opportunity.

An important moment came early. For anyone trying to navigate the world, trying to rise, there will come that first time you have to step forward and make a consequential decision. Accepting responsibility means accepting blame when things go wrong. Some turn away at the key moment. They can't take the pressure. This person might be the greatest in the world at their job, but they can never be a boss. Others—and it might be the last person you'd expect—step forward and risk the consequences. These people will run the world.

When the moment came for me, it was a question of weather. We'd set up the cameras and crew on a street in Midtown Manhattan. The actors were waiting in their trailers, the cameras ready on the dollies. Then the clouds rolled in, dark and threatening rain. I asked one of the assistants for a weather report. Will it rain? He put the odds at fifty-fifty. We could go inside to film, losing half a day in prep time. Or we could stay outside and lose an entire day if it rained, which would break the schedule.

Get Paul Kurta on the phone and let him decide—that was my first thought. But how could Paul be expected to make a better decision when he wasn't even there to see the sky and feel the wind? And hadn't Paul hired me to run the set, which meant making just this kind of decision?

"Okay, everyone in their places," I said. "We're going."

In other words, I made the call.

It was coming down in buckets by the time we got the final take, but the scene was in the can, and we stayed on schedule. It was the first big moment of my career, if only because it gave me the confidence to be a decision-maker.

Another big moment came at the end of the shoot. Working in New York was risky in the mid-1980s. There was a lot of chaos on the city streets. We were filming at Cafe Luxembourg, a French bistro on the Upper West Side. I'd ducked into the bathroom before the first take of the day. Suddenly, almost as soon as I got in there, someone started banging on the door and screaming: "Jon, get out here! We've got a problem."

The set had been taken over by activists who'd formed a kind of wall around the cameras. The police came and set up a cordon around the restaurant, like we were in a hostage situation. The head activist was named Mustafa. We talked out front. This was not the first film his group had shut down. In fact, this was Mustafa's regular gig. He'd taken over *Desperately Seeking Susan* and several other New York film sets. His stated cause was representation. He said he wanted more people of color working on our production. "Diversification of sets" was his phrase. If I call this a racket, it's only because his main demand was money in the form of immediate high-salaried production jobs, which his people would staff, a demand that would have been simply impossible to meet at this point on the production.

I pulled the actors off the set and called our producer Mitchell Maxwell from a pay phone at the back of Cafe Luxembourg. I was looking out at the black-and-white tiles and cloth-covered tables. A movie set is fantasyland, and Mustafa and his army had just punctured our dream. That's why people hated filming in New York.

Mitchell and I spoke for about ten minutes. After I'd given him the rundown, he asked what the other studios were doing. I told him that most of them were making the payoff.

"Okay," said Maxwell. "Let's do that."

I told him I didn't want to do that. It'd be like making a deal with the devil. Mitchell thought I was being unrealistic, hysterical even. We argued until he gave up, saying, "Fine. Handle it how you want. But whatever happens, it's on you."

I called for Mustafa to join me, and we sat in the back of the restaurant.

"Look around the set," I told him. "Our crew is already diverse."

He said he didn't notice and didn't care. It went on like this.

I asked him for his terms: "What do you need to clear the set?"

He gave me a list of jobs he wanted to staff along with salaries, which were double what our people were making.

I told him that we only had two weeks left to shoot. "Let us finish, then, as we move into postproduction, we will create a paid internship meant only for people of color," I said. "You can send candidates our way, but we get to interview them and decide."

He agreed, possibly because this particular shakedown was taking too long and not going as he'd planned. It was a question of time invested versus money returned. He'd be better off moving on to a production with a bigger budget and a more amenable coordinator. When filming wrapped, I reached out to him as promised. I told him he should send over his internship applicants. I never heard back.

I did agree with his goal, though. We do need more diversity on film sets. Not only is it right, but it makes for a better product. This is something I learned on *Beat Street*. The more kinds of people, the more varied the experiences, the better the movie is going to be. Gender, race, culture—I've tried to be cognizant of all of it in every film I've worked on since. It remains a work in progress. We still need to break down old barriers. That's why internship programs are valuable. On the Avatar sequels, we've offered thirty-six paid internships in a multitude of live-action filming disciplines. You diversify the cast and crew by building the talent pool. It's the only way.

SHORTLY AFTER *KEY EXCHANGE*, I started working on *F/X*, a sleek little thriller. I won't go deeply into the plot because it's just twist after twist. The simple version is this: A Hollywood special effects artist is hired by the Department of Justice to stage a fake hit on a mobster going into witness protection. It was directed by Robert Mandel, starred Bryan Brown, and featured terrific character actors, including Brian Dennehy and Jerry Orbach. We filmed in and around New York.

Best of all, Julie had been hired on the movie, too. She was the Orion Pictures representative overseeing the accounting department.

I was a production manager, hired by Michael Peyser, whom I had met when Julie worked with him on *Desperately Seeking Susan*. Julie and I walked to work together almost every day. They say you should never work in the same business as your spouse, let alone on the same project. Julie had actually vowed to never marry anyone in the film business—a promise she fortunately broke. This has to do with the danger of professional rivalry, jealousy, or maybe just the need for distance. But I did not find that conventional wisdom to be true in our case. For us, it made for a wonderful marriage—we understood each other's jobs, the long hours and late nights. We shared work colleagues and friends. Besides, working with Julie was a blast.

I learned an important lesson on *F/X* about being in a managerial position. One morning at the beginning of our filming schedule, it was time to start shooting, and the set was not ready, nor fully decorated. Delays always cause great problems—reputations are sometimes on the line, and tempers and budgets inevitably rise. Our production designer, Mel Bourne, was livid. He started yelling, blaming this person and that. I stepped in and said, "Mel, I'm responsible." I knew I needed to redirect his anger and allow our teams to finish their work. Mel turned all his venting on me. When he calmed down a bit, I said, "I'll help solve it. Now, let's go fix the problem." And that's what we did.

There is so often a human need for a scapegoat—a person to blame, someone to bear the brunt of others' anger and anxiety. But scapegoating is never productive. Later in the day, Mel came over to me and said something I've never forgotten: "Responsibility rolls uphill when there's a problem." I understood what he was saying: Leading means standing up and stepping in when it matters.

I took that wisdom with me into all my work. Be accountable. It's not taking credit that makes you a leader. It's accepting responsibility. I earned the trust and respect of the crew by doing that. For the first time, I truly understood what it meant to be a producer, even though I did not yet have the title.

THERE WAS A hilarious postscript to my work on *F/X*. The production had purchased an old postal truck that the production designer converted to be the lead character's special effects truck in the movie—his rolling headquarters, tricked out inside and with a giant graffiti F/X on the outside. Rather than let it be junked after the shoot, I decided to buy it as a gift for Julie's father. As he was an electrician, we thought it would be a fun and unique work vehicle for him. So here I am, driving this truck out to Lindenhurst on the Long Island Expressway. Anyone who has ever been on the LIE knows the scene: cars and car horns, tractor trailers and pickups with muscleheads hanging out the windows telling you where to get off. And they don't mean which exit. As I clank along, black smoke begins to pour from the dashboard. By the time I get to the shoulder, the truck is on fire. I scramble out and get clear. I'm standing thirty feet away when the police and firefighters arrive. A cop comes over, so I tell him the deal with the truck. We are standing there watching the fire when I suddenly remember that I didn't clear out all the movie props. "Hey," I tell the cop, "you better let the fire guys know, there's a fully clothed mannequin in the back."

By now, the truck is engulfed in flames. A line of rubberneckers has formed, lookie-loos catching sight of the inferno as they make their way home or to the Hamptons. It seems like the traffic stretches all the way back to Manhattan. And the cop just stands there, laughing. "Let's not tell them about the mannequin," he says. "I want to see what happens."

I HAD A reputation for finishing any job I'd been assigned. Love it or hate it, nightmare or dream—I was going to complete the task. This put me into a select group of movie producers, problem-solvers who can be tapped when a picture is over budget or a director is causing trouble. Such directors also tend to be the best filmmakers, the auteurs, the visionaries. If they weren't great, no one would put up with them. Their careers would end. Making a name as a whisperer for the hard cases guaranteed I'd always have work and that it would always be interesting.

I came by this reputation in 1986 when I was brought in to oversee *Manhunter*, directed by Michael Mann. The line producer had bailed, or been fired. Either way, something had gone wrong. That's always a warning sign, a flashing red light. The Italian producer Dino De Laurentiis, who was a legend, was one of the people behind the project, along with producer Richard Roth and Sony Pictures. But I didn't meet with any of them before I got on a plane to Chicago, where the movie was six weeks into production.

Manhunter is based on the Thomas Harris novels, which feature lawman Will Graham (Bill Petersen) as head of the FBI's Behavioral Science Unit, a division that uses dazzling new techniques to track down psychos and serial killers. The movie marked the first appearance of the flesh-eating villain Hannibal Lecktor, who, in this film, was played by Brian Cox.

We filmed on location in Tampa and Chicago, where Michael Mann grew up. He'd been a student at the University of Wisconsin when he saw Stanley Kubrick's *Dr. Strangelove*, which changed his life. He gave up his plan of being a novelist and plunged into filmmaking instead. With Kubrick as a North Star, he seemed to seek not the workaday world of mundane Hollywood but the status of auteur. In a genius, eccentricity is forgivable—that's what Michael Mann believed, especially about himself. As a true artist, he said, he was allowed to paint outside the lines. Unfettered creativity is what lets him break down conventions and get to the heart of a thing.

Mann had already directed *Thief* with James Caan. He had filled the cast and crew with actual career criminals. For authenticity.

You do not ease into the world of Michael Mann. You do not meet, exchange ideas, then get slowly started. It's *bang*! You're in!

I experienced several classic Michael Mann moments on *Manhunter*, experiences I learned from and never want to repeat. On a plane from Chicago to Tampa—the entire cast and crew were flying down together—Mann announces that he's going to shoot a scene on the plane. On this commercial flight! The scene will show the FBI agent going through evidence en route to a crime scene. Michael said there was no faking the hum and the ambience of a commercial flight. He didn't want a studio setup; he wanted the real thing.

He had not prepared me for this—he probably figured I'd either say no or check with the airline and they'd say no. Better to ask forgiveness than permission—Michael lives by that.

The flight attendants, whom you'd expect to be up in arms, were instead starstruck. They loved the idea of being in a movie. They let us film even as we blocked the food and beverage service. Michael stood in the aisle, directing in a whisper. The cinematographer rested a camera on the back of a seat. Actor Bill Petersen was full method, reading under the overhead seat light as life went on around him.

Go back and watch the scene. It's amazingly real. We filmed through the descent and landing and wrapped only when we reached the gate.

That was the thrilling side of Michael Mann. I saw the terrifying side a few days later, when we were filming on Sanibel Island. Once again, Michael was after authenticity. In the scene we were filming, the actor Tom Noonan was to shoot out a house window with a shotgun blast. The special effects team had set it all up. The gun had blanks, and a charge would be tripped when Noonan pulled the trigger, shattering the window. However, back then, there was no way to do it without seeing the wires on camera. We didn't yet have CGI technology that could remove the wires in postproduction.

Michael decided he had to use real bullets, something that would absolutely not even be up for consideration today. Too dangerous, too risky. It made me very nervous, but Michael barreled ahead. He set up with the cameraman in the trees. The scene was to take place in the half-light of dawn. Michael was rushing, trying to beat the sun. At the same time, there was a stunt performer with a small explosive rig that would be triggered remotely elsewhere in the scene. All of our walkie-talkies had to be turned off because their signals could set off that squib prematurely, so we couldn't quickly spread the word that Michael had decided to use live ammunition.

I walked the whole area, making sure the set was clear—that no one was anywhere near the action. Though nothing was supposed to happen until I gave the all-clear sign, I heard the assistant director Herb Gains shout, "Michael! Michael!" then saw Herb dive.

In that split second, Noonan turned and fired his shotgun. The *ping, ping* I heard was the sound of bullets ripping through the trees. I had not given the all clear. People were still too close to the line of fire.

But Michael wanted to get his shot. The fact that nobody was hurt, or worse, is a miracle.

I took Michael to breakfast the next morning.

We had to talk about what he'd done.

"Nothing like that can ever happen again," I said. "Never. Never. Never."

I was at fault for getting talked into that setup—there's no reason to ever use live fire. It could've been a life-altering moment for everyone.

On any film, safety is number one. You never want anyone to get injured, let alone seriously. So, as you walk the set each morning, you examine and question everything. If a director gets caught up in the moment and figures, *What the hell, it's worth the risk, the scene demands it*, you have to be the voice of reason. The one who pulls the plug. You can't be afraid to say no. There is nothing more important than the care, safety, and well-being of others. And that does not just apply when producing a movie.

Michael and I developed a tight relationship by the end of the movie. He actually asked me to take over as producer of his TV show *Miami Vice*. I considered it; *Miami Vice* was a huge hit. Then I said no. Television had never been the dream. I'd always wanted to work in movies.

Me and Dino De Laurentiis—that was a different story. Dino was an industry legend, one of the great independent producers. He had a nose for talent and had invested his money in some of the best directors and projects. Dino was behind *Death Wish* with Charles Bronson, *Three Days of the Condor* with Robert Redford, and *The Shootist* with John Wayne. But he was a mercurial man, difficult to work with and unbothered by that. He'd been using an Italian crew on *Manhunter*. None of them spoke English, which meant all communication went through an interpreter. While telling them what was wanted and needed was difficult, actually getting them to do it was nearly impossible. And it had nothing to do with the language barrier. So I replaced them.

I was in my office one morning, and a man walks in and starts screaming at me. I can't understand what he's saying because the words are coming at me so loud and rapid-fire. It's Dino De Laurentiis. And he's shouting: "You fired Italian crew? Nobody fire Italian crew. Why you fire Italian crew?"

"Well," I say, calmly, "they wanted more money."

"Good, I am glad you fired Italian crew," he says. "Those bastards never work for me again."

AFTER JULIE AND I were married, we worked together on a movie called *Making Mr. Right*. The shoot was in Florida. Susan Seidelman was the director, and it starred John Malkovich as a reclusive scientist who builds an android—his doppelgänger—to go on a long-term space mission. Ann Magnuson played the public relations expert who falls in love with the robot.

But it's not the plot I remember so much as being in Miami with Julie, the fun we had on set, the epic cast and crew softball games, which bonded the group and lightened the weight of the work. I gave in to the mood, which was cool and relaxed. It was while working on *Making Mr. Right* that I bought my first Hawaiian shirt. Unless absolutely necessary, I've rarely worn any other kind of shirt since. Julie even got to do a stunt on this movie. She was the perfect height to play John Malkovich when his robotic head was detached from his body, so she got to be the headless Malkovich who walked into a couch and flipped over it.

In the period after that film, I found that I'd plateaued at middle management and decided I wanted my next job to be one that would put my name alongside the key players in the credits: "Produced by." That opportunity came in 1987 with a movie called *Campus Man*. It was not a tour de force, not Hitchcock or Wilder, Frankenheimer or Donner, but a flick for the youth market, a classic summer comedy. The plot? An entrepreneurial college student, finding himself short of the money he needs to finish school, decides to make and sell the first all-male sports calendar, with each month featuring another Speedo-wearing member of the Arizona State swim team.

When David Korda, an executive at RKO, asked if I wanted to work on the movie, I jumped at the chance. That's the game: You go from gig to gig, making your way as a kid makes his way across the monkey bars. Many of these early jobs were little more than the means to the next job.

David had hired Peggy Fowler to produce *Campus Man*. She'd been an assistant to a studio executive for years. This was her big chance. Because I had more experience, I was hired to help. We ended up sharing producing credit and responsibilities. This meant setting up a Hollywood office, revising the script, casting, and so on. This is when Julie and I began to make the move to LA.

Location scouting took us to the campus of ASU in the cactus land outside Phoenix. That was where we would shoot the movie.

We arrived in the middle of the spring semester. The quads were filled with kids playing Frisbee, kids in tank tops, shorts, bathing suits. I was not much older than many of the students; I could vanish into a fraternity house just as easily as I could head into a production meeting. Maybe it was the atmosphere that caused me to sharpen my practice of the practical joke on that movie. Or maybe it was because I had reached a position of responsibility, knew that a bit of levity on a set could bring the cast and crew together, and could get away with it. There can be a tedium to life on set—take after take, shot after shot—that can be alleviated through good humor and good fun.

Practical Joke, Part I: RKO had sent an executive named Marc Platt from LA to keep an eye on us. Marc has had a tremendous career since *Campus Man*, but he was then still a newcomer mostly interested in not making mistakes. On the very first day of filming, he paced the perimeter like security, seeing to it that everyone was doing their job. We had not even started filming, yet he'd appear at my side every thirty minutes to ask, "How's it going?"

I said, "Look, Marc. We won't really know how it's going until we see the first dailies."

On a film, the cast, key crew, and execs get together each night to watch the newest footage—that's the dailies.

"Okay, fine," said Marc. "Just let me know how it's going when we get the dailies."

Before we actually started filming, I asked the film's director, Ron Casden, and the director of photography, Francis Kenny, to do me a favor: Shoot the first few takes off-kilter, with just part of the actor's face in frame.

That afternoon, as soon as we wrapped, Marc was at my side: "How'd it go?"

I just gave Marc a look, and, before I could answer, he nervously said, "I know, I know, we will see for ourselves when we look at the dailies."

We had set up a screening room at the Holiday Inn, and we all gathered there after dinner. You could hear the check-in bell at the front desk. You could smell the chlorine from the pool. Marc was pacing in the back of the room. The first scene appeared. It was all askew, with the sky where the ground should be.

"What the hell!" Marc screamed. "What's going on?"

"Oh my gosh," I told him, "the lenses must've been set off-axis."

"What does that mean?" asked Marc, beginning to panic. Beads of sweat appeared on his face.

"It means today is ruined," I said. "We'll try again tomorrow."

He ran out of the room, cursing. It took a while to calm him down enough to return to the screening room, where he could see that the day had, in fact, gone perfectly. We all shared a good laugh.

Practical Joke, Part II: Marc plotted his revenge. I mean, there really is no better way to respond to a practical joke than with a practical joke. But I had loyalists in the cast, eyes and ears everywhere. In this case, it was the director, Ron, who told me that Marc was going to prank me by saying the studio has decided to fire him—Casden—and bring in a new director. Marc probably told Ron in case word of the joke got around and Ron believed he'd actually been fired.

Early the next morning, Marc pulled me aside, and, in a dour voice, said, "Jon, we need to meet in your office today right after wrap."

"Is it serious?"

"Yes. Very."

At the end of each week, we intentionally expose the film we are not going to use. I asked a production assistant to collect several reels of the exposed film and bring it to my office, where I set it up to look like the dailies. I was at my desk, surrounded by this film, when Marc came in to tell me that Ron had been fired.

I stood up and shouted, "But Ron Casden is a genius! If he goes, then all of this work"—I motioned to the reels of film—"means nothing."

At which point, I began opening and exposing the (already exposed) film.

Marc got me in a bear hug and pulled me to the ground. "It was a joke, Jon! It was just a stupid joke!"

Another laugh was shared.

MARC'S PRANK SERVED as a kind of prophecy. Ron did end up leaving the picture. Not because he was fired, but for personal reasons. I don't think he ever directed another movie. RKO, who was managing the project for Paramount, wanted to bring in another director to finish, but we were so close, with the last few shots all set up and everyone knowing what needed to be done. So that's what we did—we finished it. From there, we went straight to postproduction while RKO was still looking for a new director. I worked with the editor, Steve Polivka, who'd been on *The Muppet Movie*. James Newton Howard, who's gone on to have a great career as a film composer, wrote the music. *Campus Man* was one of his first scores. I supervised the post-production to the very end, and the film was in the can without the need for another director. This whole experience gave me a much better understanding of the process: what the editors need, the importance of music, and more.

Campus Man ends with shots of various divers—guys from the calendar—executing pikes and twists and gainers off a three-meter board. It's a sequence that plays beside the closing credits. In the last shot—most of the audience will have left by then—a diver who is different from the others steps out onto the board. He's not quite as muscle-toned as the rest, nor as lean. He is, in fact, a little plump. This is me. We had a pool in Riverdale where I'd experimented with every variety of a flip. It had been a long time, but it all came back when I went out on the board at ASU just for fun after a day of filming. The cameraman filmed those dives without telling me. In the end, I decided to use my backflip at the end because it was funny and because it served as a kind of signature. It was like Hitchcock catching a bus in *The Birds*.

MEANWHILE, JULIE AND I had made the move to Los Angeles. It happened in the most natural way. Since we were spending some time there while I worked on *Campus Man*, I suggested Julie look at houses, in case we ever decided to relocate. On her first day looking, Julie found a modest house on a beautiful block she loved in Sherman Oaks. She decided I should look at the house. I loved it, too, and we put a bid in, thinking we'd be unlikely to be approved for a mortgage. In one of those lucky surprises, we were approved. To have enough for the down payment, we both had to get several weeks' paychecks in advance. But that didn't bother us in the least—we were thrilled to be homeowners and to be building a life in LA. With almost no furniture but a bed, and no money to change that anytime soon, we celebrated our first Christmas with Chinese food on snack tables— and loved it. I figured this home would just be a starter house for us. We'd get a bigger place when the time was right. We ended up staying there for thirty-six years.

WORKING IN THE film business means working on many projects, in many stages of development, at the same time. This was certainly the case for me. Always hustling. Always looking for the next break.

The next green light. While there are too many projects to write about, ones that got made and ones that didn't, there are a few worth noting. Not for the celebrity or box office, but because I learned something important through both my wins and losses.

One of those projects was *Dead Poets Society*. Losing *Dead Poets* is, in fact, one of my few professional regrets.

Disney sent me the script, written by Tom Schulman, and I loved it right away. In our version, with Jeff Kanew as the director, the teacher has been diagnosed with cancer and returns to teach at his old boarding school to secure his legacy. For me, without this detail, which was later scrapped, the motivation of the main character resonates less.

We got as far as building a set at Berry College near Rome, Georgia, and casting most of the parts. We had Ethan Hawke as the charismatic kid and Jennifer Connelly as the love interest. She turned down *Mystic Pizza* to work with us—the role that made Julia Roberts a star. We wanted Robin Williams as the teacher, but he was committed to another project. We instead offered the part to Liam Neeson, who would have been great, and were set to go with that. Then one week away from starting principal photography, Jeffrey Katzenberg, who was then chairman of the Walt Disney Studios, had what he felt was a better idea. It's such "better" ideas that sometimes sink projects.

Jeffrey wanted Dustin Hoffman as the lead, and sent him the script. Hoffman said he liked it, and might do it, and dangled that *maybe* in front of the studio execs just long enough for the other actors to move on to other jobs. When Hoffman finally came back, it was with a rewritten script and a demand to star and direct. That was enough to shelve the project. When it reemerged with new producers in 1989, it had Peter Weir directing and Robin Williams, who'd become available, as the lead. Ethan Hawke was still involved. Alexandra Powers had become the love interest. The movie is very good—a critical and financial success. And the one that got away.

I learned something important during that process. You should do the right thing, but not for external praise or to please others. Doing the right thing is, in and of itself, the right thing—always. That may sound obvious, but it is not always easy. Jeff Kanew, coproducer Steven Haft, and I did everything we possibly could for the studio and the film. Strong screenplay. Great director. Amazing cast. I have no regrets, because our choices were made for the right reasons—the excellence of the movie.

I was just beginning as a producer at that point. Few people had seen any of my pictures. No one knew who I was. In meetings, when asked to introduce myself and share a few of my credits, I'd say, "Have you seen *Top Gun*?" And the other person would say, "Yeah! I saw *Top Gun*!" And I'd say, "Well, I didn't do that one, but wasn't it great!"

In other words, though at this point in my career I tried to limit myself to good projects, I often found myself taking whatever was offered. This probably turned out to be a good thing. The variety of projects and problems I faced as a result was ideal training. A good example is *Honey, I Shrunk the Kids*, which Disney offered as *Dead Poets* was falling apart. It was then being called *Teenie Weenies*. You know the plot: A mad scientist of a father (Rick Moranis), experimenting with a new invention, accidentally shrinks his kids to the size of little green army men, forcing them to navigate a wilderness of shag carpet, dangerous dogs, and monstrous insects.

I was fascinated by the special effects being used to make the movie. Though I didn't realize it at the time, *Honey, I Shrunk the Kids* was preparing me for *Avatar*. In both pictures, we had to create an alien world and populate it with real actors. The guru behind the effects was Tom Smith. He was the executive producer of *Honey, I Shrunk the Kids*, and it was his innovations at Industrial Light & Magic (ILM) that laid the groundwork for everything I would do with James Cameron. I was coproducer on the movie.

Tom had written a book called *Industrial Light & Magic: The Art of Special Effects*. I read it on the flight to the set in Mexico City. I did this because I genuinely wanted to learn more about the topic and also because I wanted to make a good impression on Tom, who was said to be tough. I've found that to be the case with many special effects people. They have no patience for the standard Hollywood small talk. Tom scowled when I told him I'd read his book.

"Please don't," he said. "Everyone says they read it, but no one really has."

"I suggest you look at page 212," I told him. "You've got a typo in the second paragraph."

Tom grinned as he checked. He kept a copy on his desk. Finding the typo, he laughed and said, "Son of a bitch!"

The lesson?

Only say you've done the reading when you've actually done the reading. This applies to your homework as well, and I don't mean that in academic terms. Be prepared. Thoroughly and thoughtfully.

If I haven't done the reading or have done it and still don't understand the big idea, I have no problem saying so. You should always be willing to stop a conversation and say, "Excuse me, can you please explain that?" I do it all the time. If someone uses a word I don't know, I'm not embarrassed to ask for a definition. I am learning all the time from those around me. I'm lucky to be able to say that.

And so, right from the start Tom knew I was not going to bullshit him. It was the basis of what turned out to be a fantastic relationship. By the end of the project, he had taught me pretty much everything a layperson can know about special effects. *Honey, I Shrunk the Kids* opened my eyes to the power of that world.

Chapter 3

L ife is like a movie. There are highs and lows, moments of action and moments of rest, scenes set to music and scenes that play in silence, times when it seems as if nothing is happening and nothing ever will. Then something does. Then something else. Moments that feel endless while you're in them are the blink of an eye in retrospect. Focus shifts. What had been foreground becomes background. What had been distant comes close.

In fact, the projects I worked on in those next few years exist in my memory less as professional achievements than as markers, ways to date the events that truly mattered—the birth of our two sons.

Movies had been my key driver for most of my twenties— everything else was periphery. But that all changed at the end of *Campus Man*. Why *Campus Man*? Because as we neared the completion of postproduction, we found out Julie was pregnant. Since I was about to start work on *Honey, I Shrunk the Kids* in Mexico, I had it written into my contract that I would fly back to LA as soon as Julie went into labor or a delivery date was set. (As luck would have it, Julie delivered a week late, and we had already wrapped.)

Julie's parents came to LA toward the end of her pregnancy, which was a tremendous help to her and great relief to me while I was on location. These were people who did not like to stray from Lindenhurst. They seemed wildly out of place in California. Julie was funny about it. She made them T-shirts that said "If lost, return to . . ." and put our address on Longridge Avenue.

Boy or girl?

We decided not to find out beforehand. You have to leave some mystery for the delivery room. Since we didn't want to refer to the baby as "it," we began speaking of "shim"—a combination of *she* and *him*. We knew we wanted the baby's name to start with a *J*, and to work for either a boy or a girl. So the name Jamie was perfectly suited. We gave him the middle initial *S* for, you guessed it, Shim. To this day, when Jamie walks into a room, I think, *Shim!*

Friends had decided to throw Julie a baby shower. She was almost eight months pregnant at that point and really starting to look it. I was still on location in Mexico working on *Honey, I Shrunk the Kids* but decided to fly back to surprise her at the shower. When I came in, she was so shocked that she did a double take, stepped back, and flipped backward over a couch, almost like she did in *Making Mr. Right*, but this time it was not a stunt. I have that on film. It was hilarious once we knew Julie was okay.

Why do I mention it?

Because when Julie went in for a checkup a few weeks before delivering Jamie, the doctor told us the baby was breech, feet first, which would complicate the delivery. Luckily the doctor was able to use his hands to put pressure on Julie's abdomen to rotate the baby, so that when he was delivered, he came out headfirst. But we always smiled at the idea that perhaps it was that backflip over the sofa that put him upside down in the first place.

We had lived in Sherman Oaks for about a year by that point. We were happy in our house and were making it our own bit by bit, but it still didn't feel truly like home. It would take the children to do that.

As soon as we brought Jamie home, I realized what had been missing from the house. With Jamie in his crib and Julie standing over him, I was overwhelmed by a feeling of completeness.

SOON THEREAFTER, I found myself heading up Coldwater Canyon to meet with Warren Beatty.

For the movie studio, Beatty could seem impossible. He spent years on what they felt should have taken months. He went over budget, shot and reshot. But for me, this meeting was a dream. Warren Beatty meant *Bonnie and Clyde, Shampoo, Heaven Can Wait, Reds.* Warren Beatty was one of the greatest actors and filmmakers alive.

Warren was meeting candidates to produce his next movie. Disney sent me as one option among several. I just hoped to make a good impression. The house was on top of a hill off Mulholland Drive. The sun was glinting off every surface when I arrived. The city stretched below.

Warren came out to meet me. He had thick, tousled hair and a million-watt smile. We shook hands and sat in the kitchen. We talked for hours. It can happen like that sometimes—an immediate connection. He told me about his new project; he was adapting the classic Depression-era comic strip detective Dick Tracy for the big screen. The setting would be half the story: the dark streets of the metropolis, lowlife crooks and politicos, gangsters, torpedoes, and bums.

He was already thinking about colors, the palette of the movie. He'd recruited the widely admired Italian cinematographer Vittorio Storaro to shoot it. Vittorio had come with a big idea, a sort of philosophy of color. Dick Tracy would be seen only in yellow and red because yellow and red mean heroism. The streets and the villains of the city would be purple and emerald, as that would show the world as confusing and dark.

I believe I'm a creative executive. I'm not there just to balance the books. I'm there for the artistry, too. I figure out what can be done to help fulfill the director's vision. A producer with an imagination, who can see the big picture and help build it, adds value—that's what I want to do for a movie. All this talk—colors, concepts, schemes—thrilled me. I really wanted this job. I was in a mood of excited anticipation. That's what's great about the interval between projects. There's nothing to do but dream about what comes next. But people started congratulating me as soon as I got back to the studio.

"What for?"

"You're working on the new Warren Beatty movie."

A few minutes after I left the house on Mulholland Drive, Warren had called the studio head, Jeffrey Katzenberg, to say he wanted me on *Dick Tracy*.

Warren asked what credit I wanted. He was producing, so it would have to be something else. I surprised him by asking to be the coproducer. He thought I'd go for executive producer, but coproducer sounded better. That way, whenever Warren introduced me, it sounded like I was his partner.

We met for hours every day. He loved to talk and also loved to listen. He had a way of focusing his attention that was deeply gratifying. He's a sponge—that's a big part of his brilliance. He takes in and retains everything. His intellect functions as a filter, admitting what he can use, rejecting what he can't. And he has true confidence in himself, in his work and ideas—that's what lets him accept advice. He has no problem changing course when convinced another idea is better than his own. It never challenges his ego.

One day, Warren asked what I thought was a tough question. "What is your best attribute as a producer, Jon?"

I thought about it and said, "That I give one hundred and ten percent?"

Warren said, "No, try again."

"That I'm the first one on the set and the last one to leave?"

"No, it's the fact that you dream about this project every night," he said. "I know this because you come in with ideas each day and ways to implement those ideas."

It was true. I did dream about *Dick Tracy*, as I later dreamt about *Titanic* and *Avatar*. The problem your waking brain cannot solve can be fixed by your subconscious at night. I believe that.

Casting *Dick Tracy* was fun. Just think of the names of all the characters! Warren would play Dick Tracy. But from there, we added Al Pacino as Big Boy, Dustin Hoffman as Mumbles, Paul Sorvino as Lips Manlis, Mandy Patinkin as 88 Keys, and James Caan played Spuds Spaldoni.

Warren seemingly called every starlet in Hollywood to audition for the part of Breathless Mahoney. One after another they came: Michelle Pfeiffer, Kathleen Turner, Kim Basinger, Sharon Stone, Sheena Easton. He even auditioned Princess Stéphanie, the youngest child of Prince Rainier III of Monaco and Grace Kelly. In the end, he cast Madonna, then at the height of her fame.

One day, we were at Western Costume looking for the right somewhat-revealing outfit for Breathless, and Warren called me into the dressing room for an opinion. Madonna was sitting there in a completely sheer outfit. She might as well have been nude! When I averted my eyes, she said something like, *It's okay, Jon. You can look.* I don't have to tell you what shade of red I turned. I confirmed the outfit definitely went too far, and we agreed to dial it back. After all, we were aiming for a PG rating.

Production began, and Warren and Madonna were soon dating. She decided to throw a surprise party for his birthday. We set up a ruse where it seemed like just the four of us—Madonna, Warren, Julie, and I—were going to have dinner at Madonna's home. Julie and I picked up Warren and drove to Madonna's. We knocked on her door. In her foyer, many of Hollywood's A-list were waiting to yell "Surprise!" Dustin was there. So were Jack Nicholson, Tom Cruise, and many others. At public events, that kind of fame is expected, but at such an intimate party it blew me away.

Madonna's backup singers came to sing for Warren. They stood around a piano belting out "Summertime." Joining with them was Julie Landau...and she sounded as good as the pros! Incredible. Watching her singing with Madonna's crew that night—that was one for the memory books.

Now and then, Warren tested me, but always with good intentions. We still needed to cast some of the tangential roles. These were minor characters known only for a single physical characteristic. You know, comic book characters. If you get them right, you create a world. If you get them wrong, it all falls apart. We were having trouble finding someone to play Little Face Finny, a tough hood who reprimands other mob members when they screw up. He had a big head and a tiny face in the comic strip, hence the name. We looked and looked. Nobody. Nothing. Then, one day, while we were having lunch at a sushi place near the office, Warren leaned over to me and whispered, "Look at that man eating over there. He has the smallest face I've ever seen."

As we got up to leave, Warren said: "You say you're a good producer? Okay. Get that man to be in our movie. Then I'll *know* you're a good producer."

I took a deep breath and went over. I asked the man with the little face—he was eating alone—if we could talk. This put me right back in my sweet spot of talking with strangers and making connections. He invited me to sit down. He turned out to be a studio executive who sometimes acted named Lawrence Steven Meyers. When I offered him the role, he jumped at it.

All those months of preparation resulted in a brisk shoot. My job was to keep things running and be on the lookout for big problems—creative issues—that Warren, absorbed in the vital details of realizing his vision, might otherwise miss. For example, to make the actors look like comic strip characters, we relied heavily on prosthetics. I'd hired the makeup artists we used on *F/X*. They built fake chins, fake foreheads, fake noses, and so on. These had to be lit a certain way or they'd look crude. But Vittorio Storaro, though a brilliant cinematographer, had no experience with this kind of task. In some of the dailies, the actors seemed silly. Warren was shocked when I told him this. Vittorio was a legend—it was blasphemy to critique his lighting. But Warren never watched the dailies, so he didn't really know. When he finally looked, he agreed. It presented Warren with a problem. He wanted to fix the lighting without insulting Vittorio. I learned an important lesson in Warren's handling of the delicate matter.

Warren invited a group of people to watch the dailies, including Vittorio, his assistant, and me. He asked for a particular scene. It featured a character named Flattop, who didn't look good. Warren had asked me in advance to express my doubts about the lighting. As soon as I was done talking, Warren scolded me: "Jon! Don't you understand that Vittorio has the toughest job on the movie? How can you question him?"

"No, no, wait a second," said Vittorio. "Maybe Jon is right. Maybe I can light it differently."

"All right, Vittorio," said Warren. "If that's what you want to do."

Warren actually made Vittorio think that adjusting the lighting was his own idea—brilliant.

As I've said, Vittorio made bold use of the palette in the movie. It was all primary colors. This worked well for the interiors, which looked like the panels of a Sunday newspaper comic, but not so well for the exteriors, the New York–style brownstones that formed our backdrop. The stoops and the alleys looked like a candy-colored fever dream. It took you right out of comic-land.

When I told Warren, he said, "Talk to Dick Sylbert." He was the production designer. He ended up painting all the exteriors dark blue, changing our city into Tracyville. That's what I mean by keeping my eye on the big picture. With everyone so focused on their own piece of the puzzle, you can sometimes miss the overall goal. That's the job of a creative producer.

Dealing with the lighting and the sets is easy. Dealing with people— that can be tough. About two weeks into production, I realized Sean Young, who had been cast as Tess Trueheart, wasn't working. As the character's name suggests, Tess is supposed to be virtuous and chaste, to embody the purity of womanhood, to be a port in the storm. She is the cosmic balance to Breathless Mahoney, who is all temptation. Therefore Sean Young had to play the flip side to Madonna. But Sean, who was fantastic in *Blade Runner* and *No Way Out*, was too alluring for the assignment. On-screen, she was just as sexy as Madonna. We were in danger of having two Breathless Mahoneys.

Where was Dick Tracy going to find refuge?

It was a real problem.

Warren was skeptical when I expressed my concerns. Sean was so great in each individual scene, it was hard to see that her overall portrayal—not just what she was doing, but how she was doing it, how she was—was throwing the story off-balance. When I finally got him to watch the dailies with this in mind, he saw it right away. This was not a matter of coaching or character refinement. We needed a different actress. I offered to explain the situation to Sean, but Warren insisted on talking to her himself. Being let go in the middle of a picture is awful. But Warren knew how to handle it, how to make it so Sean could leave with her head held high.

Jack Nicholson—one of Warren's best friends—was around all the time. He always referred to Warren as "the pro." As in, "When is 'the pro' getting here?" Or, "Can you get a message to 'the pro'?" At first, I figured this was about Warren's skill as an actor, director, and producer. Only later did I realize Jack was referring to Warren's ability to bring out the best in people, to get them to do what they might otherwise consider unpleasant or impossible. That's how he handled the Sean Young situation. Like a pro.

We cast Glenne Headly as Tess Trueheart. If you know Glenne Headly, it's probably from *Dirty Rotten Scoundrels* or *Mr. Holland's Opus*. Whereas Sean Young was dark, mysterious, and sexy on-screen, Glenne Headly was soft and warm, the girl next door. The picture took off as soon as we reshot the Tess Trueheart scenes with Glenne. All of a sudden, the pieces fell into place and the picture came together.

Dick Tracy was released on June 15, 1990. Critical response was solid; the grosses were better. The movie took in nearly $20 million on its opening weekend and broke all kinds of Disney records. And yet, because the movie cost nearly $100 million to make, Disney, which projected it to do as well as Tim Burton's *Batman*, was disappointed. For me, it was a lesson in the dangers of big-budget production. The more the studio pays, the more they want and need. That's the reality of the system. Every big picture is supposed to break records. For this reason, a hit can seem like a flop in the executive suite, a success but also a failure. This is something I'd remember when I worked on *Titanic* and *Avatar*. Big rewards are achieved via big risks, and big risks court disaster. It's the studio's money. And you'd better not lose it.

An amazing thing happened as we were wrapping *Dick Tracy*. Warren offered me a full-time job running his production company. I would find properties—stories, screenplays—secure rights, pitch studios, and produce pictures. It was an immensely flattering offer, but I knew I couldn't accept it. This was not about Warren. I loved working with Warren. It was about me. I wasn't even thirty years old, still at the start of my career. There was so much I wanted to experience. I wanted to work on every kind of picture and get to know every aspect of the movie business. If I took a job with Warren, I would work on maybe one movie every four years. And they'd all be Warren Beatty movies; wonderful as they'd be, it seemed limiting. I was too much in the mood for *everything*. So I turned down the offer and continued on my freelance way. Excited to see where the adventure would lead next.

✧ ✧ ✧ ✧

JULIE AND I started thinking it might be time for another child. We thought, *Wouldn't it be nice to have a girl this time around?* We had heard about a procedure called sperm spinning. I won't go into the details; it's enough to tell you they required a sample, which they would "spin" to increase the odds of the desired gender, in our case a girl. If it sounds like a story from a weird Hollywood movie, I guess it was. But that's how determined we were to control the outcome. I didn't yet know, as I've since learned—sometimes joyfully, sometimes painfully—that all the important things in life are, in fact, beyond your control.

My sperm samples—there'd been two, each retrieved in the dark with Julie in the privacy of our bedroom—had proved inadequate. The collection or transportation . . . whatever it was, I was doing it wrong. They said I'd have to give my sample in person. That's how I ended up in the back room of a medical office with a dirty magazine in front of me and my pants around my knees. I was distracted. The task seemed impossible, but I kept trying anyway. Determined. And suddenly, finally, I felt the hint of something. All at once it felt as if the earth began to move.

Then, from outside my little cubicle, I heard someone shout, "Earthquake!" So, the earth had *actually* begun to move, and I was in the exact wrong position for a natural disaster. I pulled up my pants and ran out, totally shaken. All the nurses were outside my room giggling and told me to return to the cubicle and get back to work. But the interruption had snapped me out of this cockeyed dream. And just like that, I realized what I really had known all along: I didn't care if our baby was a boy or a girl. I just wanted us to have another child. All to say, our beautiful son Jodie was born nine months later. His middle initial is *E* for "Earthquake."

I think that Julie and I had always known that two would be our limit. With Jodie, our family was complete.

The moment I put Jodie in his crib was monumental, as was the moment I moved Jamie into his "big boy" room down the hall. To me, it was beautiful and a little bit heartbreaking. Just like that, it hit me— that's life. With each day, these two amazing boys would change and grow, until one day they would go out on their own. I knew my theme all at once, even if the storyline had yet to unfold.

Having two kids is different than having one. It's the difference between juggling two balls and juggling one, which isn't even juggling. I became aware of my responsibilities as role model, provider, and protector. That might explain my extreme reaction to the Northridge earthquake, which struck at four thirty a.m. on January 17, 1994, almost two years after Jodie was born. The quake, centered in the San Fernando Valley where we lived, registered at 6.7 on the Richter scale. Having been through smaller quakes, it was immediately clear to me that this was different. I remember being awoken. It was still dark out but there were flashes of light, explosions. It turns out that transformers were blowing up all over town. Everything in our house was falling, shattering. We heard none of it because the earthquake itself was so loud. Instinct kicked in, and we ran for the boys. Amazingly, Jodie was still asleep. Jamie was sitting bolt upright in bed when I got to him. His eyes were wide and his voice was pinched. "What's happening?" he asked. I had no answer because I hardly understood it myself. We brought them back to our bedroom to ride out the quake there. The walls of the house shook and shook. Parts of the roof caved. In some areas of LA, the ground rose more than two feet. Rifts and gulches appeared, glimpses of the abyss. There were over three thousand aftershocks. The worst of it was over in minutes, but those minutes felt like hours.

I remember walking through the house in the weird gray aftermath. It was a disaster. The fridge had moved across the kitchen. There were cracks in the walls, broken glass all over the floor. I was different after the earthquake, consumed by my need to protect my family. Realizing I had no control changed me in a profound way. I'd been shook, and stayed shook knowing how tenuous life could be and how little I could do to stop anything bad from happening to Julie and the boys.

Even after the house was fixed, I had trouble sleeping there. I was too anxious. This house, which I'd loved, now felt dangerous. This went on for months. It was only with the help of Julie and a therapist that I was able to comfortably and consistently sleep back at home.

Chapter 4

I decided I needed a regular gig, steady work that would keep me closer to home. It was time to shift from freelance work to a full-time job. Figuring out what that looked like was my next problem to solve. That meant having a lot of conversations with a lot of people.

I had an awkward early meeting with a production exec at 20th Century Fox. She called me in for an interview as a line producer. It was strange; here was someone roughly my age who'd already worked on fifty-six movies in-house at the studio. As an independent, I could keep going as I'd been going until I was ninety and still never get close to fifty-six movies.

Looking over my CV, she asked, "How did you handle Michael Mann?"

"With a sense of humor," I said.

"No, I mean it," she said. "How did you handle him?"

I stared at her.

"First, I don't 'handle' a director," I said, "especially a great director like Michael Mann. I am his partner, not his parent. I help him realize his vision in a way the studio can afford. Second, even if I did 'handle' him, which I didn't, I wouldn't go around telling stories about it."

A month later, after many meetings at many production companies and studios, I became her boss.

I'M NOT EXACTLY sure who recommended me for that job. A town like Hollywood, a one-industry town, is like that. It might take a while, but if you do good work, people notice. Reputation is all you have, and you build it picture by picture.

It was Tom Jacobson who called me in for an initial meeting. He was the president of worldwide production at 20th Century Fox. He'd produced two John Hughes classics, *Ferris Bueller's Day Off* and *Uncle Buck*, and would go on to oversee huge franchises: *Die Hard*, *Home Alone*, *Speed*. Fox was looking for someone to take over physical production—a sort of eye in the sky to keep watch on every picture shooting or about to shoot.

That meeting went well, and a week or so later, I found myself in a second meeting, this time with Tom Jacobson and his bosses, Roger Birnbaum, the president of production at Fox, and Joe Roth, the chairman. The only person above them was Rupert Murdoch.

Joe Roth—always referred to by his full name—had done so well with directing and producing that Rupert made him head of the movie studio.

So what did he need from me?

Well, as good as business had been at Fox, there was a kink in their internal process. The bosses were green-lighting more pictures than were getting made. There was some sort of disconnect between the office in LA, where the money was handled and the decisions made, and the production offices and sets, where the actual filming was happening. My task would be to untangle the knots, ramp up production, and bring Fox back to the top of this very competitive industry.

"You're awfully young for this job," Roger said at the end of my second interview for the job.

I said, "Roger, you know you're not allowed to ask about my age."

This was the era of memos from legal—don't ask about this or that, pregnancy status, marital status, etc. I was just goofing with him. Roger was, in fact, making a valid point. I was probably too young for the job. But, as I've said, I tend to say yes and figure out the rest later. Besides, there are some jobs you can only learn how to do by doing them.

Roger blushed at my answer—he did not know me well enough to know I was joking—then said, "Well, what I really meant was, are you married?"

"You're not allowed to ask about that either," I said, "but yes, I am married, and I am only twenty-eight turning twenty-nine, and I think I'm ready to tackle this job."

I got the offer a few days later: senior vice president of physical production at 20th Century Fox.

People ask, "Why did you take a studio job?"

What they mean is, Why not one at an independent and creative production company? Why become a "suit"?

It seemed to go against the way I had navigated my career, which was as a maverick, a freewheeler, a problem-solver in a Hawaiian shirt. The answer is simple. I wanted to learn the business from the inside. We are in a studio-driven industry, and I wanted to see how it worked from the other side. I wanted to learn the business from the studio's perspective, from the green-lighting of a picture to the production oversight to distribution and marketing.

I had three bosses at Fox: Peter Chernin, who was the chief operating officer of the film group; Joe Roth, the chairman of the company; and Rupert Murdoch. My brief was to ramp up production. To do that, I had to create a new system. Fox had big projects in production when I arrived, but many were a bit of a mess. Over budget, behind schedule, and so on. I addressed this by getting more involved than most were used to, holding line producers accountable, being in communication with directors. Most directors would like to take the studio's money, vanish, then reappear a year later with a movie. Before that, you'd hear from them only when they ran out of cash. I knew that needed to change.

I imparted a new philosophy on the physical production department. I explained it this way: There's no such thing as a separation between physical and creative—production is production. Over time, a wall had been erected between the creative and physical aspects of production. It needed to be torn down. What you're doing on one side impacts everything that happens on the other side.

I started by changing the routine, the daily way of managing production. Sometimes change, in itself—the sense that a new wind is blowing—is enough to reinvigorate people caught in a rut. Even before my first day at Fox, I showed up at an audience advance screening of one of the studio's big new movies. Some execs were shocked. That's just not how they'd done business in the past; everything had been compartmentalized, and advance screenings stood on the other side of the wall from where I, in my new role, would stand.

"What are you doing here?" That was the question.

"If we need to fix problems raised by the audience," I explained, "then we need to include all members of the team, including those involved in physical production. Whether it's editing, remixing, reshooting, or audience screenings—we all need to be part of it."

This was a new way of doing business, but the execs began to embrace it when it became clear our presence added value. Rather than taking away their autonomy, we brought new perspective, different ways to solve familiar problems.

To achieve my goals, I had to build a sense of teamwork. Some people were more worried about controlling their fiefdoms than making movies. Some executives had lost sight of the goal, the bigger picture—they had confused the progress of their careers with that of the studio. "Don't forget why we're in this business," I encouraged. "We're here to make movies—and the best ones possible!"

Fox held a corporate retreat in Palm Springs a few weeks before I was scheduled to come aboard. I went, even though I wasn't technically part of the staff yet. That's where I first met the department staff. It was a cold beginning. I felt like an interloper. Elliot Lurie, who was the head of the music department, was the only person who made me feel genuinely welcomed.

Of course, people had every reason to be wary. When a new boss takes over, they usually start by cleaning house and installing their own team. You need a brain trust, a core group you can rely on. You also need to identify who among the existing staff is willing to give you a chance, who will buy in and support the new program. Find and retain those people, and you will have champions among the old guard. Ask them for help. If you put your trust and fate in their hands, they will have an interest in making you a success. You don't earn trust by demanding it, but by offering it. Show trust, and you'll usually get trust in return. Just as important: Identify the malcontents, those who resent your presence, and if they cannot get on board, cut them loose swiftly.

In hiring, I looked for people who shared my philosophy and commitment to tearing down the fences. The idea was to assign each of these people a slate of movies in the Fox pipeline. I reached out to Kim Cooper, whom I'd worked with on *Campus Man*. She'd always been an incredible problem-solver. I lured her away from RKO—that was one of my first moves. She joined Fox in 1990 and stayed until 2018. Ultimately, she served as a studio rep as we began production on the Avatar sequels.

That sort of longevity is the definition of a successful hire. It means I brought someone to Fox who did not merely help me rebuild a department but added value well beyond my tenure and her original tasks. I'm as proud of that hire as I am of anything. Ditto the producer Fred Baron, another early hire. He worked at Fox for over thirty years and went on to become their executive vice president of feature production.

Just as important was finding the right person to head post-production. This turned out to be Ted Gagliano, who'd been a junior executive at Paramount. Ted went on decades later to become president of feature postproduction at 20th Century Fox.

With a team in place, I began making changes bit by bit, a few more each day. The point was not to create a violent rupture but to remake the environment so gradually that one day, while sitting in your same old office, you'd suddenly realize you are working somewhere new.

Some of the changes were mundane, which did not make them less important. In a company, and life for that matter, it's the little things that form the bedrock. At Fox, the computer system is an example. The entire studio was using IBM machines when I arrived. I told them that our teams needed to switch to Mac. If you looked at where the industry was heading, it was Apple—the Mac just offered more creative tools. It took a lot of explaining, demonstrating, and a bit of arm-twisting. Getting people to make that change was not easy. That switch is not the sort of thing that appears in a corporate history, but it was crucial in two respects: One, it put us on a better system. Two, it demonstrated that new, forward-thinking leadership was in charge. And it wasn't just my department of physical production. We brought other divisions along, especially postproduction. Putting everyone on the same system was another way of tearing down the wall and making it clear that we were all on the same team.

Off-site gatherings and company retreats, which many dismiss as a boondoggle, played a critical role in my big team-building project. I knew the power of getting our people out of the office, out of their regular lives, and into a new environment, where they could form bonds across the company.

Where do you get fresh ideas?

It's often the chance elevator encounter or lunch meeting between people in different units, people who, had it not been for a retreat, would never have met each other. This was part of building an ecosystem within Fox, an environment of fluid cross-department communication, the sort that leads to breakthroughs and growth.

Our white-water rafting trips were legendary. No conference centers or hotel meeting rooms for us—let's put people on a boat in the rapids. Nothing creates a bond like facing thrills and a bit of danger together.

One afternoon, soon after I arrived at Fox, Peter Chernin called me and said, "Jon, we've got a meeting on Wednesday morning. Can you be there?"

I said, "No, I can't."

He said, "What about Fred Baron? Can you send him in your place?"

Again: Nope.

He asked for this one and that one.

Nope. Nope. Nope.

Exasperated, he finally asked, "What the hell's going on?"

I told him that on Wednesday the entire department would be rafting on the Kern River.

He got it, and the conversation ended there.

We spent hours on the water. By the end of the day, many people had tapped out. The rapids had gotten bigger and bigger, leaving just the foolhardy on that last ride. Ted Gagliano had brought along a video camera and was filming from a hill above the final bend, where the river got rough. As we took that big turn, several people got dumped into the drink. The rest of us fought like crazy, and successfully, to get them back into the rafts. The bus had a video player, and we watched the footage all the way back to the city. It was our own private action movie. People hooted and cheered. Bonds were forged. Trust was developed. That's team building.

Even in a business like film, which sounds exciting, life falls into patterns and routines, which can become the sort of grind that turns up in the product. People who are having fun, who are engaged and connected, do better work. So that was a goal—infuse life at the office with some spontaneity and some good old-fashioned fun. We're not in the semiconductor trade. We make movies!

One day, I announced a surprise twenty-four-hour trip to Las Vegas. I said, "The bus is waiting outside." We left the lot in the afternoon, got to Vegas at dusk, spent all night at the tables, had breakfast together at dawn—some counting their winnings, some lamenting their losses—got back on the bus, and were back in the office for lunch.

Real change came as a result of this new atmosphere and the new practices implemented, ideas that affected the output and the company. Word spread. At one of Fox's corporate retreats, a woman from accounting complained that it was hard for her to work extra hours with kids at home. She said she wished Fox offered childcare, not just for mothers but for all parents. I raised her concerns to Rupert Murdoch. A few days later, a memo came from on high: Funds were being allocated for the creation of a new childcare program. Rupert, always the laser-focused businessman, realized that an employee who does not have to rush home to meet a school bus or rely on childcare elsewhere will spend more focused time on the job.

One of my favorite ways to enliven the workplace is celebrating Halloween. We made a big deal of Halloween every year. Costume wearing was strongly encouraged. Candy, treats, and a few tricks were always in good supply. One year, I had the makeup/prosthetic people turn me into a caveman—makeup, costume, club, and all. I met with Barry Diller, who served as chairman and CEO of Fox between 1984 and 1992, in that getup, setting my club down on the table to shake his hand—and the result was one of the best discussions we had ever had.

We tried to lighten up the mood at budget and sales meetings, too. One year, Peter Chernin, head of 20th Century Fox filmed entertainment, who was tasked with presenting a *State of the Company* report for Fox executives, asked if I could create a video to open the meeting as well as a product reel showcasing our upcoming slate of films. Challenge accepted. The meeting was being held town-hall style on stage sixteen on the Fox lot. We waited for everyone to get seated, then let several minutes go by with nothing happening onstage. Waiting for Peter onstage was Bill Mechanic.

Bill's cell phone rings. He picks it up. It's Peter's assistant, Sandi. Her voice plays over the big speakers. She says, "I'm so sorry, Bill, but Peter's running late. He'd liked to be video conferenced in."

And there is Peter, on a giant screen that fills the stage. He is in a black Jaguar chasing the bus from the movie *Speed*. He says, "Hello, Bill. I am really sorry, I tried this carpool thing, and I left my speech on the bus. I'm trying to catch up with the bus right now." The next frame cuts to the speech sitting on a seat on the bus next to a bouncing cup of coffee. We see Peter drive alongside the bus and call for it to stop. It's now clear we are looking at a spoof of the movie *Speed*, which had been our biggest hit the previous summer. In *Speed*, a passenger in the Jaguar holds up a sign that says BOMB ON BUS. In our version, the sign says SPEECH ON BUS. Like Keanu Reeves in the movie, Peter jumps from his vehicle onto the bus, where he pulls out a business card instead of a police badge, and shouts, "Peter Chernin, chairman, 20th Century Fox!" He then directs the driver: "Go left! Go right! Turn!" The bus smashes through a closed gate and onto the Fox lot. It turns toward stage sixteen, where we are all watching the film. Suddenly, the actual bus bursts through the stage door and screeches to a halt on the stage. Then, live, Peter runs out of the bus with the speech in hand. Before the assembled have even stopped cheering, a new film comes on—the product reel. It shows a cleaning lady at work in Peter's outer office. A book falls. She opens it, and the pages come to life, each one showing a trailer for an upcoming film on the Fox calendar. The cleaner rushes to the inner office. Peter is in his chair, turned away. The cleaner tells him how much she loves the movies. The chair turns. It's not Peter, but Keanu Reeves! He says, "If Peter can do my job, I can do his."

I made a lot of these short films during my tenure at Fox. One of my favorites was the one I made when Fox was going to Lucasfilm to try to sell them on distributing the upcoming Star Wars prequels. I came up with the idea of doing *Episode VII: The Distribution Wars*, a short film about the battle for the rights of the next trilogy. I utilized footage from the Star Wars films and inserted Tom Sherak, head of distribution at Fox, in a blond wig to make him look like Luke Skywalker. Howard Roffman, head of licensing at Lucasfilm, knew we were doing this. I'd shared our script with him, and he'd given us the okay. It was still nerve-racking when the time came for our presentation to George Lucas up at his Skywalker Ranch in Marin County, California. But we went for it. Up on the big screen came our spoof. One of the most flattering things that I've had happen to me is that after we presented it, George asked me for a copy to keep in his Star Wars archives.

I absolutely cannot take any credit for it, but eventually Fox did win the rights to distribute the next trilogy.

THE FACT THAT I was unconventional occasionally got me in trouble. As hard as I might have been on people who worked for me, I think it was harder to be my boss than my employee. I did not care very much about precedents or traditions. If the rules were unfair, I changed them or ignored them when they interfered with the greater goal or good. One time, I received a terse note from Bill Mechanic scolding me for missing a sexual harassment prevention seminar. The exchange went something like this:

"That you did not see fit to attend one of these sessions is just not acceptable. Do not let this happen again."

The curtness didn't sit well with me.

"Bill, I actually missed two of those meetings," I wrote back. "The first because I was on location with Jim dealing with *True Lies*. The second because it was on the day my grandmother passed away, and I feel my first responsibility is to my family, so I was with them. Should a similar thing happen again, I will make the same decision."

Bill responded: "I frankly don't think the attitude you are displaying here is one you should be displaying."

No condolences, nothing. I went into Peter Chernin's office and quit. Just like that. "I don't want to work for a person whose first words aren't condolences," I told him.

Peter talked me off the ledge.

He said, "Let me figure it out with Bill."

He came back the next day to say he'd talked to Bill.

I asked what happened.

"Bill has learned that you and he are going to disagree on a lot of things," Peter told me. "And this is just going to have to be one of them."

WE NEVER WANTED our people to forget the object of all our effort: the movies themselves. With this in mind, whenever a big new feature was released—ours or another studio's—I'd buy a hundred tickets for opening day, and we'd all play hooky at three p.m. and go see it with a real crowd at the Cineplex in Century City or the Avco in Westwood. This is how we'd remind ourselves that we were making pictures for this audience—the people who can't wait to see and feel the special magic that happens in a movie theater on opening day.

My life at Fox could be written as a series of short stories, each built around one of the colorful characters I encountered along the way.

There was Joel Silver. You had to be more careful with him, because Joel had real talent. A brilliant producer, he'd made *48 Hrs.*, *Lethal Weapon*, *Road House*, and *Die Hard* before I arrived. But he was impossible—famously tantrum-prone and rebelliously independent. At times, it actually seemed he would betray his own interests to stick it to the studio. No compromise, no communication—none of it. He took the money, then vanished, leaving you to pray for his return. The same qualities that made him a great producer—perfectionism, arrogance, bravado—made him a challenging partner.

Joel had two troubled projects going at the studio, *The Adventures of Ford Fairlane* and *Die Hard 2*, when I got involved.

A movie shoot is scheduled and budgeted for a certain number of days. Each hour over that schedule results in overtime fees, the bane of a studio balance sheet. Additional days means paying extra to the actors and crew—who might have been committed to other projects— to stay on. It means hanging on to sets and equipment and security. It can even mean dealing with shifts in the weather, if you are on the cusp of a change in seasons.

After he'd gone over schedule on *Die Hard 2*, Joel stopped returning our calls. He wanted the money without the input. Finally, after getting the runaround for days, I got on a plane and flew out to Sault Ste. Marie, Michigan, where they were filming. It was in that beautiful little Midwestern town that I got the full Joel Silver treatment, complete with the bluster and bravado. Yelling, threats, tantrums. Was Joel talented? Yes, very. Was he smart? Yes, brilliant. But he was equally difficult. Because he did not want anyone from the studio around, he pretended he didn't have time to meet with me and avoided speaking with me at all.

The movie was set in the snow, but because Joel had run so over schedule the season had changed. Winter had become spring. The snow was melting. We needed to find a new location to film the last few scenes, and do it before the whole state turned green. In short, Joel had this problem, but would neither solve it nor let me. Meanwhile, the meter was running. I finally figured *to hell with it*, and chartered a helicopter to go in search of snow. Joel and his assistants stood there, watching me take off. I think he was hoping I'd never make it back—not crash and die, maybe, but get lost in the woods and never be found. There was something so great about hovering over the trees in the helicopter. It suggested the ideal point of view of a producer: the eagle eye. The set and its problems shrank down to a manageable size. It took no more than twenty-five minutes to find the snow we needed to finish the movie. It was just over the hills in a town called Alpena.

As I was about to head back to LA, Joel decided to speak with me and pulled me aside. He was giving me one more blast of bravado. It went something like this:

"When you get back," he said, "do me a favor and tell Joe Roth to go fuck himself."

"Joel, if you want to tell Joe that, you call him," I said. "That's not for me to do. I'm here to try to make this work the best we can."

We got through the movie and—needless to say—I did not work with Joel again.

Then there was John Hughes—I had trouble with him, too. If you're thinking, *Hey, Jon. You had trouble with this one and trouble with that one. Maybe* you *were the problem*, let me explain. First, I was adjusting to a new role. Up to this point, I'd been the line producer on the set, dreading a visit by the studio executive. Having moved to the other side of the counter, I was still learning how to navigate the dynamics of the job, how to perform effectively and inspire confidence. Second, I only got heavily involved with a movie when there was a problem. By definition, these were exceptional experiences. Yes, I occasionally pissed off a director, because that's the nature of the job. You have to say no more than yes, and people don't like that. Understandably.

Sixteen Candles, The Breakfast Club, Ferris Bueller's Day Off, Home Alone, Uncle Buck—John Hughes had already made great movies. He'd built his own mini studio in an abandoned high school in the northern suburbs of Chicago. He was prepping for *Baby's Day Out*, a kidnap caper with Joe Mantegna and Lara Flynn Boyle. It was a modern screwball comedy. John was not directing—he was moving away from that—but it was his production in every way. He'd written the script, chosen the actors and the director.

We met in his office soon after I arrived, then went to his house for dinner. I was giving him notes—what needed to be added, what needed to be cut. I thought it was a warm, friendly conversation. The next day, I woke up to a call from the studio telling me that I was barred from the set of all John Hughes movies. I was persona non grata. Some people welcome input, others revolt. Say what you want about Joel Silver. At least you knew where you stood with him. John Hughes took me by complete surprise.

It took me nearly a year to understand my role at Fox. At times, it was a struggle, but I never stopped learning. From every picture, I tried to take a lesson. In those early days, I worked on a movie called *Sleeping with the Enemy* about the ultimate husband from hell. It starred Julia Roberts, the biggest star in Hollywood. That meant a big budget. Roger Birnbaum, president of production, asked me to find ways to cut costs. In a lot of studios, such savings would come out of the sets, costumes, locations. You'd trim whatever you could and try to make the same movie for less. But if done thoughtlessly, such cuts harm the movie, and if you're not willing to pay to do it right, why make it at all? The truth is, on some projects, there are no good cuts. I learned that on *Sleeping with the Enemy*. It cost what it cost. If you wanted to cut away at that, you'd get an inferior movie. I tried to explain this to Roger, but he didn't want to hear it. He told me to look again. Finding nothing after the fifth read through, I walked into Roger's office and handed him the script.

"What's this for?"

"You want us to reduce costs, right?"

"Absolutely. We have to."

"Fine, take five pages out of the script."

"Which five pages?"

"It doesn't matter," I said. "There's no miracle, Roger. What we've proposed to budget is what it's going to cost. If we cut, no matter what we cut, it'll weaken the movie. It might as well be random."

Roger backed off, and we got the budget approved. For me, this experience was important because I'd drawn a line. I'd told my bosses what sort of compromises I was not willing to make, and it gave me the room to make decisions and lead production the way I wanted going forward. Sometimes you can spend less without getting less. Sometimes spending more gets you more. Neither is always true. Movies are expensive. There's no way around it.

I GOT MY first real insight into the strange life of a big-time celebrity while working on a movie called *Shining Through*, a World War II flick with Michael Douglas and Melanie Griffith. At their level of fame, you have to be mindful of everything you do in public. I became aware of this in London, where the movie was being shot, when I flew over to check on the progress. I went to dinner one night with Douglas and

Griffith. Someone had leaked the details. Paparazzi were waiting outside the restaurant when we arrived.

"Hey, Jon," Michael asked, "can you stand between me and Melanie when we get out?"

"Why?"

"If I'm seen standing next to Melanie," he explained, "the tabloids will be filled with rumors of an affair tomorrow."

Melanie threw a dinner party in London during the shoot. Seat cards with first names were placed at each table setting. My seatmate had not arrived when I sat down. His name was Mike. *Who could that be?* I wondered. I knew it wasn't Michael Douglas; he was already seated. Then, halfway through the first course, my seatmate showed up. It wasn't Mike. It was Mick. As in, Jagger! We talked all night, me and Mick—an incredible conversation. He took me back to my hotel in his blue Rolls-Royce, the two of us and a driver. I got on the phone as soon as I was in my room. I had to tell Julie's brother, Chuck. He's a huge Rolling Stones fan.

Now and then, I worked with a director who'd known me in my previous role as an assistant or a line producer. Getting such a person to accept you in this new position is a challenge. I experienced it with Michael Mann. We'd last worked together on *Manhunter,* when I was an underling running interference with the studio. Now I *was* the studio. This would be as much of an adjustment for me as for him. I had to find a way to make us both comfortable with this new dynamic.

He was shooting *The Last of the Mohicans* in North Carolina. This was Michael's adaptation of the James Fenimore Cooper novel, a classic set in upstate New York during the French and Indian War. That novel had, in some sense, been the first Western. It created a genre that became a staple of the motion picture industry. Michael approached it with great ambition. He had Daniel Day-Lewis in the lead as Hawkeye and Madeleine Stowe as Cora Munro, a British officer's daughter enraptured by the American wilderness personified by Hawkeye. As a rule, the larger the directorial ambition, the greater the challenges and chances that control will be an issue. The creation of a masterpiece is an elusive thing. As Michael was chasing that dream, there were significant overruns. Four weeks in, and already two weeks behind; $30 million budgeted, $40 million now estimated—it was that kind of production.

Some directors seem to think the harder you push people, the harder they will work, when, of course, the opposite is more often true. I think half the crew had either quit or been fired by the end of the first month. It quickly became clear that here was a movie in serious need of supervision. In the end, I had to head out there to see what was happening for myself, and possibly get very hands-on. And that could mean tangling with Michael, which would be no small thing.

I did catch a lucky break, though it did not feel lucky at the time. I broke my jaw just a few days before I was supposed to fly to North Carolina. It happened at a coed company softball game, one of my team-building outings. Fox was playing against Disney, and I'd been caught in a rundown between first and second base. A guy from the Disney team delivered a hard tag as I slid into second. "Safe!" I could hear the crack as his elbow hit my jaw. In all my years competing in youth, high school, and college sports—football, basketball, baseball, ice hockey—I'd never been hurt. And here I was, laid out in a studio softball game. Julie laughed when I told her I was calling from the emergency room. That's the price paid by the practical joker. But she was an excellent caregiver and milkshake-maker throughout my recovery.

My jaw being wired shut when I arrived in North Carolina turned out to be a good thing, as it forced a different kind—and tone—of communication. Michael had to lean in close when I spoke, which made him listen carefully. And for the most part, he responded in kind. There was no yelling in either direction. I suddenly understood the power that quiet can have. It comes off not as an expression of weakness but as an expression of confidence.

I had to establish the fact that I'd come with good intentions—not merely to control the budget but to help Michael make the movie he wanted to make. "It's your vision," I told him. "But I can help you realize it." If Michael thought I'd come to crack the whip, he'd tell me to buzz off. If he thought I'd come to lend a hand, he'd be open to my input. Great directors—and Michael Mann is a great director—want any ideas that can help the picture, no matter the source. It's important to establish your value to the creative process, not just the production process. To understand the vision, not just the numbers.

I did that on my first day on set. Michael had been shooting Daniel Day-Lewis in a cabin in the woods. Because no take ever seemed quite right to Michael, he fell further and further behind schedule. It was Friday afternoon. The crew would be off for the weekend. If he couldn't get his shot by sundown, we'd have to come back to the same location on Monday, which was unplanned and would cost us money. When it was nearly dark, Michael said, "I have an idea. I know how we can do it now and not come back Monday." He told me his plan, but I thought it would compromise the scene. I said, "Don't do that, Michael. Let's come back here on Monday and we'll deal with the schedule and the budget later. The picture has to come first."

That interaction set the tone for our relationship on the picture. From that moment, Michael knew I wouldn't diminish the movie to save money. If I wanted to do something a certain way, he knew it wasn't just about the budget. He might disagree with me, but he didn't see me as an enemy. I wanted to help realize his vision—not compromise it.

"After all, that's what we believed in and bought," I told him. "Your vision."

That does not mean we didn't fight. We did fight. All the time. It's often a fight with Michael. I think it's part of his artistic process. Perhaps that's what gives him the signature energy that drives his work. Our biggest battle did not take place until after the wire had been removed from my jaw. He wanted to yell, and, for that, he needed me to be able to yell, too.

The wire had just come off. We were shooting on a set made to look like a colonial-era town that we called Huron Village, from the book. Michael was shooting take after take of Hawkeye walking down a street. If there was a difference between one shot and another, I couldn't see it. Finally, after more than two hours of the same shot again and again, I said, "Hey, Michael, I think we got this."

"Okay," Michael said. "Just give me two more takes."

I sighed and agreed. Fine. Two more takes, but then we're really done. We shook on it. After the second of those two takes, he said, "Okay, one more take."

"No way," I said. "We had a deal."

He said, "I'm going again."

Then, as he was calling everyone back into position, I yelled—it was beautiful to hear the roar of my own voice—"Lunch!" Then I shut down the shoot. And so Michael and I stood in the middle of that fully realized colonial-era town yelling at each other. The director and the studio exec fighting—you've never seen a movie set clear out so fast.

We finally settled down and talked, but neither one of us was willing to back down.

He said, "Jon, we're not going to be able to finish the movie this way."

I said, "You're right, Michael, we're not."

We stared at each other until we got tired of staring, then worked it out: He admitted that he didn't need another shot of Daniel Day-Lewis walking down the street. I agreed it was his movie. When the air cleared, we were able to establish a new schedule and new rules. The production proceeded smoothly after that. I finally felt it was okay to return to LA.

Michael was shooting a scene in a cave when I was getting ready to leave. He agreed to wrap it up after two or three more takes—he said he'd already gotten what he needed anyway. A car took me to the airport. I was seated at the gate when they announced that the flight had been canceled. I rebooked for the next morning, then, as I had nothing else to do, went back to the set. Four hours had elapsed since I'd left, but there was Michael, still shooting the same scene! The lesson? You can institute every kind of rule known to Hollywood, but, in the end, Michael Mann is going to be Michael Mann.

David Fincher was another director with tremendous passion. Fox hired him to direct *Alien 3*. It would be his first feature. He'd made his name in music videos and TV commercials, and his work was visually stunning. There was a competition among studios to produce his first feature film. We enticed him with Alien. It was a major franchise. The first two films had been directed by Ridley Scott and James Cameron, respectively. Quite the lineup to step into. We were taking a risk by putting the property in his hands. Not only did he seem unfazed by that, but the fact that he had been pursued by so many studios almost made it seem like he felt he was doing us a favor.

He had quite an ego. Supposedly another studio had said to him, "David, do you really think we're going to give you fifty million dollars to direct your first feature film?"

David's response was apparently "No, because I don't think you want half a movie."

And then there is the lore about the exchange that occurred when Fincher was leaving for London to shoot the movie, and Roger Birnbaum, who was overseeing *Alien 3*, wished him luck, saying, "David, go and make me so proud that we will want to work with you again."

Fincher's supposed retort? "Roger, you're not going to be able to afford to work with me again."

Of course, Fincher ran into trouble right away. Directing a big-budget feature is nothing like directing a TV commercial or a music video. The scale of every element involved is different. The weight of the pressures and responsibilities are, too. The director of the big-budget movie has to deal with so many actors, so many details, so many egos. It's a machine with a million moving parts. And the element around which everyone needs to come together is the script—it's story-telling that launches it all. Unfortunately, David had gone to London with a weaker script than hoped. He knew it, and could have fixed it, but he was out of time. When the studio sinks big money into a picture, they want it for release on one of the major calendar days. Memorial Day. The Fourth of July. Thanksgiving. That means a hard deadline backed by a production timeline to meet it.

I went to London to help manage the production, which was not going well from a scheduling and budgeting standpoint. (Are you seeing the pattern here?) David had been reworking the script on location, and the dailies looked beautiful—but the production was in jeopardy due to overruns. David resented my presence; to him, I was like the school principal who has come to watch the new teacher work with students. We fought and fought. He actually talked about those fights in *Premiere* magazine, saying, "We have had amazing, amazing bouts, with screaming and spitting, cat-scratching, the whole thing. It's his job to control costs and my job to get the shots. It was a bloodbath—a constructive bloodbath."

Finally, when it was clear that he could not finish the movie, I said, "David, we're pulling the plug here on Friday."

"Are you firing me?" he asked. "Because I won't be done by Friday."

"I didn't say *you* were going to be done on Friday," I told him. "I said we were going to be done *here* on Friday. We're going back to LA. We'll edit the picture in LA, see what we've got and what we still have to do. If we need to reshoot scenes, we'll do it later." That did not go over well, but it's what had to happen.

We rescheduled the release and took a two-month break, which was what everyone needed, including David. Sometimes, more than a new scene or a different soundtrack, what you really need is time, distance, and perspective. Three things not often afforded on a big-budget film, especially one on which the "big" has only gotten bigger. We ended up doing six weeks of reshoots. It was on this film that I first worked with Sigourney Weaver, who played Commander Ripley. I hated that she first knew me as a studio heavy—never my favorite role. She rightfully and thoughtfully took the side of her director during those months of filming. When we started working on *Avatar*, I worried that her image of me would be tainted, but I was wrong. Sigourney was a pro. She was a major advocate for our work together on *Avatar*, and she was a friend. When she was getting her scuba certification for *Avatar: The Way of Water*, she stayed with Julie at our home in the Florida Keys. There are moments when past and present, work and family, come together in unexpected and wonderful ways. This was one of them.

By 1993, I finally felt comfortable in my role at 20th Century Fox. I knew how the place operated, where I could make a difference, and where I'd just get in the way. I had learned when to get involved and when to back off. We had an amazing team and the result was a great run of success, with hit after hit. It was a golden era at the studio.

THERE'S A HOLLYWOOD of clubs and parties, but I never wanted to be part of it. And neither did James Cameron. The fact that we both saw ourselves as operating outside of that helped us form a connection. Even when I was the cost-cutting studio executive and he was the headstrong director—roles our jobs required us to play—there was mutual respect and recognition. At some level, I knew even then, well before we established our partnership, that Jim was going to play a major role in my life. I divide my career in two sections: before Jim, and with Jim.

We first met in 1993 at Fox when he was directing *True Lies*, a movie with Arnold Schwarzenegger and Jamie Lee Curtis. Arnold was playing Harry Tasker, a secret agent living a dual life: that of a spy fighting the bad guys and that of a timid, boring salesman married to Jamie.

Jim had set up the financing for the movie through his own production company, Lightstorm Entertainment. He sold the foreign rights to European distributors and the American rights to Fox. This split distribution deal is not uncommon and is called a negative pickup. At some point, as is often the case with Jim, his ambition surpassed his budget, and he was running out of money. He came in for a breakfast meeting at Fox with Peter Chernin and asked for an infusion.

Chernin agreed to invest more, but said that the studio was going to have to get much more involved. That's where I came in. I was told to go out to the set and try to manage James Cameron, as best as possible.

Why me?

Because I'd worked successfully with Warren Beatty and Michael Mann, two of the strongest (in both will and artistry) directors in the industry. James Cameron was said to be in the same rank, both creatively and temperamentally.

Jim came into the movie business via special effects. As a physics major at Fullerton College, he made extra money building scale models for the producer Roger Corman and fell in love with filmmaking in the process. He started out as a writer, then, in order to fully realize his vision of what the movies could be and have control over his work, he went into directing. By the time we met, he'd already made a quadfecta of sci-fi classics: *The Terminator, Aliens, The Abyss,* and *Terminator 2: Judgment Day.*

Jim was pissed at the demand and the studio, but was willing to give me a chance. Here are three secrets to a successful career in the film industry: Number one, don't blame the individual for the institution. Number two, don't make enemies unnecessarily. Number three, do look for a way to turn an opponent into an ally.

In our first meeting at a conference room at Fox, Jim walked past the studio heads, his producers, even Arnold, and went straight over to my chair. Standing over me with his six-foot-three frame, he said, "So, Jon, I understand we are either going to get to be pretty good friends . . . or bitter enemies."

"Pretty good friends, I hope," I responded.

Thirty-plus years later, I don't have to tell you which one was the case.

That doesn't mean we haven't had our arguments. I quickly got to see firsthand both the brilliance and the stubbornness of Jim. There are often dueling agendas between the studio and the director, but for me, it is never about taking sides or being someone's messenger. It is always the best interests of the movie that motivates me.

We were filming in Providence, Rhode Island, when I spoke to Rae Sanchini, executive producer on *True Lies*, about the opening action sequence of the movie that would be shot later in the schedule. It seemed to outweigh some of the action later in the film. Too much up front, including a helicopter slaloming down a ski slope with Arnold at the controls. I thought the story would be better served by allowing the action to build throughout the film. Of course, it didn't hurt that cutting back on the big stunts would save the production time and money, but that wasn't why I believed the scene should be changed. It would help the storyline.

We were shooting at night and broke for dinner, when I approached Jim and asked, "Did Rae mention to you that I wanted to talk?"

"She mentioned it, and the answer is no," Jim said. "That was a short meeting, wasn't it?"

"Yes, Jim, but can we have a follow-up meeting?" I retorted.

Jim brought me into his trailer. It was small. (He never has an ostentatious trailer.) I tried to get my point across, and I got a lecture in return. There was no resolution. But six weeks later when we were in Tahoe, ready to film the opening sequence, the phone in my hotel room rang at six a.m. It was Jim.

"Jon, I don't know that we need to shoot Arnold skiing down the mountain on the helicopter," he said. This time, I half-heartedly argued to keep it in, but he insisted he had a better, smaller-scale version of the scene in mind now—an idea that would really work. There was no resentment and no ego. His only concern was, and is, the vision for the movie. Jim doesn't care where a good idea comes from. I joke that I know this because he takes credit for my ideas all the time.

It was a revelatory moment for me. The idea that you can plant a seed, and over time that seed grows and, eventually, blossoms with someone else. It is that way with Jim. If you come up with something that works, great. If it doesn't work, he'll let you know, and sometimes loudly. But you should never take it personally. That's what I learned on *True Lies*. It's not personal, but it is passionate.

During the shoot, Jamie Lee Curtis had invited me to a dinner at her apartment. Jim and I had just bickered, and I knew he'd be at the dinner and I didn't want to make him feel uncomfortable.

I said, "Look, Jim, if you'd prefer I not go, I'm happy not to go."

Jim's face transformed. He said, "Jon, I leave this shit at the door."

Jim is a puzzle. I eventually figured him out, but not on my own. It was only with the help of Rae that I came to understand and adeptly navigate the world of James Cameron. A film and television producer, Rae was president of Jim's production company, Lightstorm Entertainment. Over time, she became a singular confidante and one of my best friends. Our relationship was founded on a shared belief: the brilliance of James Cameron. Alongside others who have changed the course of motion pictures, Jim is one of the great filmmakers of the era. It's his movies that people will still be watching in a hundred years. We wrapped *True Lies*, and I returned to my work at Fox, but my career would never be the same.

Chapter 5

My father, Ely, died on November 4, 1993. He was seventy-three when he passed from complications of the catastrophic stroke he had suffered ten years earlier. In a wheelchair and left with diminished mental capacity—of which he was keenly aware—Ely's life had been severely limited throughout that decade. Edie had, in many ways, been trapped by Ely's illness as well. Theirs had been a grand love affair, so her feelings of loss were tremendous, but so too was her relief for him. No more suffering.

Ely's health had begun to take a serious downturn, and he was hospitalized when I was working on *True Lies*. I'd actually flown back to LA to see him the night before he died. Kathy, Tina, and I were tag teaming to be at the hospital with Edie. Kathy had been there for several days and had taken the red-eye to New York the night I arrived. Tina arrived the morning I was heading back to Florida, where *True Lies* was filming. I was at LAX waiting to board my flight when I got the news.

Ely was buried at Hillside Memorial Park in Los Angeles. Edie requested we get one hundred multicolored helium balloons for the graveside service. Needless to say, we all thought she was a bit crazy and lost in her grief. But one hundred balloons there were. You can imagine what the funeral director thought when those balloons were delivered to the cemetery. For Edie, the balloons were an important symbol. In heaven, Ely would be able to rise out of his wheelchair and soar once again, just like the balloons.

As the gravediggers in their dusty gray overalls lowered the casket, Kathy, who was sitting next to Edie, leaned over to me and whispered, "Edie wants to know why they couldn't have dressed a little nicer?"

"For another five thousand dollars," I told her, "they could have been in suits."

We all started to laugh. It was a quintessential Landau family moment.

My father's death made me ask certain questions. What was I working on, and why? What did I want from my life and career? That's what happens when a parent dies—you recognize, in a way you never did before, that time is limited. I knew more clearly than ever that I wanted my life and work to have meaning.

I left Fox in 1995, after five-plus years. I had been promoted from senior vice president to executive vice president. I had learned and accomplished a lot during my time at Fox. I had grown and so, too, had the members of my team. That has always been important to me—to bring people along. But I felt I had gotten everything out of the job that I could. Maybe it was because Ely and Edie had been independent producers, or maybe it was just my nature, but running a studio was never my goal. You have to know when to stay and when to go. It was time to go.

I'd always seen the job as a stepping stone, and this was my moment to take the next step. I'm only happy that I recognized it when it came. Some people wait too long, until after they have lost interest or the opportunities have faded. Or, worse, they never stop waiting. Waiting for "the right moment." Waiting for external forces to propel them forward.

For about two minutes, I considered trying my hand at directing. I had watched some of the greatest directors at work, had learned a lot from them. Though I was not in the same league, I believed I could do the job behind the camera, and might even enjoy it. I'd finished movies when the director quit or was fired. I'd directed all those spoofs for sales conferences and pitches and was proud of them. But in the end, I realized directing would be a mistake. I had found what I loved— producing, focusing on the big picture. And it also happened that it was what I was good at. If you are lucky enough to find something you both enjoy and can actually do well, keep doing it until they make you stop, and then find a way to keep doing it anyway. That's my mantra.

I was actually offered three different jobs when I announced my departure from Fox. These offers came from directors I had worked with before—that has to be an ultimate vote of confidence. One came from Warren Beatty. He wanted me to produce his next movie, the political satire *Bulworth*. One was from Michael Mann. He wanted me to produce his potential next movie, *Flight of the Phoenix*, a remake of a Robert Aldrich movie about a cargo plane that crashes in the desert. One was from James Cameron. He wanted me to produce his next picture, which was then going by the code name *Planet Ice*. This was *Titanic*.

How could I say anything but an exuberant yes to James Cameron and *Titanic*? A cast of hundreds, period costumes and machinery, the building and sinking of a massive ship, the ice-filled ocean at night, a riveting screenplay (a feat when everyone knows the ending)—it seemed impossible to pull off, which is one of the reasons I took the job. The size of the challenge was irresistible. The other reason? Simply put—James Cameron. Jim is a genius and a visionary. Working with him can be tough, but it also means being part of something bigger than the making of a movie.

Rae Sanchini was instrumental in convincing Jim that I was the right person for the job. If all I had ever gotten out of taking that job was the chance to work again with Rae, who was our executive producer on *Titanic*, it would have been more than enough. Over the course of the last thirty years and throughout all of our endeavors, Rae has been an exceptional partner, for which I am grateful. But I am even more grateful for her extraordinary friendship.

All we had for *Titanic* was a scriptment, a document—written by Jim—that is halfway between a novella and screenplay. While Jim wrote the full script, we went out to partner with a studio to make the movie. To any self-respecting studio—Hollywood executives tend to be risk averse—*Titanic* would look like a money pit. As I've said, Jim's job is to dream the dreams, and my job is to make them happen. That was how Ely always described his partnership—in business and in life—with Edie: He dreamed the dreams, and Edie made them happen. After ten months of rewrites, we had the epic we wanted to bring to life on-screen. The script was both intimate and grand.

Jim and Rae had set up the picture at Fox, but the bosses began to gripe at the ever-rising budget forecasts. Fox decided to bring in a second studio to share the burden. We all thought it was a done deal with Universal Pictures, when Jim got an out-of-the-blue call from Sherry Lansing, chairperson and CEO of Paramount. According to Jim, Sherry said: "Hi, honey. I'm excited to be in business with you!"

We had no idea Fox had separately been pitching to Paramount—but, of course, we were genuinely happy. Fox? Universal? Paramount? It didn't matter where the money came from; we knew the picture we wanted to make, and we knew the deep pockets it would take to make that a reality.

The deal was supposed to be a fifty-fifty split between Fox and Paramount. You put up half of the cost, get back half of the gross. But as it became clear that the budget that had been written in the contract was fantasy, Paramount began to balk. Rather than lose a partner, Fox agreed to add an addendum to the contract. There would be a budget cap. After it was reached, Fox would cover all additional costs. In exchange, the payout was changed. Paramount would get 50 percent only until their original investment had been recouped, after which it'd be a sixty-forty split in favor of Fox. To recoup the original investment, *Titanic* would have to do unprecedented business: $800 million at the box office. It ended up doing $1.8 billion. What looked like a risk-minimizing win for Paramount turned out to be a huge payday missed.

As anyone who has seen *Titanic* knows, one of the stars of the movie is the ship. And, like with casting our leads, we had to get it right. We had historical images to go by, along with Jim's vision and immense research, but from there, we actually had to figure out how to build the ship. And not just the ship, but a ship that would accommodate the needs of filming without compromising the authenticity or feel. We also had to build the sea in which the ship would be sunk and raised again and again throughout the shoot.

So that was the biggest task: Find a location, build a ship, create an ocean. We needed a large self-contained environment where we could control conditions. It took us a year just to scout locations. We went all around the world. For a minute, I thought we'd found an answer in an old dry quarry in Poland near the Gdańsk shipyard. I'll never forget that trip. This was right before Christmas. We met with a local production company, then went to their Christmas party, which was held on the first floor of an office building. They had to keep the curtains closed because it was not long after the Soviet era, and they had to hide the fact that they were celebrating a religious holiday.

In the end, we found an ideal spot in the most unlikely of places: Rosarito, Mexico. Unlikely because, whereas the *Titanic* went down in the ice-filled waters of the North Atlantic, Mexico is the land of sunshine. I visited the forty vacant acres on the edge of Rosarito, a resort town in Baja California. If you used your imagination, you could almost see it: the build that would be the ship and the ice-filled sea. The *Titanic* steaming toward destiny as Rose and Jack fall in love.

I walked those forty Mexican acres looking, thinking, planning. We could build a massive water tank here—that'd be our ocean. We could build the Southampton dock, the gaming house, and the seaside tavern, too. There'd be space for the interiors of cabins, steerage, the engine and dining room, the parlors. I sat with a napkin and sketched what I imagined down to the smallest detail. I knew I'd found our location. Now for the hard part: to convince Jim.

We ran into a hiccup. Jim refused to go down and see the site until the studio had given us the green light, but the studio would not give us the green light until we'd finalized the budget, which we could not do until we'd settled on a location. It was a catch-22: Fox wouldn't give the okay until Jim made the trip; Jim wouldn't make the trip until he got the okay. Someone had to blink, and, as usual, it was not going to be Jim. But we made use of the extra days. By the time Fox finally signed off, Geoff Burdick, senior vice president at Lightstorm, and his team had set up a twenty-foot-long model of the *Titanic* that we had built, so that way Jim could see it in context when we got him down to Mexico.

We stayed in a hotel twenty minutes outside Rosarito. I'd planned to get to the site before Jim. I wanted to make sure everything was ready for a presentation—ship and diagrams, how it would be done, how it was going to look. Jim tends to go with his gut, to decide fast, and, once he's decided, it's hard, though not impossible, to change his mind.

I got up at dawn, and, of course, Jim was already up. No matter how early you wake, Jim wakes earlier. We drove down to the proposed site together. Jim hopped out of the car and raced over to study the model of the ship. He started shouting: "Landau! Landau!"

"Yes, Jim?"

"What were you thinking? There are lights over there. There's a hill over there! How the hell is this going to be the middle of the ocean! Send everybody back to Los Angeles! This is not gonna work!"

A crew member pulled me aside and said, "Jon, that's exactly what you said he'd say."

Jim has a process, which I'd come to understand. First he balks, then he reconsiders. He needs to get his hands in there; his fingerprints need to be on any and every decision. He took twenty minutes to shift the model of the ship ever so slightly, then suddenly looked up and shouted, "Landau! It's perfect! It's the only place we can make the movie!"

The crew began building the set, and we went back to LA for casting. We, of course, wanted young, beautiful stars for the leads—Rose and Jack—but more importantly, they had to be great actors, too: tough and willing to deal with an arduous schedule and long days of shooting in the water.

We decided to do old-fashioned screen tests. We'd found a period set for this purpose and shot over the course of a long weekend. We put three actresses under test/option deals, but we never really got beyond the first actress, Kate Winslet, a young Brit who'd been in a handful of period pictures. At twenty, she was already typecast. People called her "Corset Kate."

Jim ran her through several scenes from the *Titanic* script, asking her to play it this way and that. It soon became clear he could not get enough of Kate. We were using real film, and all of a sudden, we realized Jim had shot an entire one-thousand-foot-load of film stock on a single take with Kate. And we only had fifteen thousand feet for the entire weekend and all the screen tests.

We tested various actors for Jack, but Matthew McConaughey was at the top of the studio's list. In 1995, he was still unknown and trying to break into the big time, handsome with that famous Texas twang and cocky grin. He was young, with a handful of roles on his résumé— some commercials, a music video, and a scene-stealing part in Richard Linklater's *Dazed and Confused*.

That cockiness was no act—I felt that Matthew McConaughey was really like that. We brought him in to do a scene with Kate. You want to check for chemistry, not just how people look on film but how they interact. Kate was taken with Matthew, his presence and charm.

Matthew did the scene with the drawl.

"That's great," said Jim. "Now let's try it a different way."

Matthew said, "No. That was pretty good. Thanks."

Let's just say, that was it for McConaughey.

Someone suggested Leonardo DiCaprio. He'd been a child actor, a breakout on the TV show *Growing Pains*. He played opposite Robert De Niro in *This Boy's Life*, which made it clear he could act, as did his performance with Johnny Depp in *What's Eating Gilbert Grape*. At first, we thought he'd be too young—too slight, too small—for the part of Jack, but, when we got him in the room with Kate, it was obvious that we'd found the relationship that would drive the movie. People are awed by special effects, by spectacle, but it's the actors and their chemistry together that make people forget about the effects and lose themselves in the story. In the end, a good movie is about people, which means you have to get the casting right. As soon as the screen test was done, Kate exclaimed, "Even if you don't cast me, you have to cast Leo."

As we assembled the cast and crew, the set was being built—and it was a *big* build. For me, a person who is all about physical production, this meant splitting my time between Los Angeles and Mexico. Rosarito began to feel like a second home. It was thrilling to watch that world within our script be built into existence. A movie set is a feat of extraordinary magic. Fleeting—it's here, then gone. But oh, the wonder it leaves behind.

The scale of this build made it feel more permanent. We weren't just building a set for *Titanic*. We were building a city. We needed to bring in phone lines from seven miles away. We needed to bring in over a thousand workers to construct the giant water tank—seventeen million gallons!—indoor stages, screening rooms, office buildings, and more. And we needed to do it all on a deadline.

There comes a point in every big production when you think, *No way, we can't do it, we can't build it, we can't square it, we can't pull it off. Impossible.* Defeatism can spread like a virus. I knew I had to stop it and instill confidence. I had to go back to the lessons I had learned as a coach—inspire, bring people together, set a goal, and create a strategy to meet it.

This is when I gave out those copies of *The Little Engine That Could*.

Meanwhile, we started filming the contemporary scenes. *Titanic* is told in flashback. We began by shooting sequences that take place in the present, which bookend the main story. These center on Rose, a one-hundred-year-old woman choppered out to the deck of a recovery ship anchored over the ruins of the *Titanic*, where she is asked to identify a priceless diamond found in the wreckage, the so-called Heart of the Ocean. We filmed in Halifax, Nova Scotia, on a six-thousand-ton Russian research vessel called the *Akademik Mstislav Keldysh*. Much of the work was done on open water, with the wind whipping and the waves crashing and the actors and crew hanging on for dear life. The underwater sequences, which take you into the ghostly wreckage of the actual *Titanic*, had been shot by Jim from his own vessel before we got the green light.

In the movie, the treasure hunters also find a drawing of the young Rose. (Fun fact: The drawing of young Rose, done with great tenderness in the film by Jack, was in fact drawn by James Cameron, who'd sketched Kate Winslet in a bathing suit.) The older Rose, played by Gloria Stuart, the octogenarian former starlet of the 1930s, identifies herself as the subject of the drawing and begins the tale of Rose and Jack.

FOR ME, THIS entire experience was new. I had worked with Jim as a Fox executive, but now we were partners. The first surprise came early, on the first morning of the first day in Halifax. I'd always been an on-set presence in my work. I wanted to be on the scene, tackling problems as they came up. We weren't on the water yet—just setting up at the dock, planning for the shoot—when Jim pulled me aside and said, "Jon, how long have you been on the set?"

"What? Today?"

"Yes. Today."

"I don't know. I don't keep track like that."

Jim said, "Look, Jon. I have a rule. My producers, even if I'm married to them, are only allowed on the set five minutes at a time."

I laughed. Genuinely.

Me: "What? Really?"

Him: "Yes, really."

I'd always seen my role on a movie as akin to that of a backstop, a problem-solver. I wanted to be there to resolve issues as they arose. Even better, to identify potential ones and prevent them from occurring. But Jim had this rule. Presumably, he also had his reasons. I just had to deal with it.

I was back out on the set a few days later to deal with some issues. Jim saw me and knew why I was there, but came over and asked how long I'd been there anyway.

I said, "Four minutes, Jim. I have been here for four minutes."

I'd been there half an hour at least, but Jim had made his point. I finished up, resolved the problem, and got out of there fast.

With time, Jim accepted that I was there not to watch over him but to watch out for him. When we finally moved to the big set in Rosarito, he said, "Okay, Jon, you can now be on the set for ten minutes at a time." That was my opening. From there, I was able to win Jim's trust and convince him that it was to his advantage to have me close. I was another set of eyes and ears for him, not someone with an agenda of my own.

About a month into production, having already fallen behind schedule, I got a call from Fox. I was being summoned in from Halifax for a meeting. I knew what this meant. I had been on the other side of this equation—representing the studio's interests, riding herd on a movie that already had signs of going dangerously over schedule and over budget; that's how I'd met Jim in the first place. And here I was now, the one being called in for those very same concerns. The meeting was to be held in the big conference room. I was greeted by an assistant and escorted to a seat at the table to wait. Tom Rothman, the president of the studio, was late. I stared at his empty chair for thirty minutes. I knew this was part of the game. Rothman was letting me know who was in charge.

When Rothman finally came in, he was livid. He waved a printout of the proposed new budget and schedule and shouted, "You're a fake. You're a fraud. You and Jim Cameron are liars." You get the picture.

And to think, at that point, we were only three days behind schedule.

I said, "Look. We have to keep building the set in Rosarito. We have to keep shooting in Halifax at the same time. We know it's costing more than projected—we all know the reasons for that. And we all also know that we have to keep going to make our release date. Calling us names won't get us there any quicker."

I agreed to not fall further behind in the scheduled shoot in Halifax, and booked a flight back there, where Jim and the crew were shooting some of the scenes with older Rose. We trudged forward with the shoot. By the time I arrived on set on what was meant to be our very last night in Halifax, Jim did not look well. His eyes were red, his complexion pale. At first, I assumed something had happened to one of the actors or stuntpeople. I thought he was angry or sad. But no. He said it was his stomach. He thought it was something he ate, probably the seafood chowder they'd served at dinner. I called for the medic—there's a doctor on the set at all times. Jim asked for something to induce vomiting. "Get this thing out of my system," he bellowed.

Then other people started feeling sick to different degrees. First a few, then dozens. We pulled everyone together, actors and crew, and asked all those not feeling well to raise their hand. Almost every hand went up. Food poisoning? Because I had eaten before arriving on set, I had escaped the wrath of whatever was sickening everyone.

We took more than fifty people to the hospital. We filled the emergency room. This had started out weird and continued to get weirder. Everyone was sick in a different way. Some people couldn't breathe. Some wept uncontrollably. Some became deliriously happy. Some were nauseous. Some had vertigo. Some formed a conga line and danced. It was beyond bizarre and deeply troubling.

Meanwhile, as I'm watching this, deep in the back of my mind was the meeting with Tom Rothman and my promise to the studio. But right now, the priority was to take care of the cast and crew afflicted with this strange illness. With great care from the doctors and nurses, people soon began to feel better, acute symptoms started to fade, and things calmed down.

I called Tom Rothman, got his assistant, and said, "We have a situation." I told him what was happening, and said, "We are going to have to adjust the schedule."

The local police came in to investigate because circumstances had been so perplexing and suspicious. What the hell happened? It seemed less like a case of bad seafood than an intentional poisoning. They narrowed it down to the chowder served at the buffet and ordered a toxicology report. The results were shocking. The chowder had been spiked with PCP—angel dust! Our dinner! Someone put angel dust in our dinner! We never figured it out definitively, but the best theory pointed to a crafts service guy, disgruntled because he'd recently been fired.

Two things for which I am very grateful: Everyone recovered with no lingering side effects, and Gloria Stuart had been taken out to dinner that night and did not have the chowder.

We started shooting in Rosarito, Mexico, in September 1996. By October, we had entered the dog days of production. The actors were homesick and tired, the crew wiped out, but Jim kept pushing.

The schedule originally had us shooting for 138 days, but that number quickly came to seem absurdly optimistic. Days were added, then weeks. In the end, the shoot took us 160 days, with each incremental hour adding to the costs. Our accounting department later said that we were burning through a million dollars a day.

There are many reasons a picture goes over schedule or over budget. Problems with the script. The location. The weather. Our biggest obstacle was the set itself. A monumental and unprecedented building project, it took much longer and cost much more than anyone anticipated. We built an entire ocean for the shoot, not to mention the life-size ship itself. That was a particularly daunting task—Jim wanted to get every detail right. He rejected the idea of using a scaled down version in the shoot. Not authentic. We searched the archives of Harland & Wolff, the company that had built the *Titanic* in 1910, and found the original blueprints and designs. He wanted our *Titanic* to be as close to the real thing as possible.

For the long shot exteriors—the ship seen from a distance, the ship listing and wounded in the wine-dark sea—we did use scale models.

These can be seen in the private museum we keep at Lightstorm. The onboard sequences—Jack hanging over the rail at the prow, Rose at dinner with the Unsinkable Molly Brown—were filmed on a set nearly as big as the actual *Titanic*. It was designed with handmade period pieces—chandeliers, furniture, doorknobs—that would send audiences back in time. If a single detail was off, if a single anachronism crept in, Jim knew the spell would be broken.

But even when striving for perfection and historical accuracy, you still need to be practical. After all, with ballooning costs, we had to look for any opportunity to save money and make the best use of any given environment. In building the *Titanic* replica, we made the decision to build only one side of the ship. This saved us millions in construction costs. We decided to build the starboard side of the ship to best utilize the prevailing winds down in Mexico, which would blow the ship's funnel smoke toward the stern. With the smoke blowing toward the stern and the Pacific Ocean as our backdrop, we were able to create the illusion of the ship moving forward on open water.

This setup, however, created a problem we needed to solve. Our story included an important scene on the dock in Southampton before the ship sets sail. Historically, the dock was on the port side and not on the starboard side. So how could we possibly film the port side if we hadn't built it? Our solution: Film the starboard side and flip the footage horizontally to create a mirror image that would accurately appear to be the port side. What made this a challenge was that flipping the image would make any lettering appear backward. So all signage along the dock was written backward, and Deborah Scott and her team needed to make two of each costume, one normal and one reversed, with buttons, coat pockets, and "White Star Line" lettering reversed. When we flipped the footage, everything appeared completely normal.

As we filmed the sinking of the ship, Jim spent most of his time up on a crane, zooming in and out of the shot, first near the ground, then an eye in the sky. He would bark his direction over a megaphone. Some members of the cast and crew thought he was demanding to the point of being mean. They recognized his brilliance and passion, but also knew he had a temper that matched. From my perspective, day in and day out, I was always impressed by Jim. No matter how big the crane, no matter how many extras, he always focused on the performance. For him, the scale and the spectacle weren't important; it was the drama and the performances he was able to get from the cast that mattered.

Jim, warm and thoughtful away from the set, was driven by his singular perfectionism while shooting and often turned into an impossible taskmaster within sight of the cameras. To some, these two sides seemed irreconcilable. The crew came up with a name for his alter ego. They called it Mij, the mirror image of the otherwise friendly Jim.

Even under the best of circumstances, shooting days can be grueling. Now imagine spending days on end in a seventeen-million-gallon tank with water rushing all around. That's what it took to get those dramatic final scenes on the ship. The actors had to spend hours at a time in the water—the ship has hit the iceberg, the ocean is rushing in. The water in our tank was heated, but, as the hours passed, the temperature dropped. And tempers rose. We were on a deadline and had to keep pressing on.

Rumors about chaos engulfing our set—accidents, poisoning, infections—spread through the industry. A September 1996 *Entertainment Weekly* story ("PCP-Laced Chowder Derails *Titanic* Filming") was followed by a *New York Times* piece headlined "As Problems Delay 'Titanic,' Hollywood Sighs in Relief."

Fox did what the studio does, what I had done myself when I was a studio exec and there were problems on a set—they sent a rep to Rosarito to keep us in line. Other people from the studio came down as well: to visit the set, or watch the shoot, or talk to Jim, who really had no patience for that. Remember the five-minute rule? If they persisted, he'd tell them that the only way they'd get what they wanted, which Jim believed was to get him to make a cheaper—and therefore lesser—version of his movie, was to get him off the set, and the only way to do that was to kill him.

So they spoke to me instead. Flak catcher—that was a big part of my job.

The Fox rep told us that he was concerned with a particular scene that we had on the schedule. He talked to Jim during a break and Jim, who, as I've said, has no patience for studio interference, gave him an answer even I found fairly shocking. Not something I would repeat here—let's just say the Fox rep was stunned.

He said: "Jim, I'm just trying to be your friend."

"I choose my own friends," said Jim, "and I don't choose you."

After a few of our stunt performers had injuries during filming, the Screen Actors Guild issued a statement. It suggested our set was unsafe. This stung. Jim and I always put the safety of our cast and crew first. But a certain amount of risk is inherent in the filming of any action sequence. That's why we have trained stunt performers.

The guild sent two of their own people to do a safety check. Imagine having to finish an epic-size production—we employed eight hundred people—deal with false rumors and newspaper articles, then, in addition, focus time and attention on explaining it all over and over again to union reps who've never seen the likes of this scale of production before.

I talked to them in my office. I told them what we were doing, how we were doing it, and the safety measures in place. We had a medical airlift helicopter available at all times, as well as our own doctor and medical staff—precautions we imposed on ourselves. And then I said, "Go and take a look around. Go anywhere you want and you will see what I mean." I gave them free rein.

Later, when they issued a clean report, they said that had been the moment—when I gave them the freedom to go everywhere and talk to everyone—that they knew they'd not find anything unsafe on the set of *Titanic*.

Between all of our stunt performers, if you added up all of the days they worked, we shot what was the equivalent of six thousand single stuntperson days. Jim would tell you if you stretched these days out among just one stuntperson, it would be equivalent to their spending nearly seventeen years doing stunts every single day.

When I was a child, I always looked forward to visiting Ely and Edie on location when they were making their movies. I have amazing memories of getting to explore the sets, sitting quietly in eager anticipation of "Rolling!" being shouted, and a hush falling across the soundstage. I loved watching my parents, and everyone else, at work. And, of course, I was thrilled meeting the actors, who were always larger than life to me.

Because I could only go home occasionally for a day or a weekend during the filming of *Titanic*, Julie and I decided to take Jamie and Jodie out of school for a week so we could all spend time in Mexico together. We all needed that. Plus, I loved the idea that they, too, would explore and observe and absorb.

Turns out that while they were there, we needed more stunt children for the upcoming scenes we were shooting of the sinking. Jodie was too young and too shy, but Julie and Jamie took some stunt tests with the stunt coordinator, Simon Crane. Passing with flying colors, they were soon off to the costume department to be fitted. The first day they were filming, they were to hang via harnesses from the poop deck, which was engineered to tilt in order to achieve the effect of the sinking ship. Unfortunately, that day the poop deck actually got stuck, and everyone was hanging there for hours while the crew tried to fix the malfunction. It turned out that Jamie and Julie didn't even realize it was stuck and simply had a great time "hanging out" with everyone. You can see them in the movie when the poop deck is at ninety degrees and the ship is going down . . . if you look *very* closely.

The family affair even extended to another generation. Julie's mother, Kathryn, had passed away several years earlier and her father, Marshall, was living alone and about to retire. When we created our core group of extras, background performers to fill out all the ancillary characters on the ship, I asked Marshall if he would want to come be an extra in the film. He thought I'd said it would be for six weeks, not six months! He ended up loving the experience, creating lifelong friendships with the other extras, and can be seen looking quite dapper as a first-class passenger many times throughout the film. For me, having my family on set was one of the highlights of my time down in Rosarito, and I loved seeing them be part of the bigger *Titanic* family.

Given the high-profile nature of the project—and the high budget— Fox continued to send people down to the set. Most were there to exert some oversight. A few came down as a friends and allies. Tom Sherak was one of them, a real salt-of-the-earth guy. He'd worked at Fox since 1983. He distributed *Aliens, Die Hard, Home Alone, Mrs. Doubtfire,* and *Independence Day.* He was the president of domestic distribution at

Fox when we first met. If I linger on Tom, it's only because I came to love him. (He died of prostate cancer in 2014.) Tom was unique, one of a kind. He embraced the film industry as a whole and, most importantly, the people who worked in it. He loved what he did. We developed a strong relationship, a bond. Tom was someone I could turn to. He was always there as a sounding board, a confidant, and a friend.

He couldn't stop laughing as I walked him around the set in Rosarito. At the scale of it, the ambition, the audacity. He said, "I don't know if we're crazier for letting you do this or if you're crazier for thinking you can." I took a lesson from that: Everyone thinks something's impossible until it's accomplished.

Tom said something that I will never forget. While talking about all the trouble we were giving the studio with *Titanic*, he said, "Jim Cameron walks a finer line between genius and insanity than anyone I have ever known." Jim is a *genius* in the truest sense of the word. He dreams the impossible and pursues it obsessively.

Another crisis came late in production. Because we were so far over budget, Peter Chernin decided to again send someone to the set, this time someone Jim could not just blow off. This was my old friend Bill Mechanic, who'd risen through the ranks to become the chairman of Fox Filmed Entertainment. The studio believed the movie was coming in too long—close to four hours of screen time. Bill was supposed to swoop in and suggest scenes that the studio thought could be cut from the script. If you ask Bill, he'll tell you it was a sensible list. If you ask Jim, he'll say it was three single-lined pages of absurd cuts, half of which we'd already shot. Jim refused to even engage. He said, "That is not the movie I envisioned." Jim shut down the shoot and went back to his rented apartment.

This was in the middle of a scene.

Bill found Rae and me, and said, "That did not go well."

I asked what had happened.

"Jim ordered everything shut down and went home."

Bill was heading back to LA and said he'd call in the morning. The first thing we did after he left was to get assistant director Josh McLaglen on the walkie-talkie and tell him to keep working. No way we were shutting down. Rae and I went over to Jim's place together. He was enraged. We talked. He vented. But we got him back to the set. There was not another mention or consideration of the studio's notes. We would finish the film on our own terms.

The studio doesn't always understand the value of a scene if it's not driving toward something specific, and obviously so. A great example is the scene in *Titanic* when Jack teaches Rose how to spit. We got notes from both Fox and Paramount to cut that scene, but it becomes important later when Rose uses her new skill to spit in her fiancé's face. When you parse things out on paper, looking only at numbers—page count or budgets—it's easy to lose sight of the bigger picture. The emotional ties. The subtle moments that connect characters and scenes. The threads that weave together to form the heart of the story.

Relief came in the form of a call from Peter Chernin. He said, "Jon, I'm really annoyed. You know how upset we are about the course—and cost—of the production. Well, I just saw your dailies, and goddamnit, they are some of the best dailies I've ever seen."

As I said, relief. But also, vindication. Most of the people who were bad-mouthing *Titanic* had not seen so much as a minute of film. They had no notion of Jim's accomplishments.

✧ ✧ ✧

FOR ME, A big task was keeping up everyone's spirits as we finished the shoot. It was an arduous shoot, long and hard, but that did not mean we couldn't also have—didn't also *need* to have—fun. I've always believed that good work and good fun are vital to success in all endeavors. It's a serious role for the producer: Open the windows, let in some air.

I did this in my usual way—goofball antics, practical jokes. And I went all out for Halloween. I'd always liked to dress up at work and encouraged everyone to do the same. And as with most things, I like to go big.

I asked the costume department to turn me into Mr. Potato Head. There I was all day on the set, a life-size, walking, talking Mr. Potato Head. We had a big meeting at the end of the day about the scene in which Spicer Lovejoy chases Jack with a gun through the dining room of the sinking *Titanic*. Any scene with a gun is a serious safety issue. But Jim couldn't stop grinning as we—Jim, David Warner (the English actor playing Lovejoy, the man with the pistol), and I—talked. Finally, right in the middle of the discussion, Jim smiled and said, "Hey, Jon. Let's do this later. I can't talk gun safety with Mr. Potato Head."

We shot the scene without any hitches.

There is a giddiness that comes in the last days of a production, especially when it's been an arduous shoot. You've suffered in the course of the work, had setbacks and triumphs, and, in some sense, become a family. You love those people, and now, just like that, it's all going to change. Each person will go on to their next project. This particular group, in this particular configuration, will never come together in the same way again. *Melancholy* is the word. You came together and built this world and now—*poof!*—it will dissolve. But there's happiness, too, and a feeling of accomplishment and release. Excitement to share the finished work. Gratitude.

As a way to mark the occasion, I decided to put myself in one of the last scenes. I did it with the help of our visual effects studio, Digital Domain. I went in and had myself scanned, and they created a digital model of me and made me the character who jumps off the sinking *Titanic* and hits a propeller on the way down. A little different than my high dive in the closing credits of *Campus Man*.

WE SPENT MANY months in postproduction. Entire plot devices, scenes we took great care to shoot, fell away as we pieced together the film. All the while, the press continued to hound. Reporters would infiltrate and ingratiate in search of scoops. Rumors spiraled. Articles reported we'd spent $200 million. Others speculated we'd spent even more. They compared *Titanic*, still months away from release, to *Ishtar*, *Waterworld*, and *Cleopatra*, the most notorious flops in Hollywood history. Whenever you try for something great, you risk everything. Your reputation, your career, your livelihood—important things are on the line.

The buzz inside the studio was just as bad. It, too, was all rumors. They said the movie was too long. They said the effects didn't work. They said the acting was weak. None of it was true, but gossip takes on its own life. Perception becomes reality. You end up chasing phantoms, which can be deadly. But at Fox, one person mattered most. Rupert Murdoch. Jim and I ran into him in the hallway at the studio during the darkest days of postproduction. We stopped and talked.

I said, "I guess we're two of your least favorite people in the world right now."

Rupert had a perfect answer. Without missing a beat, he said, "I'll wait until I see the movie, then I'll let you know."

We had decided to hold an advance screening at the Mall of America in Minnesota. Jim went out to scout the venue early. Rae and I flew east on the Fox plane with Tom Rothman and Peter Chernin a few days later. Tensions and pressures were high. There was a lot riding on the screening. A lot on the line.

Rothman sat up at the front of the plane. Rae and I went toward the back and sat side by side. Peter Chernin came back with us.

"So, Jon, what do you think?" Peter said, somewhere over the middle of the country. "Do you think there's someone at Universal Studios right now going, 'Hey, let's hire that producer Jon Landau, who just went one hundred percent over budget'?"

I said, "No, but, Peter, do you think there's someone at another studio going, 'Let's hire the chairman who green-lit that movie'?"

That was the relationship I had with Peter. We bantered. Sometimes we sparred. Cared deeply. I respected him greatly and still do.

The movie had been challenging from the start. Now we were going to find out just how well we'd conquered those challenges. "Let's see how people react," said Peter. "We are going to know a minute after the film starts if we have any chance at all."

Here's how advance screenings work: People line up at the box office for a free preview; they only find out what movie they're going to see as they enter the theater. We arrived early and sat in the back—Rae, Peter, Tom, and me. Jim snuck in and took an aisle seat as the lights dimmed. Then the movie started. *Titanic* came up in huge letters on the screen. This was met with silence from the audience. One minute in, two minutes in, three minutes in—silence.

We started whispering to each other. *Oh my God! We're dead, we're dead.*

Then the mood changed. The audience got caught up in the action.

A favorite photo of my mom, Edie, and me, 1960

Photo courtesy of the Landau family

With Dexter Scott King,
Martin Luther King III, and my
sister Kathy on Montauk, 1971

Photo courtesy of the Landau family

In my Jonny the Jock days
at Riverdale Country School, 1975
Photo courtesy of the Landau family

As an extra with Robby Benson on the set of *The Chosen*, 1980
Photo courtesy of the Landau family

One of the happiest days of my life—when Julie and I were married, 1985

Photo courtesy of the Landau family

Dancing at our wedding with my father, Ely, 1985

Photo courtesy of the Landau family

The day I became a dad—Jamie's birth, 1988

Photo courtesy of the Landau family

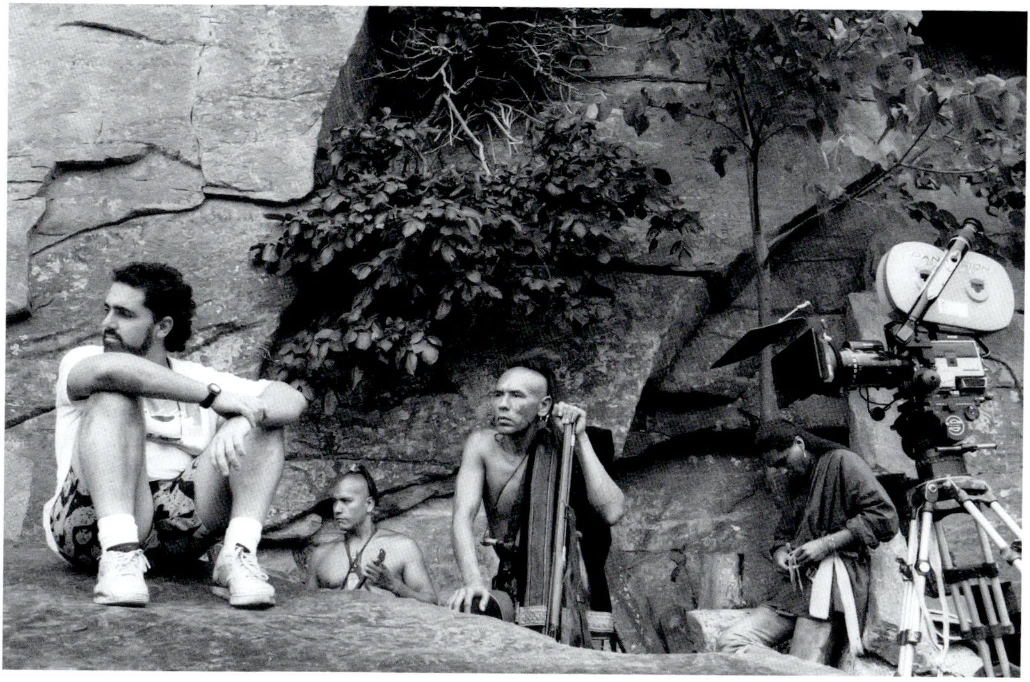

With Wes Studi on the set of *The Last of the Mohicans*, 1991

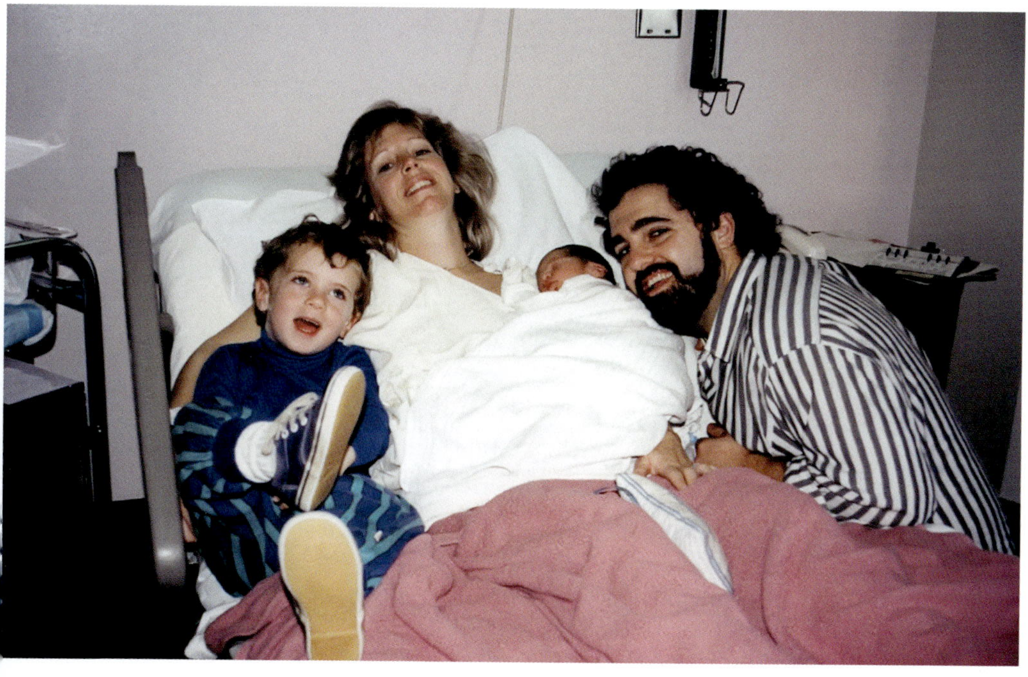

The day our family was complete—Jodie's birth, 1992

Photo courtesy of the Landau family

Team building with the Fox physical production department, 1994

Photo courtesy of the Landau family

With Ted Gagliano and Peter Chernin on the set of our *Speed* spoof, 1994

Photo courtesy of the Landau family

On the set of *Titanic* in front of our 90 percent scale replica of the ship, 1996

With James Cameron and Rae Sanchini on the set of *Titanic*, 1996

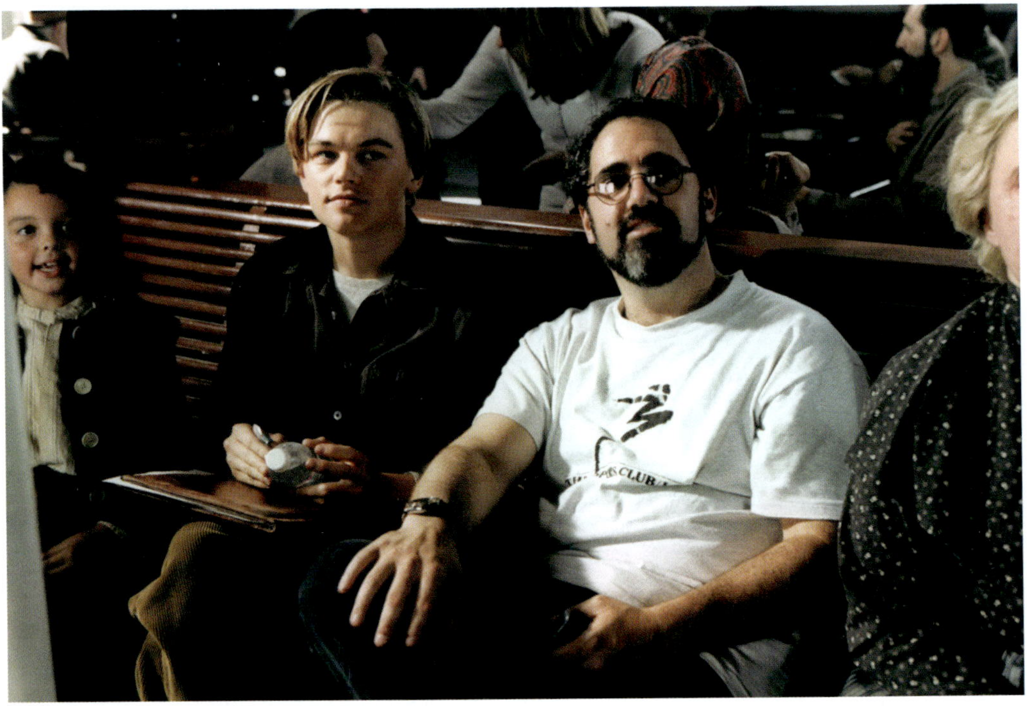

With Leonardo DiCaprio on the set of *Titanic*, 1996

A night to remember—
the Oscars after-party, 1998

Photo courtesy of the Landau family

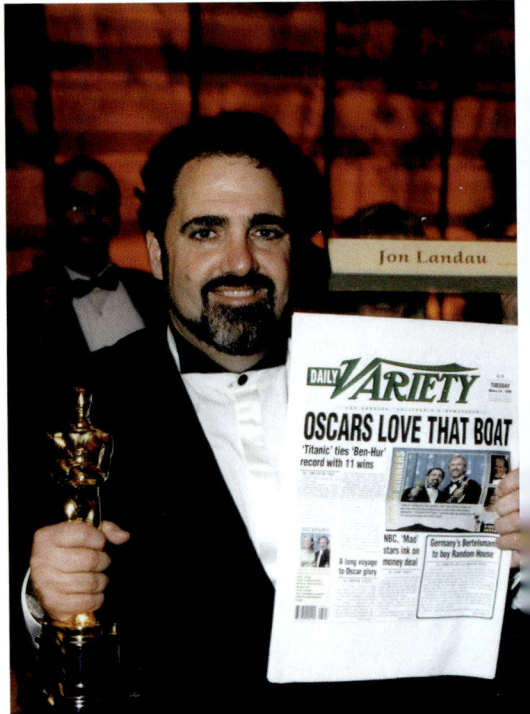

Celebrating with Julie and Jamie the moment
after *Titanic* was announced as Best Picture
at the Academy Awards, 1998

*Photo copyright © Academy of Motion
Picture Arts and Sciences*

Playing around with Sam Worthington and Zoe Saldaña during
(e)motion/performance capture filming on the set of *Avatar,* 2008

Set photograph from Avatar copyright © 2009 20th Century Studios, Inc. All rights reserved.

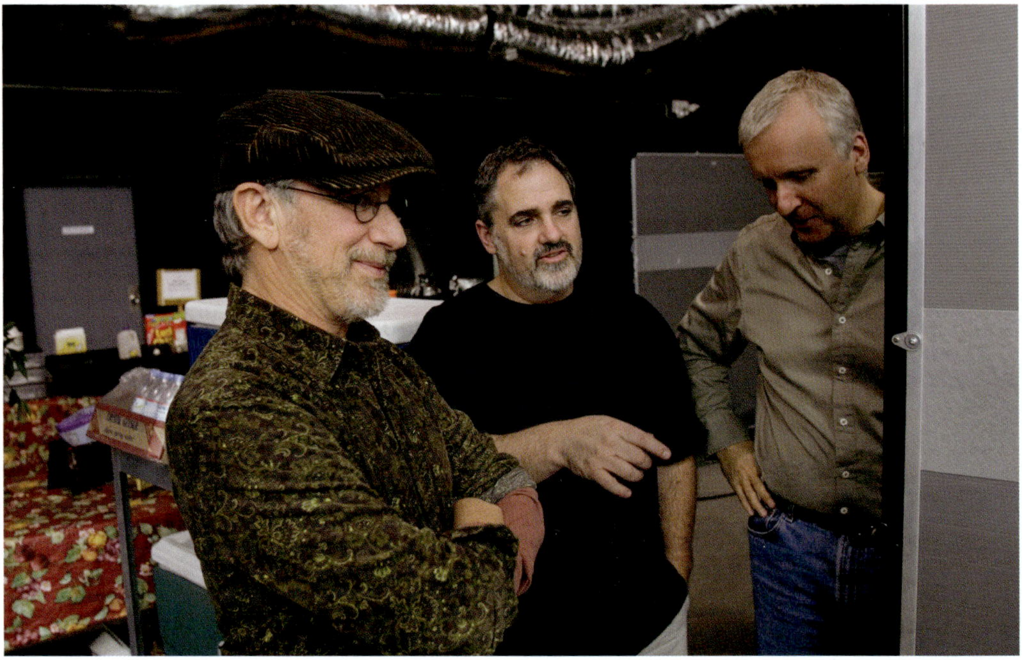

With Steven Spielberg and James Cameron on the set of *Avatar,* 2008

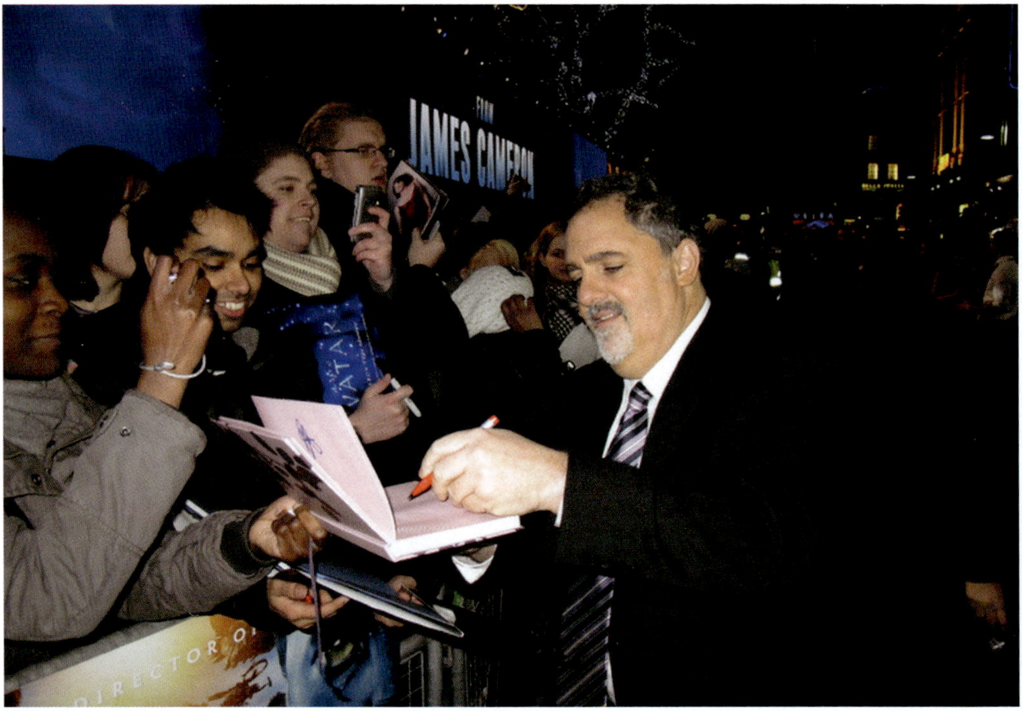

Signing autographs at the world premiere of *Avatar*, London, 2009

At the Los Angeles premiere of *Avatar* with my family
and dear friends Rhea Perlman and Danny DeVito, 2009

Photo courtesy of the Landau family

Onboard the U.S.S. EISENHOWER nuclear aircraft carrier
January 26, 2010
(somewhere in the Persian Gulf)

Fox Team
AVATAR
Thank you
FOR MAKING
AVATAR
#1
OF ALL TIME!

AVATAR

With Michelle Rodriguez, James Cameron, Stephen Lang, John David Cameron,
and military personnel aboard the USS *Dwight D. Eisenhower*, 2010

With Julie the day we bought our piece of paradise, Bali Hai, in the Florida Keys, 2010

Photo courtesy of the Landau family

With the cast of Cirque du Soleil's *Toruk–The First Flight*, 2015

Photo courtesy of the Landau family

Me as a hot dog on Halloween with director of photography Bill Pope and
director Robert Rodriguez on the set of *Alita: Battle Angel,* 2016

Opening day of Pandora—The World of *Avatar* at Walt Disney World Resort with James Cameron,
CEO of the Walt Disney Company Bob Iger, and members of the cast of *Avatar,* 2017

One of the many joyous Christmases spent at Bali Hai with family, 2019

Photo courtesy of the Landau family

Flying to New Zealand with James Cameron to shoot during the covid-19 outbreak, 2020

Photo courtesy of the Landau family

My friendly covid
safety reminders
to the crew, 2020

*Photos courtesy of
the Landau family*

Having a bit of fun with Jack Champion, 2020

Set photograph from Avatar: The Way of Water *copyright © 2022 20th Century Studios, Inc. All rights reserved.*

With my family at the Los Angeles premiere of *Avatar: The Way of Water,* 2022

Photo courtesy of the Landau family

A magical day—the ceremony in front of the TCL Chinese Theatre in Hollywood, 2023

Photo courtesy of the Landau family

They were shouting and weeping by the end. So what the hell happened during those first three minutes?

After the movie, during the audience Q and A, the Fox person running the session asked, "Did anything confuse you?"

All hands shot up. Somehow, in spite of the fact that audiences are not supposed to know what film is being shown at an advance screening, everyone had been told they would be seeing *Great Expectations*, another Fox new release. For the first three minutes, they thought they were watching a trailer for *Titanic*. That's why they were so quiet. It took five minutes for them to realize what was going on.

THERE IS A beat at the end of *Titanic* that Rae and I had talked to Jim about before we even started filming. Older Rose goes out on the deck of Brock Lovett's ship to drop the necklace—the Heart of the Ocean—into the water. In the script, Lovett, played by Bill Paxton, stops her, and they talk. Lovett convinces Rose to let him hold the necklace just for a moment. He turns it over in his hand, then gives it back to Rose, who, with the salvage crew watching, drops it overboard. We wanted that changed. It seemed like something Rose should do alone—she should stand by herself at the rail as she stood with Jack at the beginning when she was young.

Jim didn't go for it.

Around the same time as the advance screening, we held a screening for friends and family. Afterward, I sat with Steve Quale, a protégé of Jim's who'd done second unit directing on the film. I wanted to get his thoughts. He said the ending was off. That night, he told Jim that Rose should be alone when she throws the necklace overboard. Jim agreed and made the change. To this day, Jim credits Steve with making that crucial suggestion. Sometimes, all it takes is the right time and the right messenger.

You can take all the time and spend all the money in the world, but, in the end, it's the small changes, those that reflect on character—Rose was independent and adventurous; that's what she got from Jack and that's why she had to act alone—that make a film.

By the time Jim decided to reshoot the ending, the sets had been taken down. We still had the Russian ship to shoot Rose at the rail, but we had nowhere to show the necklace spiraling down into the sea. And so we shot that scene in my swimming pool in Sherman Oaks. When the camera looks back toward the surface of the water, you are, in fact, seeing my backyard.

People often ask what happened to the diamond—the Heart of the Ocean. In movies, a prop can become a talisman, a magic object that captures the imagination and becomes a cultural touchstone. Think of Dorothy's red shoes in *The Wizard of Oz* or the DeLorean in *Back to the Future*. The Heart of the Ocean is currently in our private museum at Lightstorm alongside the model of the ship and many other props. I love watching people try it on—a costume jewelry prop that's returned a billion dollars in pleasure.

FOR ANY MOVIE, the first trailer is hugely important. It's the best chance you will have to capture an audience. You have two and a half minutes to convey the movie's story and feel. Those 150 seconds are everything, and like so many things on *Titanic*, they became the subject of a major battle.

Translating a three-hour-and-fourteen-minute (or two-hour-and-seventy-four-minute, as I like to say) movie into the standard ninety seconds is not easy. We navigated our way to a four-minute-and-two-second cut and sent it to the studios—remember, we were working with both Fox and Paramount—then waited. About two hours later, Rae got a call from Rob Friedman, the head of distribution and marketing at Paramount. "I saw your trailer," he apparently told her, "and I'm throwing up all over my shoes."

Paramount had taken the same footage and made their own shorter trailer. We called it the John Woo trailer. It was all flash cuts and pounding music, gunshots, and screams. It made the movie look like an action flick that happened to take place on the *Titanic*. It was not our movie. We went back and forth with Paramount, first reasoning, then screaming. We ultimately convinced Sherry Lansing, Paramount's chairperson and CEO, to veto her own distribution department and let us test our trailer at ShoWest, the conference of the National Association of Theatre Owners in Las Vegas. These are the people who really matter. By choosing what movies to book into their theaters and deciding how many screens to dedicate to them, they serve as arbiters, a link to distribution.

Our trailer was long. To us, it seemed proportionate to the length of the movie. And necessary. It was the first footage almost anyone outside the studio and production team had seen of *Titanic*. The stakes were high. Everyone was tense. We'd spent five years and $200 million. At times, it seemed like the whole world was rooting for us to fail. *Time* magazine ran a *Titanic* cover story with the cover line "Glub, Glub, Glub . . ." The sound of the big ship sinking.

Rae and I sat at Paramount's table at ShoWest with some of their top executives and biggest names, including Kurt Russell, the star of their upcoming film *Breakdown*. I sat nervously as our trailer played in that banquet hall in Las Vegas, and just as it ended, Kurt Russell loudly announced, "I'd pay ten dollars just to see that trailer again." With that, we got a special dispensation from the Motion Picture Association—trailers were supposed to be 150 seconds, max—to release a four-minute-and-two-second trailer to audiences around the world.

And from that day on, every negative article about the film ended with the sentiment that the movie might actually be good. It was a real turning point.

TITANIC WAS ORIGINALLY scheduled as a summer movie—a July 2 release. When it became clear this date seemed impossible, Fox gave us a little extra time and pushed the release to August. But even August became unrealistic. There were still too many visual effects to be completed, and those alone could take months. We told the studio we could get them a version of the movie for August, but it would be too long and we'd have to cut key visual effects shots. Tom Sherak, going against the rest of the studio executives' desires, was instrumental in encouraging us to hold out for a December release. Summer was traditionally the time for blockbusters, and the studio was sure they had lost the window in which they could make anything close to the box office they needed to recoup their investment, let alone make any profit. Tom had convinced us that a December blockbuster could exist. In that Christmas holiday window, everyone is off from work and school. If we could catch on then, we could play well into the new year.

We decided to hold the premiere of *Titanic* at the Tokyo International Film Festival. The screening was scheduled for November 1, 1997. Jim Gianopulos, the president of 20th Century Fox International—he'd been a big supporter of the project since I had first shown him Jim's underwater footage of the real *Titanic*—believed Tokyo was the right place, too. Paramount didn't want the movie shown at the Tokyo International Film Festival. They thought it was too early; it was still six weeks before the general release. But as they had such low expectations of our prospects for success anyway, they were not hard to convince.

Julie and I went to Japan with Leonardo DiCaprio a week before the event. Leo was just twenty-three, but any chance for a life of anonymity was behind him. Baz Luhrmann's *Romeo + Juliet* had made Leo a heartthrob, and the excitement around the release of *Titanic* pushed him into superstardom. There were swarms of adoring fans (mostly women) waiting to meet him at the airport and follow him everywhere he went. Images of the Beatles flooded to mind; "Leo-mania" was real. That is a lot to deal with at such a young age.

Kate was also catapulted to stardom. And she was a workhorse when it came to the press. She sat for every interview, answered every request. She talked a lot, and very honestly.

The film festival was held in an old opera house. We put in special projection equipment to show the movie at its best. Once the decision to premiere in Japan was made, we had to have Japanese subtitles, which meant we had to find a translator who could work fast. We hired two companies—one was directed to work from the start of the movie to the end, and the other was told to work from the end to the start. That way, if the work took longer than either had expected, they could meet in the middle.

Both companies completed the work on time. We watched the movie with the subtitles from the first company on the morning of the premiere. We were startled to find that the opening credits had been changed. The main title card now went not to Jim, Leo, or Kate but to the translation company itself. In huge letters it said: "Subtitles by." There was no way we could let the movie screen like that. We quickly unspooled the final reel of 35 mm film off the projector and Jim cut out the "Subtitle by" frames and spliced the footage back together himself. Jim's name—plus everyone else's—was exactly where it was supposed to be.

Evening rolled around, and the movie premiered. The crowd loved it. The standing ovation went on and on. Then Leo, Kate, Jim, and I went up onstage to take questions. Jim made sure I spoke first. He always did that. He wanted me to share the spotlight and was afraid if he spoke first that wouldn't happen. A lot of directors ignore their producer when it comes to festivals and award shows. Not Jim. He is very generous that way. A true partner.

There was a second premiere—the so-called Royal Film Performance—held in a theater on Leicester Square in London. This made thematic sense. *Titanic* was a British ship. Southampton, England, turned out to be its only port. It was a black-tie event. The evening started and ended with a standing ovation: the first when the then Prince Charles arrived; the second when the credits came up at the end of the movie. We still didn't know how it was going to play in theaters—release was weeks away. As we gamed out the possibilities, we thought we'd be lucky if we had another *Dances with Wolves*, a three-hour film that would be critically acclaimed and do decently well at the box office.

The movie opened on December 19, 1997, a Friday night. It was seventy degrees in Los Angeles, with a breeze from the west, an offshore wind that scattered a skyful of fair-weather cumulus clouds. *Teletubbies* was the biggest thing on TV that year. The Backstreet Boys were all over the radio. The Lakers, at 18–6, were scheduled to play that night, but, in our world, there was one thing that mattered most: opening weekend.

No doubt, journalists and newspapers were ready with headlines such as "Titanic Sinks at the Box Office" and "Studio Execs Go Down with the Ship."

No one could have predicted the phenomenon it became, especially when I tell you the movie only made $28 million its first weekend. The miracle was that in week seven—by which time most movies, even the successful ones, have faded away—*Titanic* was still making over $20 million a weekend. In fact, our biggest day did not come until the ninth weekend: Valentine's Day. *Titanic* is a perfect date movie. We eventually found out why the numbers did not drop— diehards were going back to see the movie a second, third, or even fourth time.

People often ask, "Well, with a movie like *Titanic,* a movie that makes that much money, do the reviews even matter? Do you really care about them? Do you even read them?" The answer is yes, yes, and yes; they do matter because you want the artistry and hard work of your cast and crew to be recognized.

On *Titanic,* one of the first reviews we got was from Kenneth Turan in the *LA Times.* It was just terrible, so bad it was followed by weeks of dueling letters and op-ed pieces. *Ken Turan shouldn't be writing reviews*—many letters went like that. Jim wrote an article commenting on the review, the comments about the review, and the comments about the comments. What I remember best from the Turan piece— because it stung—is what he said about our dialogue, which he dismissed as clichéd.

When Jim wasn't nominated for Best Screenplay for *Titanic* at the Academy Awards, William Goldman, the godfather of modern screenwriting, responded to the snub with a piece about all the criticisms of the script. Scriptwriting is not just dialogue, William explained. It's structure. It's the journey of the characters. And, when it comes to dialogue, one man's cliché is another man's archetype. That's something I'll never forget.

Ten weeks after the release, Rupert Murdoch called up Tom Sherak and asked: "Is this movie really going to make a billion dollars?" No film had ever come close to that. We were in new territory. *Titanic*, in its initial release, brought in $1.8 billion in ticket sales.

Here's something else that people only pretend doesn't matter: awards. To most of America, movie awards mean the Oscars—or maybe the Oscars and the Golden Globes. But, when you're out running the gauntlet, you experience awards as an entire season, a winter of anticipation, possible heartbreak, and hopefully success.

The Golden Globes, which were at the time given out by the Hollywood Foreign Press Association, are the harbinger. That event will generally tell you who is going to win at the Oscars. If you lose at the Globes, check your expectations. People say merely getting nominated is good enough, and it is definitely good, but winning is certainly better. Winning an Oscar is the pinnacle in our business.

The Golden Globes took place in a ballroom in the Beverly Hilton, a few blocks from where I now live. Sitting in my kitchen, I can look out the window at the hotel as if looking back in time. What a night! Christine Lahti, who was up for Best Actress in a Television Drama for *Chicago Hope*, was in the bathroom when they called her name as a winner. Timing is everything in life.

Titanic was nominated for eight Golden Globes and won four. Best Original Score went to our composer, James Horner. Horner and Will Jennings, the lyricist, received Best Original Song for "My Heart

Will Go On," performed by Céline Dion. Best Director went to Jim. We also won Best Motion Picture–Drama.

Meanwhile, the Oscars were approaching. The competition was fierce. It had been a great year for movies. There were five Best Picture nominees: *As Good as It Gets*, *The Full Monty*, *Good Will Hunting*, *L.A. Confidential*, and *Titanic*.

I vividly remember walking with Julie onto the floor of the Shrine Auditorium. We sat with the *Titanic* team in front, next to Edie and our son Jamie. Kathy and her husband, Michael, had flown out for the occasion and were also there.

Although the first award did not go as we'd hoped—Gloria lost to Kim Basinger—the tide shifted. Our teams won Best Editing, Best Song, Best Original Dramatic Score, Best Costume Design, Best Art Direction, Best Visual Effects, Best Cinematography—all those categories that make a movie a movie. Helen Hunt, for *As Good as It Gets*, beat out Kate for Best Actress.

The biggest awards come at the very end of the show. It was particularly thrilling to hear: "James Cameron, Best Director!" Jim went up, said his thanks, and was back in his seat in time to hear the nominees for Best Picture. Then Sean Connery called my name. I knew Ely would've been proud—I'm sure of that.

Jim and I made our way to the stage and stood there side by side. As they put the statuette in my hand, all I could think was *Is this for real?* and *Be sure to hold on to this.*

After we spoke, we were escorted backstage for photos and interviews. On our way there, I said to Jim, "When we pose for photographs, let me stand between you and Sean Connery. Otherwise, they'll crop me out of all the pictures."

When asked to pose for some shots alone, Jim gave me his three

Oscars. This left me holding four statues in total. The awards are given without plaques—these are added later. They do have numbers, though. These tell you where in history your Oscar falls. The first went to William A. Wellman in 1929 for his silent movie *Wings*. To date, more than three thousand have been given. I checked the number of each of our statuettes. One was emblazoned with the number 2929. I'm not normally into numerology, but that struck me as a good number. Easy to remember, and it went well with my phone number, which was all twos and nines. So I kept that statuette, and it sits proudly on my shelf beside my desk.

I felt a tremendous release after the Oscars. We'd been in high gear since preproduction—over two years of peak stress. There had been battles, reversals, doubts. It took me back to the moment when I'd called Julie from the set after our last day of shooting and burst into tears.

"What happened?" she asked. "What's wrong?"

"We did it," I told her. "We made *Titanic*."

Chapter 6

When I look back, I'm amazed by all the people I met and places I traveled. I met Bill Clinton. I met Hillary Clinton. Barack and Michelle Obama. I met Ronald Reagan, George H. W. Bush, and George W. Bush. I met the president of Israel, Shimon Peres. We hosted a dinner for the prime minister of New Zealand, John Key, at our home in LA, and later we met another of New Zealand's prime ministers, Jacinda Ardern.

As interesting as these encounters could be, they often felt performative and perfunctory. Dog and pony shows, or handshakes and small talk, and I was craving something more. It did not take long to realize I really only wanted to be in one place and with one group of people: at home with my family. I desired less whirlwind, and more time with Julie and the boys. More everyday life. It wasn't the big moments I missed—birthdays, anniversaries, and the like. I had made it to almost all of those. It was all the little ones in between—school drop-offs and pickups, homework, sports, school plays, sleepovers, game nights—that I was craving. Firsts, lasts: I wanted to be there.

Edie was a part of it all, too. A big part. She was a constant in Jamie's and Jodie's lives and an active participant. She took them to the theater, exposed them to different music, taught them 500 rummy and mah-jongg, read them poetry, brought them on trips—everything. In the end, it was less the details, sights, and sounds of those trips that enriched the kids than the time they spent with her. The bond was strong and beautiful. To this day, I see so much of her in them.

Jamie was a kid who always loved music. He was drawn to it. He could sing before he could speak. I have amazing videos of him at the age of two in his car seat, belting out Madonna's song "More" from *Dick Tracy* from beginning to end. He was in school plays and local theater productions. In high school, he and four talented friends started a rock band called Discovery Zone that went on tour after graduation. Jamie was the lead singer. Rob Cavallo, a top guy in the music industry, produced one of their songs.

Jim even used that song, "Bless the Plague," for a scene in *Avatar*. Jim didn't do this for me. He would never sacrifice quality for sentiment. We presented Jim with multiple song choices, and he chose Jamie's. It was a great song with environmental themes kindred to those in the movie. Unfortunately, that scene was cut from the theatrical release of the film, but was later included in the extended edition. I never would have thought that Jamie would eventually put music behind him and follow my path in film production, though he ultimately did.

Jodie's first love was ice hockey, and it became a big part of our lives. From the time he was eight years old, he played. He was a natural—fast, scrappy, and competitive, in the right proportions. I had played as a child, and those years spent with Jodie at practices and games brought me back to happy memories with Ely. Hours and years spent with him at the rink—him lacing up my skates before I could do it on my own, our packing up the car and heading off to games, hearing him cheering from the bleachers. Jodie and I spent hours on the road, traveling to tournaments around the country and world. Fargo, North Dakota. Littleton, Colorado. Montreal. San Francisco. And even Prague. People at work would see me leaving the office early on a Friday with a cell phone, a beeper, a hockey bag, and a stick. I loved those trips—they grounded me. They connected us to each other and to a whole world outside of Hollywood.

When he got older, Jodie swapped hockey for music. Musically, he always seemed to be drawn to what I would call the avant-garde. Even in high school, Jodie, who always marched to his own drumbeat (yes, musical pun intended), was fascinated by eclectic jazz and contemporary classical aesthetics rather than the standard teen fare. For a senior project, he wrote and performed a suite of songs. As a performer, Jodie sings and plays various keyboard and percussion instruments, my favorite of which is the harpejji, an instrument that is a mix of a guitar and keyboard and is as unique as he and his music are. Jodie has performed in renowned venues around the world—from Carnegie Hall and Lincoln Center in New York to the Walt Disney Concert Hall in Los Angeles, the Barbican in London, the Philharmonie de Paris, and more. He has recorded albums, both his own and as part of ensembles. He's performed in operas, composed for and sung in dance performances, and worked with composers on film scores. And he created an autobiographical solo show, *Performance of Self,* that debuted in New York in March 2024.

Seeing your kids find themselves and follow their passions—on the ice, onstage, on set, and in the world—is about as thrilling as it gets.

Yes, even better than a packed house for *Titanic*.

TO CELEBRATE OUR family, Julie and I went all out on our annual holiday cards. Viewed side by side, the cards tell our story.

It started soon after the kids were born. I liked to tinker with Photoshop and always wanted the cards to be memorable—sometimes useful, sometimes intended just to bring a smile, sometimes a treat. When you recalled or looked at them years later, we hoped you would see more than just a photo of us—you'd get a sense of that time in the life of our family or moment in the world.

One year, we sent out a miniature 3D chocolate mold of ourselves inscribed with "Sweet Holidays." Another year we sent wine bottles with the four of us on the label and a card that said "May you have nothing to wine about throughout the holidays or the entire year!" Another year, we sent a card that said "What you realize at the holiday season is that it's the people who make up the parts of your life who make your life special." It came with a mosaic of Jamie and Jodie made of 1,500 tiny photos and was accompanied by a magnifying glass and a cheat sheet that identified everyone in those little pictures—all the people on the mailing list. In the first year of covid, we had our family photo imposed on bars of soap in a nod to encouraging people to wash their hands. There was the year of the View-Master, which came with a disc that showed highlights from the year as lived by the Landaus. We did a Rubik's Cube that, when solved, showed our faces and read "Here's to solving all of life's puzzles." We did a holiday tree ornament, a scratch-off lottery ticket, and even a magazine memorializing all the cards of years past. One year, we made a holiday CD. Julie sang "O Holy Night," Jodie sang John Lennon's "Happy Xmas (War Is Over)," and Jamie sang "Jingle Bell Rock" in a faux-Elvis voice. As *Avatar* was still in development at the time and we were looking for a studio deal, I sang, and not too well, "All I want for Christmas is a green-green light.... If only I could have a movie in production, then I could wish you Merry Christmas." I'm the only one in the family who can't sing— I like to describe myself as the world's only monotone who can sing off-note.

One year, Rae, an annual holiday card recipient, said, "Jon, can you think about doing something more traditional?" Jamie, a high schooler at the time, shared the same sentiment.

So, the cover of that year's card showed our family dressed in formal attire, with a caption above that read "This holiday season we had so much pressure from our teenage son to do a 'traditional' card, we had no choice but . . . to grin and bare it." Because traditional was never our thing, when you opened up the card there we were, in the nude, with the phrase "Happy Holidays" covering everything that needed covering. I had to photoshop Jamie's head onto my body, with chest hair digitally removed, as Jamie absolutely refused to pose nude. We actually sent out two different versions that year. Only a select few (for us, "few" meant a couple hundred or so of our far more expansive list) received the card with us nude on the inside. The other version, which the majority of our mailing list received, featured us in holiday-themed underwear, with the reluctant Jamie still in a suit and tie.

Julie ran into Peter Chernin that December.

When he saw her, he said, "Hi, Julie! I didn't recognize you with all your clothes on."

Julie was really not happy, and let me know it. "Jon, I thought those cards were only going to our friends!"

What can I say? I goofed.

Chapter 7

Avatar, which started as a seemingly impossible-to-produce fantasy, would turn into one of the defining projects of my life. But there were twelve years between the release of *Titanic* and *Avatar*. That time was not solely spent developing the necessary technology, and it was not spent sitting idle.

I had been working at Lightstorm under a limited-term deal during the making of *Titanic*, and at the same time, I had started my own production company, Blue Horizon, which had a first-look deal with Fox. Just as my term deal was expiring, Lightstorm was renewing its deal with Fox with plans to develop more films. Rae and Jim asked if I wanted to join them at the company. Rae was president. Jim was chairman. They wanted me to be their third partner.

Jim does refer to me as his partner except when he doesn't, when he'll quip, "Jon, we create the illusion of a partnership." But it is a partnership, a true triumvirate, running the company. Jim's focus at the time was on his television series *Dark Angel*, and he had gone into full deep-sea-explorer mode, making documentaries along the way. Rae was heavily involved in *Dark Angel*, but I mostly stayed out of those worlds and focused on the development of other feature films for us to produce.

Those films were all in different stages of development. What would be next? How do you top *Titanic*? You don't even try. I don't believe in chasing past successes—I believe in looking forward.

Jim always had a dozen ideas going in his head. Ideas for movies, shows, projects. Working through his list, we eased into a new way of collaborating. I believe in his vision, both for our films and for filmmaking—that grand, groundbreaking, and singular Jim Cameron vision . . . challenging as it may be.

The key to all our endeavors is to anticipate Jim's needs and identify and fix the problems before they even reach him. As the man at the center, Jim has only so much time and attention. My goal is to help save them for those things that really matter.

I have given a lot to Jim, but have been given even more. Watching him work on a script has been more educational than film school. He has greatly expanded my sense of story. From him, I have learned how an audience is captured, enthralled, and released. The goal is a catharsis that leaves people transformed and enlightened. They enter the theater in one place and leave it somewhere else.

Jim shared a key lesson that he learned early in his career: The emotional climax has to come after the visual climax. It was a truth he knew inside out by the time he got to *Titanic*, which is why the last scene between Rose and Jack is so powerful. The physical climax—the sinking—has come and gone. The emotional climax comes after, in the ocean water, where it has our complete attention.

This is true in life as well. When all the bells and whistles are stripped away, the possessions and material things, it is the people, the feelings, the relationships, the loves, and the losses that matter and move us.

When I think of all the movies we developed that never made it to the silver screen, I shudder. It's a tough business. You can have the highest-grossing film of all time as your calling card and still not get a green light on your next picture. There was our long-gestating remake of the sci-fi classic *Fantastic Voyage* and the tragic, real-life romance of free-diving pioneers in *The Dive*. And there was a script I really loved, the high-stakes thriller *Nagasaki Deadline*.

Nagasaki Deadline was a look back at the horrific events in Hiroshima and Nagasaki, but told through the contemporary lens of an atomic bomb being detonated in a terrorist attack on American soil. The screenwriters, Peter and David Griffiths, came into the Lightstorm offices and sold me on it with a two-line pitch. I brought it to Jim and Rae, and they bought in.

If I had to pick one word to describe Jim's writing style, it would be *engineer*. The man constructs movies like an architect. He anticipates everything when he writes a script, engineering each emotional response from the beginning. You might think his focus is on plot or dialogue, but, for Jim, that's just a means to an end. Every shot, every visual is crafted to elicit the emotional connection. He never forgets the purpose of each element, or what it's supposed to do for the audience. I saw this most clearly in a meeting we had with the Griffiths brothers. I remember Jim holding up their script for *Nagasaki Deadline*, saying, "If you want this to happen in the third act, you have to set it up here on page six." That's how Jim works: He identifies the desired audience response, then figures out how to get there.

All the while, Jim never loses sight of the most important question: *Why?* Why am I telling this story? And who are the main characters? What do they want? What's the intent? The motivation? What do we want the audience to leave the theater with? You cannot make a good movie if you don't understand the *why* at every moment in the process.

There were many drafts and iterations of *Nagasaki Deadline*, and in 2001 we had attached Tony Scott (*Top Gun, Crimson Tide*) to direct. Then September 11 happened—I was at the gym that morning when everyone dropped their weights, stopped their treadmills, and watched, in shock, as the live images came in from New York. I immediately called Kathy to make sure she, Michael, and their three kids were safe, then checked in on Tina, and raced home. Rae and I closed down the Lightstorm offices, and I invited all of our employees to come over to my house so that we could be together in whatever was going on. I drove to the local grocery store to grab some food and extra pallets of water and essentials because, who knows? I was thinking about those closest to me and the fate of the world when my cell phone rang. It was Tony Scott. "Well, I guess we're not making that movie," he said.

Our business can be all-consuming. The stakes and pressures are high, and our perspective might be off-kilter some days. But for me, 9/11 was a day that brought everything important into sharp focus. *Nagasaki Deadline* did not get made.

There was only one film during that period that we shepherded—developing the script, recruiting the director, getting the green light, and overseeing filming, editing, and marketing—all the way through release. *Solaris* was adapted from the 1961 novel by the Polish writer Stanislaw Lem, an absolute genius. Like Philip K. Dick or Isaac Asimov,

Lem was one of the rare authors whose work went beyond genre, becoming something like philosophy. These books are less about space travel than about what it means to be human.

That type of story has always appealed to Jim. Like Lem, Jim looks at sci-fi not just as a way to imagine the future but to see what's happening in the here and now. The use of fictional characters and archetypes lets him cloak his conclusions and admonitions. For Lem, who worked in the Eastern bloc, this was a matter of life and death. For Jim, such stories are parables. It's only by setting the action in another world that we can get a clear view of our own.

There had already been a *Solaris* movie, the 1972 Russian cult classic by Andrei Tarkovsky. But Jim, Rae, and I believed there was still room for a commercial feature that could draw people to the movie theater. On paper, Steven Soderbergh was perfect to direct. His early hits had been quirky indies, critical darlings like *Sex, Lies, and Videotape.* But in 2000 he was coming off *Erin Brockovich,* a commercial hit that won Julia Roberts an Academy Award. Having read our script, Steven came in and pitched his own version of the movie. And he promised to deliver stars, specifically George Clooney, the lead in Steven's wildly successful and entertaining *Ocean's Eleven* remake and in his adaptation of the Elmore Leonard novel *Out of Sight.*

Here's the thing about movies: It's not enough to have a great script and a great cast. If you want a big budget, you also need a big star. It's the only way a studio will risk the outlay—previous hits by an actor give the execs a way to estimate box office and justify cost, though everyone knows it's hardly a guarantee. Each movie is a new beginning, a new opportunity to lose your shirt. Or, of course, rake in millions.

We knew Steven's take wasn't going to be exactly like Jim's. We expected and even wanted that. "If we wanted Jim Cameron's version of a movie," we explained, "we'd have Jim Cameron direct." Our job was not to dictate a vision, but to support the director. But we did have to agree on the basic concept. We had to be working in the same territory. Which is how we started with Steven. He took our notes and agreed with our general concept. This would be a mainstream movie—a painting in bright colors—that would appeal to a broad audience.

A few weeks before we began to shoot, we started to get a funny feeling in our meetings with Steven. He seemed to be pulling away from us, withdrawing.

We had all agreed on the script. It had been the product of lengthy collaboration. Then, about ten days before filming was to begin, Steven showed up with an entirely different version of *Solaris*. It had become esoteric, ethereal, and far less commercial. Act three left the audience struggling to untangle fantasy from reality—maybe it had all been a hallucination. Leaving the viewer unclear, in a state of ambivalence, is very un—Jim Cameron, whether he is directing or producing.

It left all of us at Lightstorm in a quandary. On the one hand, the director side of Jim understood the importance of creative control, and he didn't want to second-guess Steven right before filming was to begin. We didn't want to bigfoot, or take over the project. This was a Steven Soderbergh movie. On the other hand, as producers, we had grave concerns about the changes, and with them, the movie's chances for success. In the end, we decided to back off, trust Steven, and hope for the best. The result was one of the few disappointments of my career. Not only did the movie fail at the box office; it was just not the picture we'd envisioned.

A few years later, when an executive at Fox was giving me a hard time about cost overruns on *Avatar*, he said, in front of a room of people, "Hey, Jon, have you ever brought a movie in on budget?"

I said, "Yes, *Solaris*."

Here's what *Solaris* taught me: A weak movie that comes in below cost and ahead of schedule is still weak. Getting it right is what really matters in the end—for the filmmakers, the studio, and the audience. Lesson learned—going forward, on any production that came under our umbrella, we would trust our judgment and retain creative control. We had done neither on *Solaris*. It still stings that the film was such a miss. I promised myself I would never let that happen again.

Chapter 8

J im has been fascinated with science fiction since he was a kid. And as a director, he loved it even more. Even skeptical viewers let their guard down when the action is set on an alien planet. You can reach people who would otherwise remain unreachable. Jim understood this intuitively. He loved sci-fi because he had an innate understanding of how it worked and the stakes involved. It ignited his imagination. By high school, he was writing sci-fi stories of his own, some of which were published in pulp magazines. His first real screenwriting foray into sci-fi came in 1978 when he cowrote and codirected a short feature film called *Xenogenesis* about a man and a woman blasted into space by an advanced civilization to find a new home for humanity. He never really stopped writing those sci-fi stories; after all, the movies that first put Jim on the map were all sci-fi. At Lightstorm, the drawers were full of wild screenplays Jim had worked on and, for one reason or another, abandoned. One of those was a scriptment that he had written in 1994 with the intention of shooting it with digital effects that would push technology into the new millennium. It would go on to become *Avatar*.

In 2005, Jim was finally ready to direct another feature and had homed in on a revised version of another sci-fi project: *Alita: Battle Angel*. That coincided with the moment I went to him and said, "Jim, I think we might be at a point where we can finally make *Avatar*."

I had first read *Avatar* when we were in preproduction on *Titanic*. Jim was one of the first directors to understand that the future of the medium was going to be in digital effects. In 1993, he had partnered with Stan Winston and Scott Ross to create the company Digital Domain. He hoped that *Avatar* could be the project that pushed the company to create an entire world and characters using computer-generated effects, instead of Stan's phenomenal puppets and prosthetics. It would be a giant leap to go from optical-based effects into full digital effects.

But as usual, Jim was ahead of his time. The effects he imagined, the effects he'd need for *Avatar*, were still a decade away in 1994. *Titanic* is probably the last of the old-fashioned epics, closer to the moviemaking world of *Lawrence of Arabia* than *Avatar*. It was made on the cusp of the revolution. If we produced *Titanic* today, we would not build the ship. We would not cast thousands of extras. All of that would be digital.

When Jim showed his partners at Digital Domain the *Avatar* scriptment, they thought he was crazy. The technology to make it simply did not exist. And so, he put the scriptment in a drawer, which is where I searched for it almost a decade later. It was not the proposed effects I had fallen in love with—it was the characters, the story, and the message. A wounded marine joins his fate to that of an endangered alien civilization. It's a love story, a war story, a story of redemption and rebirth. And, *Avatar* was an anguished cry for environmental aware-ness. There can be no future if we destroy our world in the process.

In the years that had passed since Jim first wrote *Avatar*, all kinds of new-look technology had been invented. The most relevant and exciting advancement to us was in motion capture, or mo-cap for short. The real-life movement of actors could now be recorded and transferred to a digital character. How? Picture an actor in a skin-tight Velcro suit with Ping-Pong balls stuck all over. These are actu-ally markers or sensors that can be tracked by cameras and turned into computer data. Think of it like a super-advanced version of connect the dots, where the lines drawn between each point create a form that any digital avatar can be placed over to form realistic animations.

George Lucas featured the first fully motion-captured main char-acter, Jar Jar Binks, in *Star Wars: Episode I–The Phantom Menace*. Robert Zemeckis began making entire features, like *The Polar Express*, with the technology, and Peter Jackson's *The Lord of the Rings: The Two Towers* was the first film to use a version of motion capture where the digital character, Gollum, could be seen by the filmmakers in real time as the actor performed on set. We were impressed, and our imaginations ran wild with ideas of how we could utilize the technology.

Jim really didn't know at the time whether those tools were going to be used for *Avatar* or for *Alita* first. I was always advocating the *Avatar* side of things. I'd like to think I pushed him in that direc-tion, but if I am being honest, I think Jim chose *Avatar* before *Alita* for logistical reasons. I think that he felt that if we solved *Avatar*, *Alita* would be easier to make, because with *Avatar*, our computer-generated characters are in a computer-generated world. He perceived that as easier to achieve than what would be *Alita*'s computer-generated character in a photoreal world, interacting on locations and sets with human characters. Pandora would be a world newly created—every detail designed by master artists and artisans. An entire ecosystem with no parallel in the real world, and inhabited by mythical figures.

I remember when one of our *Avatar* trailers came out, someone criticized us. They said, "That helicopter in front of that floating mountain wasn't flying properly." It's a helicopter in front of a floating mountain, guy! What's proper, what's not? But I loved that it wasn't the world of Pandora or the emotional core of the story that he was questioning—those all seemed real and true to him. It was the Resources Development Administration (RDA) helicopter. I think the idea that Pandora doesn't exist, that it is fantasy, has given us liberty in design. That doesn't mean we were careless with our decisions; Jim plots out every detail to make sure they're all as scientifically and physically accurate as can be. Years later, I was shown concepts of aerial vehicles the United States military was developing. They looked startlingly like the twin-rotor Samson and Scorpion gunships we designed for *Avatar*.

Though we would be leaving the convention of shooting on film behind, we would be echoing maybe the greatest of all Hollywood movies: *The Wizard of Oz*. When I was a child, that movie would play once a year on TV, and Edie, Ely, Tina, Kathy, and I would gather in our living room to watch it together. It was a family tradition. Each year, no matter how many times we had seen it, we would all gasp when Dorothy stepped out into that colorful land of Oz.

In our movie, our hero, Jake Sully, having lost use of his legs on earth, travels across the galaxy to a planet called Pandora, where his consciousness is uploaded into an artificial alien body—an avatar—that will allow him to live among the native, ten-foot-tall blue creatures called Na'vi. The key moment comes when Sully, in his new body, steps out into that strange, colorful paradise for the first time. The portal is a spaceship instead of a tornado-tossed house, but the impact is the same. Jake Sully is Dorothy. The world is new.

To make *Avatar*, we needed to create an entirely unique virtual production pipeline. The movie could only be made with a seamless integration of motion capture, live-action photography, and fully realized, computer-generated effects.

I think that when people hear that we waited for the technology before making *Avatar*, they are often confused. They think we waited for 3D viewing technology. That had nothing to do with it. We waited for technology that would allow us to put emotive and engaging CG characters up on the screen. Movies are ultimately about performances and close-ups. They're not about the environments. They're not about the action. They're about seeing the minute reaction in your hero's—or villain's—eyes. We needed technology that was ready to a point from which we could take it to the next level.

I tell people, *motion capture* was always missing one key letter in front of it—an *E* for *emotion*. *Motion capture* is a dirty phrase on our set. I won't let anyone on our crew use it. And you won't see me use it again either. We aimed to change it to *performance* capture. Gone were the days of only having the digital data of broad movements and big gestures; our goal, and commitment, was to put every nuance of an actor's performance up on the screen.

To make that full transition, we first broke down our major requirements—and therefore challenges—into three categories for development: face, body, and camera.

FACE

Avatar's real breakthrough, developed with the digital effects and computer animation company Wētā FX, was a front-facing head-rig camera that was placed directly on each actor to capture even the subtlest movement of facial muscles, lips, and eyes. To paint the picture of what that looked like, I'd describe it as almost like a headset mic a pop star would use.

This was a game changer. It was important for us to create a production paradigm that would allow Jim to work with actors with the same intimacy that he had worked with Kate and Leo, Jamie Lee and Arnold. We needed to make sure that technology would not get in the way of that director/actor relationship. These unobtrusive head-rig cameras allowed us to record, in fine detail, the facial performance of an actor at the same time as their skeletal motion.

BODY

One of the things that we saw very early on when testing the capture process was that when two people were standing apart, we got all the data from their bodies. However, when they came together, because some of the markers (the "Ping-Pong balls") were blocked from the cameras, we began losing a lot of the data. We would have CG characters suddenly doing the Watusi dance on-screen—all of their limbs going in different directions. We searched for solutions and found one from Giant Studios, a company, that had developed proprietary software with a biomechanical solve, which meant that if an area of a performer was obstructed from view, the software could reconstruct the actor's movements by applying real-world anatomical constraints and physics. It ensured that the digital characters moved naturally and realistically within the limits of human biomechanics. The backbone of the software was strong. Strong enough that we ultimately bought the tech outright from the company.

CAMERA

Our ultimate challenge was creating a camera that Jim could hold and move, just as he would when shooting with a traditional camera, but this one would be a "virtual" camera that functioned as his portal to the visual world we were creating. It needed to be the lens—literal and figurative—through which Jim could look at the actors standing there right in front of him and see not the actor but a crude CG representation of the character they were playing. And on a barren soundstage, he would see not the stage, but the broad strokes of the world within the movie—the world, in our case, of Pandora. I use the terms *crude* and *broad strokes* because I'd describe the virtual camera's CG images as similar to those of a 1990s video game. We worked with Glenn Derry, our virtual production supervisor, and his team to come up with the best virtual camera. The first one was round like a wheel. We tried one with a shoulder harness, except then you couldn't get low-angle shots. There were many iterations, evolutions that we spent over a year getting right. But, with a remarkable team of creative minds working to master the challenge, we eventually had just what we needed. It was a lightweight camera with an LCD monitor instead of a viewfinder, and with two flight control sticks repurposed on each side to control the different aspects of the camera. Jim could move the camera around on the soundstage and see the crude and broad-stroke environments that would later be fully realized. He could zoom in, pan left, crane up—anything that he would do on a live-action set.

Face, body, camera . . . action!

Making *Avatar* was not just about mastering performance capture. Pandora didn't exist. We were designing every element, and doing it in the most exacting detail. Every costume, every raindrop, every blade of grass. Building entire sets, characters, vehicles, and creatures, all virtually. Realizing an entire film that way would require designers, artists, artisans, craftspeople, scientists, linguists, botanists, engineers, and more—and each would need to be a master of their respective trade.

In our first year, we went through the entire ten-million-dollar research and development budget we had in our deal with Fox. Part of that went to the creation of a prototype clip of a scene from the movie—the one in which Jake and Neytiri first meet. We needed to test the virtual production pipeline and the visual effects to prove that this could work, taking the performance capture and bringing our characters and the world of Pandora to life—vibrant, photoreal life. That first test was promising, but not entirely convincing. We had to find the right visual effects company. We ultimately did—Wētā FX.

During that year, we also finished a rewrite of the script, which Jim worked on with Laeta Kalogridis, a screenwriter known for *Lara Croft: Tomb Raider* and Oliver Stone's *Alexander*. With the prototype clip, the concept art, and the script in hand, we submitted all three to Fox along with a budget. A complete package.

In September of 2006, Peter Chernin came to Lightstorm and passed on the movie. He didn't come in and say, "Reduce the budget."

He didn't come in and say, "Change the script." He didn't come in and say, "Change your deal." He just said, "We pass." And that was it. Suffice it to say, if we had been using our performance capture system that day, it would have captured a lot of emotions.

Jim and I felt we could get the film set up at another studio, and the best one for us would be Disney. The dream of Pandora, a strange, beautiful alien world, was clearly in the spirit of Disney. It is something I feel that Walt Disney himself would've understood immediately. Jim had worked on a few documentaries with Disney, *Ghosts of the Abyss* among them, and had a good relationship with Dick Cook, the chairman of Walt Disney Studios at the time. We presented all the material to the top brass. Then Dick, Alan Bergman, and Bob Iger came down to our facilities in Playa del Rey to see the work in development. Over the course of four weeks, they decided they were ready to come on board and be the studio behind *Avatar*.

During that four-week period of uncertainty, Vicki Rossellini, executive vice president of production finance and business affairs at Fox and a major champion of the film, and I went out—unbeknownst to Peter Chernin or even Jim—and we pitched to two financial partners that Fox had: Dune Capital Management and Ingenious Media. We hoped they would step up and cover more of the budget. James Clayton from Ingenious and Chip Seelig from Dune came to Lightstorm, and I did the dog and pony show. I was a full-on P. T. Barnum. It was starting to look like Disney was ready to commit, so we went back to Peter Chernin and said, "Look, we'd like you to support us for another month, and we'll have the paperwork done with Disney, and that will be that."

And Peter said, "I think we found a way to keep the movie at Fox."

Vicki had succeeded in putting together a deal in which Ingenious and Dune would step up to the plate. You know the old saying, the devil you know is better than the devil you don't. We made the difficult call to Disney.

WE HAD FOUND our studio partner; now we needed to find our cast. The best technology in the world wouldn't matter if we didn't have the right actors.

The first big question was who would be our Neytiri. The answer came quickly and resoundingly when we found Zoe Saldaña. What I didn't know at the time was that I had also found a lifelong friend.

Zoe's entry point into films had been through dance—she had starred in a handful of films, including *Center Stage* and *Drumline*. There were also a few small parts in big movies, including *Pirates of the Caribbean: The Curse of the Black Pearl*, but *Avatar* would be her first lead role in a major motion picture. (Fun fact: Since Zoe was cast first, she greatly influenced how the Na'vi spoke and moved. The rest of the cast would take their lead from her.)

Finding our Jake Sully was a much harder challenge.

We needed a certain kind of actor for *Avatar*. Talented, trusting, and they had to be able to connect with an environment that would be almost entirely virtual. We did not just want to fill out the cast with big stars. The appearance of a big star, no matter how talented—an actor who could not help but evoke images from former films—could blow the illusion. *What's* he *doing on Pandora?*

We thought we'd finally found our Jake in Sam Worthington, a successful Australian actor largely unknown outside his home country. He'd been a regular on a hit Australian TV show called *Love My Way* and had won a Best Actor award from the Australian Film Institute for his performance in the indie film *Somersault*. He had sold all his possessions and was living out of his car in Sydney when he came in to audition. On paper, he was a fit as our Jake—a skilled, charismatic actor unknown to a wide audience. But we needed to see him work, to see him with Jim, with Zoe, in the environment. And then, we'd need to convince the studio.

We put all of our potential Jakes with Zoe in a round of big old-fashioned screen tests with real sets. Two other terrific actors who went on to wild success had made it that far, Chris Evans and Channing Tatum. But it was Sam, in Jake's big speech during one of the scenes—a rallying cry to the clans of Pandora—who made the hair stand up on the back of our necks. We believed everything he was saying, and we felt we would follow him into battle to protect the world and the people we cared about. That's exactly what we needed the audience to feel. When we first tried to call Sam to tell him he got the part, we couldn't find him because he was up on top of a mountain somewhere without a phone. That's our Jake.

We made a promise to our actors that they would see themselves up there on the screen. That their performances would be fully realized and conveyed. That the beauty and subtlety of their work would not be overwhelmed by the visual magnetism of the fantastical creatures they inhabited. Well into postproduction, I invited Sam to come to our screening room to watch the scene where Jake wakes up for the first time in his avatar body: Jake awakens, and unaccustomed to walking—let alone in his new ten-foot-tall blue body—he stumbles, flails about, and catches himself. The scene started to play and Sam laughed. I glanced over nervously. *Uh-oh, what does he think?* The scene played for another couple seconds, and Sam laughed harder. He turned to me and said, "That's a good laugh, mate. That *is* me up there on the screen." A promise kept.

We decided to do a photo shoot of Sam and Zoe together before we started production. As we were setting up, Sam told me that those types of photo shoots are not something he's really comfortable with. It's not who he is.

"Sam," I said, "now that you're moving into these types of movies, there needs to be three yous. There needs to be you, the Sam we couldn't find who was up on the top of a mountain. There has to be you, the Sam who transforms into Jake Sully whenever we are filming. And there needs to be you, the Sam who's the movie star. Think of it as a part."

Years later, when we started doing press on *Avatar*, Sam said, "I'm a little bit nervous about this."

I said, "Sam . . ."

"I know," he said, and repeated back to me the three Sams.

We had our heroes; now we needed our villain. Jim immediately thought of an actor he had auditioned two decades earlier for the role of Corporal Hicks in *Aliens*—Stephen Lang. Slang (as he likes to be called) didn't get that part, but Jim always remembered his audition. I knew Slang because he played the sleazy tabloid journalist, Freddy Lounds, in *Manhunter*. When he came in to audition for Colonel Miles Quaritch, the film's ruthless antagonist, he was in his mid-fifties but had gotten his body into the shape of a ripped twenty-year-old. He even performed the dialogue in his first scene while doing a one-armed push-up. He had a deep knowledge of military history, had studied real-life military figures, and completely embodied the role.

There was one actor who we didn't need to audition. We offered the part of the lead scientist to Sigourney Weaver. That role had been written for a man, but when the idea of Sigourney entered the ether, it was as if lightning struck. Originally, her character in the *Avatar* script had been called Shipley, a little too close to Ripley—Sigourney's character in the Alien franchise—so we changed it to Grace Augustine. Jim loved and trusted Sigourney; their work together on *Aliens* back in 1986 led to her first Oscar nomination. Sigourney signed on, and we had our key players.

We filled out the supporting cast with incredible actors: Wes Studi, CCH Pounder, Giovanni Ribisi, Joel David Moore, Laz Alonso, and Michelle Rodriguez.

The bulk of our shoot, the performance capture, would be done in an old Howard Hughes airplane hangar in Playa del Rey that we had been using during the development of the project. It would be different than anything any of us—cast and crew—had ever worked on. Because of the technology, we needed to film all of the scenes in a sterile, warehouse-like space specifically designed to accommodate the hundreds of infrared cameras mounted across the ceiling, with gray building blocks put together like Lego to approximate the terrain and environments that would eventually be fully rendered on-screen. It was a tough job for the actors. They needed to believe that Pandora was real. With this in mind, we took the cast to Hawai'i to spend a few days in the rainforest. We hiked the wilderness, experienced the canopy with all those koa and ohia lehua trees, and even rehearsed a few scenes. We mostly wanted the actors to collect sense data—smell, touch, sound. We were there in the mornings, when the rainforest sounds like an aviary. On the trails with the extraordinary array of colorful flowers and plant life. At dusk, when the fading light would make the entire forest glisten. All this, they could bring back to the blank canvas that was our soundstage.

The first day there, we ran across a man in a bulldozer clearing trees. We stopped and stared. Here we were, making a movie about preserving the natural world, and here's this man clearing the rainforest. Sigourney went over to talk to him. She asked him why he was doing it. He thought for a moment, then said, "I don't know." He'd been told to clear these acres, so that's what he was doing.

It seemed to prove the urgency of Jim's vision. He'd written a rallying cry for the preservation of the natural world disguised as a story about a planet—as the Star Wars crawl says—"in a galaxy far, far away." That's what makes *Avatar* a fable: It turns the people and issues of our real world into archetypes and totems, using the power of storytelling to reflect to us our own dilemma. Movies can be a powerful window and a mirror.

People often ask me when Jim's enlightenment about the environment happened. I think it's always been who he is. You can't read the scriptment of *Avatar* and not see an environmental undertone in it. You cannot read *The Terminator* or *Terminator 2* and not see the warning. Machines versus humanity—the theme is about values and priorities, and the story is about the dangers of losing sight of them. I think that *Avatar* is the culmination of all of the seeds that Jim had been planting for himself.

We were out early one morning rehearsing in the rainforest. Jim was filming with a handheld camera. Sam was in costume—loincloth, ponytail wig, plastic bow and arrow. Sure enough, here comes a guy with his dog. He stops, looks at Sam, and says, "What the hell are you doing?"

Sam puffs up his chest: "Making a movie, mate."

"Making a movie?"

Sam says, "Yeah," and points to Jim, who is behind a tree with his camera. "That's Jim Cameron, the man who made *Titanic*."

"Boy," says the dog walker, "has he gone downhill!"

✧ ✧ ✧

BACK FROM HAWAI'I, we started production in earnest with our first six-month block of performance capture in Playa del Rey. There was still a learning curve on the sterile soundstage, but the actors found the process completely freeing. At times, it felt more like putting on a play at a black box theater than filming the most expensive film ever made. On a live-action set, you might have to act directly to the matte box of the camera while your scene partner reads lines from the other side of the room. On *Avatar*'s performance-capture set, the camera is always on you. Any take can be used later for a close-up or a master shot.

As with any movie, but here on a larger scale, we needed a tremendous number of secondary characters and extras (characters seen but with no spoken lines), and they would all need to be created through performance capture. To do this, we cast a performance capture troupe. They were a group of performers from different backgrounds—acting, dance, movement, stunts—who would stay with us throughout the entire shoot and who could play all secondary Na'vi characters.

Each scene has been designed on the computer before the actors even get involved. We know how it will all look in advance. On a traditional film you might travel to scout a real-world location; on the Avatar films, Jim is able to pick up the virtual camera and "scout" every designed location and set, making changes to the environment in real time with a few keystrokes on the computer by the stage operators. We share the locations—the look and feel—with the actors so they can imagine the setting of each scene on Pandora as they perform. We never want the actors to pantomime, so we created proxies for every prop in the film. We created proxies for the other living creatures of Pandora as well. If a character was flying on an ikran, our pterodactyl-like wonder, we would hang a full-size mold of the torso and wings of the creature up in the air and have the actor hop aboard and ride as we filmed.

Every aspect of the alien world Jim had created needed to be fully fleshed out, including the native language of Na'vi. I reached out to my alma mater, USC, and found linguistics professor Paul Frommer, who met with Jim and signed on to develop a language for the film. Jim had written about forty Na'vi words into the screenplay, which was all Paul had to go off to create the vocabulary, grammar, syntax, and pronunciation of a brand-new language. There are thousands of words to date, and I've heard that some hardcore fans have even had their weddings officiated in Na'vi.

Every costume you see in *Avatar* was actually made—not just rendered on a computer, but physically constructed. We needed to know how each outfit would look in the wind or the rain, how it conformed to the character's body. A good example is the scene of Jake jumping fully clothed into the water. We shot reference footage for that in real water because we needed to know how his clothes would look when wet. All that information was then used by Wētā FX to render the scene. Pieces of Na'vi wardrobe that would only ever be seen digitally, we made for real. Our remarkable costume designer, Deborah Scott, worked hand in hand with the artisans at Wētā Workshop to hand build or 3D print nearly every one. We also fitted and shot performance capture with each actor in a wig so Wētā FX could see how the hair moved when a character was running, fighting, swimming, or sleeping.

Word had spread that we were creating a new way of working—a new production paradigm—and we wanted to share everything we had learned and were accomplishing. So, we extended special invites to other creatives and some dignitaries to our performance-capture stage. Directors including Steven Spielberg, Peter Jackson, and Roland Emmerich. Tom Cruise, Arnold Schwarzenegger. Even the king of Jordan came to see what we were doing. I was always struck by the fact that our crew seemed unbothered by the luminaries and celebrities coming through. Then I brought down the *Fox NFL Sunday* crew—Jimmy Johnson, Howie Long, and Terry Bradshaw. And there it was—everybody went gaga. The crew all wanted autographs and pictures. I loved it.

In October 2007, we began to shoot our live-action footage in Wellington, New Zealand. People often assume we film in New Zealand for the stunning locations. Nope. We never even leave the soundstage. Well, then it must be because we want to be close to the artists at Wētā, right? Wrong. That is indeed a nice bonus. But, the truth is, it's all about the tax incentives we receive from the New Zealand government. They also happen to have fantastic crews and craftspeople there—people as talented as I've worked with anywhere.

Filming continued through March 2008, and it was clear by then that we were behind schedule and over budget. I tried to insulate Jim from the studio's dismay and anger—my job is to create a space where Jim can focus on work—but he began to feel it. It was like a drop in temperature before a storm. You heard it in the clipped tones on the weekly calls between us in New Zealand and the teams at Fox. You saw it in the Fox executives who visited the set saying that they just wanted to "take a look"—it was their money, after all, and they wanted to see how it was being spent. Jim resents that kind of interference, even if it's low-key, no more than a shadow on the wall. His temper got short.

One day on set, out of nowhere, Jim told me he wanted to fire our brilliant cinematographer, Mauro Fiore. Who remembers why? Something unimportant none of us can recall. This would have been a foolish act that would only have done damage to the film. We'd lose Mauro's whole department if we let him go. Jim and I started fighting about it in front of the crew. Not good. Jim was frustrated but did not want to show it in public. He pulled me into his trailer. We sat at the little table there.

Jim said, "When the fucking general says what he wants, the fucking colonel listens."

It's a tricky balance with Jim. You have to pick your battles. He's usually right, and always passionate. But if I thought he was wrong, I was more than capable of standing up to him and weathering his outrage. The goal was never to prove him wrong, but rather to protect him, his vision, and the movie. I finally got him to back down on firing Mauro, who went on to win an Academy Award for *Avatar*. But I'll never forget Jim saying, "When the fucking general says what he wants, the fucking colonel listens." What a line! I wish we'd used it in the movie.

IT WAS DURING that live-action shoot in New Zealand that we put our 3D camera rigs to the test. Jim had worked on *T2 3-D: Battle Across Time*, an attraction for Universal Theme Parks that opened in 1996. Jim loved the result, but hated the process. The 3D cameras of the time were behemoths; you needed two of them, and they weighed a combined four-hundred-and-fifty pounds. When they pushed the dolly for action sequences, the stunt performers had to run at half speed because the cameras couldn't be moved quickly enough; they later sped up the footage. This was not a way to make a movie.

Jim's 3D obsession blossomed after a getaway scuba diving trip that Jim and I took with two visual special effects guys, Vince Pace and John Bruno, to Chuuk Lagoon in Micronesia after releasing *Titanic*.

We dove down to incredible shipwrecks. Jim was shooting with a very early digital high-definition camera that Vince brought along. Having previously spent hours moving around heavy 35 mm camera rigs underwater on *The Abyss*, Jim suddenly found himself astonished by the exquisite footage he was able to obtain with a very small, light-weight camera. On the flight back, Vince and Jim talked about how to make a compact, digital 3D camera that would allow us to get the result that we loved in *T2 3-D*, but without encumbering the filmmaking process or the filmmaker.

Jim and Vince began developing the Fusion Camera System, which has one body and two side-by-side lenses, mimicking the way the human eyes see. This allowed for a much quieter, lighter setup. When we had our first digital 3D cameras, we went up to Marysville, California, where we shot 3D footage of a World War II bomber. Why a World War II bomber? Because nothing's ever easy or simple with Jim Cameron. The test was a success, and it was with these new cameras that we were able to do handheld and crane shots in 3D. Another challenge overcome through creative problem-solving and a strategic partnership.

So why 3D? It's about engaging audiences more in the narrative story. 3D had been used for mostly cheesy effects in the past—balls flying off the screen, a glass sliding down a bar, the fire in Vincent Price's 3D classic *House of Wax* bursting into the audience. I always tell people that, for us, 3D is a window into a world, not a world coming out of a window. The latter makes the audience notice the 3D, interrupting the suspension of disbelief that is critical to any narrative film. 3D is more important in a dramatic scene than it is in an action scene. In an action scene, in fact, we reduce the amount of 3D effects because we are cutting fast, and it can hurt the eyes. But 3D in a dramatic scene puts the viewer in that space and time, and the experience becomes immersive. 3D draws audiences further into the world of Neytiri, Jake, and Pandora. You are in there with them—flying on an ikran, walking among the woodsprites, standing beneath the Tree of Souls.

PART OF MY role on *Avatar* was to sell exhibitors—movie theater owners—not just in North America but around the world, on the idea of upgrading their projectors to be 3D compatible. I traveled across the country, and went to Spain, Russia, Brazil, France, Germany, Japan, China, and other countries, showcasing the potential of 3D and how we were utilizing it. People started to get it, to understand the type of cinematic experience we wanted to create. We homed in on emerging markets, places that had growing movie businesses and audiences, where new movie theaters were being built. This allowed us an opportunity to say, "Hey, you're in the market for new projectors and you'll want your projectors to be state of the art." Our point to them was, if you're putting in a projector anyway, make it a 3D compatible projector. There's no reason not to. Ultimately, the theaters thanked us for that, and we are thanking them. It's a two-way street.

When we started out on *Avatar*, we felt we would be happy if there were a thousand theaters that could show our movie in 3D. By *Avatar*'s release in 2009, there were closer to seven thousand screens worldwide in 3D. Now, there are over one hundred thousand.

After the success of *Avatar*, people tried to chase 3D. They pivoted in the middle of production and at the finish line. Scrambled. But that never works. When you see Martin Scorsese create *Hugo* in 3D, it's spectacular. When you see Ang Lee's *Life of Pi* as intended in 3D, that's fantastic. When somebody suddenly says, "I have two months left until release, let's transform this into a 3D movie," they're compromising quality—impacting the film, the audience, and the industry. A hasty retrofit to 3D is always an inferior product and delivers an inferior experience. When we rereleased *Titanic* in 3D in 2012, we spent a whole year converting the film properly.

MOST FILM SHOOTS are somewhat linear—you shoot and then you edit the film. *Avatar* was a Jackson Pollock painting. Production was a swirl of performance capture, live action, virtual camera days, editing, and visual effects reviews. We knew it would take a long time for Wētā to render the photoreal visual effects, so we had to feed them scenes throughout.

What we turn over to Wētā, while initially of that video game quality, contains the complete intention of every shot. We practically have our own visual effects company on the production, which we refer to as "the Lab." It consists of many departments to ensure that the performances, lighting, environments, costumes, and Jim's camera angles are all represented in what we call a template. Wētā's job wasn't to "fix" anything; it was to render the templates to look photoreal.

Here's the kicker—it took a whole year before we got our first finalized shots that would be used in the film back from Wētā. By this point, we had practically shot the entire film. All we had was our faith that it would work out and look as good as we imagined. Wētā showed us the fifty-three-second scene where Neytiri sees Jake for the first time. She holds up her bow, then a woodsprite—one of those delicate seeds from the great Tree of Souls—lands on her arrow, and she decides not to shoot. We were thrilled. Elated. We were there in the rainforest with her. The emotion was coming through in her eyes.

The energy in the room quickly vanished when we realized we had two thousand more visual effects shots to go.

Because we now truly knew we were going to have the film Jim envisioned, we invited Tony Sella, copresident of domestic marketing, to come see the clip for himself so he could start to understand the finished product he was going to have to be able to market. We watched the fifty-three seconds, and when it was over, he turned to me and said, "Jon, is there something wrong with me or is she hot?"

My answer to him was "Both. There's something wrong with you *and* she's hot."

We had been working on a rough cut as we continued our filming and capturing process. "Rough" was the perfect description—the film was a patchwork of reference footage straight from our soundstages that had not been fully realized with special effects and the finished footage we had received back from Wētā. Remember, it took a year for our first photoreal scene, and while they were steadily delivering film-ready footage back to us, the process was lengthy.

But, as soon as we were done with the actual filming, the executives at Fox wanted to watch the film. We pleaded with them to wait. They insisted. Fair enough. It was their money, and a lot of it. They came to the Lightstorm screening room in Santa Monica, where we gave all the appropriate caveats and left them to watch the early cut of the film. When it was over, their faces were ashen. Their imaginations couldn't fill in the gaps. It was all gloom and doom. To them, there were only problems and no solutions.

We held strong: "Look, give us time. Let us work on it." They came around, and we went back to work.

✧ ✧ ✧

A YEAR LATER we had our first audience preview. The movie was in much better shape. Most of the visual effects shots had been filled in, but the response made it clear to us what we had already suspected: The movie was too long. A movie can be long. That's not a problem. It's that three-letter word *too* that is the problem. The movie cannot *feel* too long. We cut a half hour out of the movie and screened it again at the theater on the Fox lot. This new version was a very different movie than we'd screened there before. But when the movie ended, the studio execs walked right by us, didn't say a word, went outside, and entered into a huddle. The statement they made with silence was loud and clear.

The studio was basically scared shitless. They didn't know how to market the film. During our final stretch of postproduction, the movie just weeks away from release, I would pull up on the Fox lot every day, driving past the iconic Fox gate on Pico Boulevard. There would be enormous billboards for Fox's Friday night television lineup and for *Alvin and the Chipmunks: The Squeakquel*, but there was not a single *Avatar* poster on the lot. I thought it was embarrassing.

The cochairmen of Fox, Tom Rothman and Jim Gianopulos, had the same notes every time they saw a new edit of the film. They wanted us to cut out the sequences of Jake and Neytiri flying on their ikran. In these meditative and transportive flying scenes, you can see our characters falling in love. But it didn't advance the plot, so they wanted them out. They also wanted Jim to cut Grace's death scene— not because of Sigourney's portrayal, but because they felt the film was too long and they simply needed cuts. This scene not only has a huge emotional impact, but actually ended up being the basis for so much of what we are now doing in the sequels. And there was an early sequence in which the forest fills with woodsprites, naturally attracted to our hero, Jake Sully. It is a sign from Eywa, the life force of the Na'vi, herself that Jake has been accepted by the Indigenous people. We were sure that the woodsprites were a cool way of introducing audiences to Pandora and the connected nature of the exomoon. The studio execs felt it was time-consuming and silly, too much hippie-dippie granola. "I've been at screenings in the field," I told our studio colleagues. "When people come up afterward, that's always the scene they want to talk about."

"You're the producer," they argued. "They're just telling you what you want to hear."

REMEMBER THE TRAILER challenges on *Titanic*? Multiply those by a thousand for *Avatar*. How do you convey the epic scale, unprecedented visual immersion, and story in 150 seconds? It's especially difficult when most traditional trailers invariably end up being watched mostly online on computer screens. At the time, people who saw our characters on the small screen regarded them as Smurfs. As they had with *Titanic*, Fox wanted a traditional three-minute trailer and to be done with it. We knew we needed to do something unconventional to capture the monumental beauty of *Avatar*. We proposed an "Avatar Day" on which we would take over a certain number of screens across the country and show sixteen minutes of footage, free of charge. When we presented the plan to Fox, they wanted to know what scenes we planned to include. When I said "the woodsprite scene," their faces said it all.

Imagine setting up over a hundred 3D screens across the country for the "Avatar Day" promotion. 3D was such an important part of the *Avatar* experience, and very few theaters were ready for it at this point. In many cases, we had to bring in our own equipment. If the last movie finished at eleven p.m., we were working by eleven fifteen p.m. On some occasions, we worked all night—screening and adjusting. Ultimately, the woodsprites worked their magic on audiences, and people felt the promise of the film in a way that no trailer could possibly convey.

A month before our release date, we again screened the film at Fox. There was not a lot of love in the building. The execs understood that some people were moved by the movie—spouses usually, or friends who had been invited along—but they did not understand why. At the screening, two people in the audience were so emotionally engaged, they started weeping. The executives didn't seem to notice or care. For me, that said everything. They gave the exact notes they'd always given. Cut all the flying. Cut Grace's death—one of the scenes that seemed to make the two people cry. Expletives flew behind closed doors, but we didn't change a single frame. The same movie they saw that day was the one that went on to earn them nearly $3 billion.

In early December, we screened the finished film for the cast and Steven Spielberg. I did not know Steven well. You might call us "hi and bye" friends, which is why I was surprised when he came up afterward and gave me a hug. Steven said that seeing *Avatar* was the best cinematic experience he'd had in thirty-three years. I did the math. Thirty-three years? That was *Star Wars*! Before Spielberg left the building that day, he stopped in to see Tom Rothman. I'm not sure what he said, but just like that, Tom went from *Avatar* skeptic to a true believer. From that day on, it was a wild ride around the world.

Avatar's world premiere took place in London on December 10, 2009. Because we had done so well there with our opening for *Titanic*, we decided to go back, only this time, instead of a red carpet, we rolled out a blue carpet, the color of the Na'vi. The evening was unforgettable—people were wowed. Awestruck. And most importantly, moved. They were amazed by the visuals but also taken by the depth of the characters. That, and not the 3D, is what made *Avatar* a blockbuster.

We opened in 3,457 theaters across the United States, and the movie was shown on over fourteen thousand screens around the world. The reviews were good, the numbers great. *Avatar* grossed $26,752,099 on its opening day and $77,025,481 on its opening weekend in the US. Ticket sales, as I've said, usually fall off after the first few days, but our grosses continued to climb. We crossed the $1 billion mark nineteen days after release. By January 31, 2010, we'd become the first movie to gross more than $2 billion. Even after two months in theaters, we were still number one in the US. The big push we had made for 3D paid off. Over 80 percent of our box office came from 3D screenings. As of our rerelease in September 2022, *Avatar* is just shy of $3 billion and remains the top-grossing movie of all time, just ahead of *Avengers: Endgame, Avatar: The Way of Water, Titanic,* and *Star Wars: Episode VII—The Force Awakens,* which is why when people say I produced three of the top five grossing movies of all time, I wink and say, "Three of the top four."

James Cameron, who broke every box office record with *Titanic,* had done it again. How? That's what people wanted to know. Success being so exceedingly rare, how did Jim do it twice?

It goes back to what I have said before: When they go to the movies, people are looking for emotion, compelling characters, and the largest of themes—themes bigger than any genre. That is what Jim delivers. He has always had the ability to key his stories to the most important themes—that's his secret. When Jim writes, he weaves in universal themes that people want to return to again and again. He creates relatable characters and, sure, sets them against extraordinary backgrounds, but when people see a Jim Cameron movie, they walk away with something bigger than plot or even story. Something lasting.

Titanic and *Avatar* work on a grand scale because they take you on a journey with characters who are not perfect, who have flaws, but who love profoundly, believe deeply, and fight passionately to protect the people and places they love. You live their triumphs and tragedies—Jack and Rose, Jake and Neytiri—and leave the theater feeling that the world is full of hope.

Jack dies in the frigid waters of the North Atlantic, devastating Rose. But we know that she goes on. She faces the unimaginable, finds her inner strength, and makes a rich and full life for herself.

In *Avatar*, Jake seems the most unlikely of heroes, a former marine without direction in life, and using a wheelchair after a spinal cord injury. Then he finds love. He finds purpose. He literally and figuratively rises out of his wheelchair to save an entire planet and be with the woman he loves. The movie ends with Jake opening his eyes. To me, that's a challenge to people in the audience, to open their eyes and see how their actions impact our world and the people around us. When he opens his eyes, it's a new beginning. It can be a new beginning for us, too—that's the message of *Avatar*, for me, and why people leave the theater inspired.

I have tried to live those lessons, particularly now as I face down the challenges of the cancer that is ravaging my body. Radiation. Chemotherapy. Surgery after surgery. Experimental treatments and drug trials. I am in the fight of and for my life, and I am doing it all for love. To continue the extraordinary adventure and life that Julie and I have built. To continue to watch Jamie and Jodie take on this world in their individual and wonderful ways. To be with friends for celebrations and milestones, and most especially the everyday moments.

To be a source of strength in the hard times. To shepherd the next chapter of our Avatar franchise through to the big screen. I am steadfast in my resolve to be there for it all. As I often say to our Avatar family/crew, "Sivako," which in Na'vi means: "Rise to the challenge."

AWARDS SEASON IN 2009–2010 felt very different than when we were running the gauntlet with *Titanic*. Perhaps it was because I had the wisdom experience affords. Or maybe it was because I had already won a Golden Globe and an Oscar. What I really cared about at this point was the remarkable *Avatar* cast and crew getting the recognition they deserved.

Best Picture, Best Director, Best Art Direction, Best Cinematography, Best Film Editing, Best Original Score, Best Sound Editing, Best Sound Mixing, Best Visual Effects—*Avatar* was nominated for nine Academy Awards. At the end of the night, we had three: Best Art Direction, Best Cinematography, and Best Visual Effects. My hope had been for each of the teams to win—they deserved to. I know I am not objective, but I am discerning, and their work was absolutely at the top of the game. What they do have, instead of a statue, is the legacy that is the film.

One of my favorite jokes actually involves my Oscar. I love pretending to drop it as I hand it to someone. You should see their faces! I tell you pridefully my Oscar probably has more miles on it than any other Oscar in the world. I have shared it with people around the globe, so much so that I've twice had to have it replated due to excessive handling. At airports, I often get stopped with it by TSA, but my guess is they just want to see it up close. I even pretend to drop it with them. I figure, why have something like that and not share it? I have taken it to schools, speaking engagements, hospitals, and, one of my favorite experiences, the Special Olympics. It's an iconic symbol for people everywhere.

When I was a studio executive, my application to become a member of the Academy was rejected—even though everyone else I knew who held a similar position was a member. Even after I won an Oscar, I was rejected again. The Academy called me up a year after *Titanic* and asked if I would speak in front of a blue-ribbon congressional panel about digital preservation.

"I would," I said, "but wouldn't you prefer a member to do it?"

"What do you mean?" they said.

"Well, I'm not a member." They looked it up. All of a sudden, my membership was approved—and I spoke in front of that blue-ribbon panel.

IF IT'S NOT the oldest question in the movie business, it's probably a close second: Would you rather win awards, or win at the box office? Of course, I'd like to do both—we had that with *Titanic*—but, if forced to choose, I'd choose the box office. It means millions of moviegoers are connecting to the work. That is the real prize—reaching people looking to be transported, to escape, to find hope in the embrace of a darkened theater. Film is a mass medium. The goal is not to win the most votes for awards. It's to connect with moviegoers, who vote by going back to the theater to see your film again and again. To me, the opening weekend numbers are less important than the numbers for weekends four, five, six, seven. Don't tell me how we did on day one. Tell me how we did on day 101.

✦ ✦ ✦ ✦

YOU NEVER KNOW what audience your movie is going to reach. No matter how carefully you game and predict, you'll be surprised. *Titanic* made a connection with young people, teenagers and those in their twenties experiencing the first taste of love. It was about two people, and also about everything—wealth and poverty, love and death. *Avatar* ended up having an even wider base. I can find myself in places all around the world, from Brazil to Korea, and locals will say, "That movie, the Na'vi people . . . that is about me. That's my people I saw up on the screen."

We also surprisingly found a devoted audience among the military. The US was then mired in conflicts in Iraq and Afghanistan, and our movie struck a chord with those serving. It is interesting that for a movie with a lot of cool military hardware, *Avatar* is anything but a pro-war film. It was still screened on bases and on ships around the globe. That opened a new world to me.

Avatar afforded me one of the most unique and rewarding opportunities of my life—a trip to the Persian Gulf sponsored by the United States Navy. Jim went for part of that trip, as did Sigourney Weaver, Stephen Lang, and Michelle Rodriguez. The USS *Dwight D. Eisenhower* aircraft carrier took us to visit troops on navy ships in the Persian Gulf a few days before they deployed to Afghanistan. It was in the Persian Gulf, while heading toward the Arabian Sea, that we got news that *Avatar* had broken $2 billion in ticket sales. We took a picture to celebrate, posing with as many of the five thousand crew members as could fit in the frame. I captioned the photo "USS Eisenhower somewhere in the Persian Gulf" and sent it with a thank-you note to everyone at Fox.

The captain of the USS *Dwight D. Eisenhower* wrote an email to his crew the day we left. It said, "As we go into battle, let's learn from the lessons of *Avatar*, and let's make sure that we are respectful of the people who are the Indigenous people of Afghanistan." The film is not anti-military; it's anti-abusive-military, a warning against the misuse of imperial forces. This captain clearly understood that.

Something bizarre happened during that navy trip, on our visit to Bahrain. We were in three cars, driving to an admiral's house outside of town. It was evening. Sigourney Weaver and Stephen Lang were with a half dozen marines in one vehicle. I was with more marines in another. An escort vehicle followed. We got off the highway, and out of nowhere a car pulled alongside and intentionally banged into us. Suddenly, the marines were on the walkie-talkies. Sigourney's car was in front. They told her driver to drive away, *leave*. We pulled off the road. Four guys in black emerged from the car that had hit us and walked toward our vehicle. They were shouting. They said we hit their car. Our vehicles were unmarked—these guys had no idea they were confronting a group of heavily armed US marines. Our escort vehicle pulled in front of the strange car, blocking it in. We received instructions over the walkie-talkie to back out and leave. We drove into the desert with our headlights off. The escort then followed.

The admiral knew all about it before we reached his house.

"How did you hold up?" he asked.

I told him that I'd been nervous.

He said exactly what you don't want an admiral to say: "Yeah, I was nervous, too."

Apparently, people had been coming from Kuwait and doing these bump-and-runs on the desert road. That night they picked the wrong car. When I wrote to Julie about the experience, I framed it as a script—exterior: Bahrain, desert night—because it felt like a scene from a movie.

✧ ✧ ✧ ✧

MEANWHILE, THE PASSING of time had brought changes in the family, too. I'd started working on *Titanic* in 1995 when I was thirty-five. Jamie was seven, and Jodie was three. They had been little boys when I won the Oscar. *Avatar* was released in 2009, when I was almost fifty. By the time of the Persian Gulf trip, they were adults.

If you asked the grade-school Jamie what he would want to get into as a teenager, he would have said music. When his band—Discovery Zone, which had the song featured in the extended version of *Avatar*—broke up, he found his way back to his early love of acting. It's what ultimately brought him further into the world of Avatar, where, in 2016, we were putting together the performance capture troupe who could play multiple characters in the sequels. Jamie came on very early as we were doing our virtual scouts. Jim saw Jamie work that first week and said, "Jon, Jamie is really doing well. Do you think he would want to be part of the troupe full-time?"

I said, "Yeah, I think he probably would, Jim."

I said it like that—hedging—because I wasn't going to be the one to hire him. If Jim wanted him, he would have to ask Jamie. And he did. After months and months of performance capture in LA, Jamie was one of only four members of the troupe chosen by Jim to travel with the crew to New Zealand. He'd become more than an actor. He understood what Jim was doing and what he wanted from a directing standpoint, which made him indispensable. He became an intermediary between Jim and the background actors. When other members of the troupe, having finished their work, were sent back to the States, Jim kept Jamie on.

"Jamie shouldn't leave," said Jim. "He needs to stay through to the end."

Jamie then became a buffer between Jim and the crew as we

worked on the virtual camera stage and during the sound mix. Jamie, who has incredible recall, would remind Jim, the cast, and the crew members about the continuity or original intention of a shot. Stephen Lang said that if Jim ever hands off the directing of the Avatar movies, Jamie could direct parts six and seven. Jim even decided to make Jamie a coproducer on the third Avatar film. I explained why I thought that was a bridge too far, but Jim wouldn't hear it. He insisted. I disagreed, but I sure was proud.

Jodie's path was more straightforward. I give a lot of credit to Oakwood School, and particularly their summer arts program, Academy of Creative Education, for giving both my boys, but especially Jodie, a unique early musical education that, in many ways, sent him on the path he's traveling. At a young and pivotal age, Jodie was able to perform with—and even have his music played by—both students and remarkable teachers, local musicians, and artists. Since the day he got his driver's license, Jodie would drive all over LA to see as many performances as he could, always making a point to introduce himself to the artists he met along the way, some of whom later became his colleagues and collaborators. Jodie didn't just focus on performing and composing. When he wanted to get better at using music notation computer programs, he volunteered to help his friend Ellen Reid with copywork—making scores and parts legible for musicians. (Ellen later went on to win a Pulitzer Prize for her opera *Prism*, for which Jodie also did the copywork. If only "Pulitzer Prize copyist" was a legitimate title.) When Ellen's work was being performed by the Los Angeles new music collective Wild Up in 2013, Jodie offered to help set up chairs for rehearsal or do whatever else they might need so he could sit in and observe the process. It turned out Wild Up needed another percussionist, and Jodie has been a part of the group ever since, as a performer, arranger, and composer, and he even took on administrative work for a few years, learning the ins and outs of grant writing and the like.

For his twenty-first birthday, we got him tickets and backstage passes to a Björk concert in Los Angeles, which is where he met the members of Graduale Nobili, the female Icelandic choir touring with her. Jodie, not being shy, invited the choir to a pool party and barbecue at a friend's house. He asked them, "If I ever write something, will you perform it with me?" They said yes. Jodie spent that year at CalArts writing music, asked other composers to write as well, and then raised the money to record an album. Jodie and Wild Up flew to Iceland to perform and record with Graduale Nobili. They recorded just outside of Reykjavik at Greenhouse Studios with Valgeir Sigurðsson, who later asked Jodie to join his music collective and label, Bedroom Community. Since then, Jodie has performed with them all over the world. Jodie later joined what I would call an a cappella group, but they refer to themselves as a vocal ensemble, Roomful of Teeth. Roomful has performed all over the world and even received their second Grammy in 2024. Jodie has started getting into film composing and working for film composers and, again, has gained entry into that portion of the music industry by being anything but shy. He got work on a recent film project by approaching the composer after a performance and saying, "I heard you're working on a film score. Would love to help any way I can, with copywork, arranging, whatever you need." He ended up working with the composer on the movie on and off for a year and a half.

Edie and Ely taught their children to "be the first one in and the last one out." I'm glad this is something we passed on to the next generation, as both Jamie and Jodie have very much taken on that spirit in their work.

I'm grateful and proud that they each pursued their passions and found careers—ones that inspire, challenge, and excite them. They have been incredibly lucky in that regard. I know that, because that has been my story, too.

IF YOU ASKED me to name my best years with Julie, I'd say, "All of them." We've had an especially great time on vacation, those times when we could get away from work and just be together.

In 1993, while working on *True Lies*, I fell in love with the Florida Keys, where the movie was shooting. The rocky inlets, the spongy bays, ships on the horizon, the causeway that strings together the islands—it was wonderful. It felt like I'd always been searching for this place, but hadn't even known it existed. Julie spent a lot of time with me there, and felt about it like I did. In 2010, after *Avatar* had been released, we went back to the Keys to fulfill our dream of owning a piece of paradise. After looking at homes from Key West all the way up to Key Largo, we found our house on Islamorada, halfway between Miami and Key West. The town is scattered across an archipelago, an Eden made of five islands—Tea Table Key, Lower Matecumbe Key, Upper Matecumbe Key, Windley Key, and Plantation Key. The seven thousand residents of Islamorada, which means "purple island" in Spanish, are a collection of fishermen, artists, everyday working people, and millionaires. It was on Plantation Key that we found our refuge; it felt like more of a compound than just a house. An estate with six bedrooms—four of which were in separate "pods" outside the main house—on four waterfront acres. There was a swimming pool, a tennis court, and beautiful landscaping. We called it Bali Hai.

It was our dream home, Shangri-la. Of course, we thought we'd moved into the ideal house. Kathy still teases me for saying, "This place is perfect. We're not going to change a thing." Three remodels later, it really was perfect. It felt like our own private resort. We added an outdoor fishpond, a hot tub (half water, half dry seating area, with a firepit in the middle), a game room, and even an apartment for Julie's father to live with us. Don't think our friends and family didn't notice. Our first year in Islamorada, we had visitors on forty out of fifty-two weekends.

(Fun fact: Bali Hai made a cameo appearance in the Netflix show *Bloodline* as the home of one of the corrupt guys, Roy Gilbert, played by Beau Bridges.)

I took up new hobbies at Bali Hai. It's where I first discovered my love for landscape design and gardening—perhaps it was inspired by the extraordinary plants, trees, and flowers of the world our team had created for Pandora. I found the joy in putting my hands in the dirt, making the winding paths that would crisscross the property, searching out the exotic trees and plants that flanked those paths, creating nameplates for each specimen and variety. The property became its own verdant utopia. We also bought a new boat—naming this one the *Bali Hai* after the house—and enjoyed fishing, snorkeling, scuba diving, and taking trips to the Bahamas with friends from all over the world. We scattered laser lights throughout the trees along our long driveway to light the leaves at night, reminiscent of the bioluminescent forests of Pandora.

Seeing as I do not drink alcohol (why would I drink it if I can't even stand the smell?), my most unexpected hobby is wine collecting. Bali Hai is where I really got into that. As with our gardens, it was the process of discovery and creating that I loved—learning about different varietals, searching for specific vintages, designing a wine room, building a digitized sommelier system, participating in auctions. I was into it all. I got feedback from Julie and others when they drank a bottle—what they liked, what they didn't like—and put all their reviews in the digitized database. And as with the landscape design at Bali Hai, the best part was sharing the collection—a pretty good one, if I may say so—with friends and family. It was there not to be admired, but for everyone to enjoy. And they did.

When people ask why a person who does not drink would do such a thing, I point to Julie—she hates when I do this—and say, "Because the more she drinks, the more fun I have." It's a joke, but there is truth to it. The ultimate pleasure for me is the pleasure that I see people, not just Julie, derive from the collection. Blowing someone away with a particular bottle—I just love that.

Christmases were great in Bali Hai. The weeks when everyone came down were the highlight of the year. Our entire family would gather, my sisters and their families, my brother and his family, as well as Julie's father and niece Amie, and Amie's family who also lived in the Keys. Edie was healthy enough to enjoy ten years of Bali Hai. When the stairs became an obstacle for her, we put in an elevator we called the Edie-vator.

When I think of those years, I remember the parties, the family events, and birthdays. The night before Julie's sixtieth birthday, I sent her and a girlfriend on an overnight getaway. Then, on the way back, she was to meet me at one of our favorite local restaurants, Pierre's. It seemed closed, so she went around back and there we were: one hundred fifty people yelling "SURPRISE!" Julie makes friends wherever she goes, and her big birthday became an opportunity to get them all in one place. Friends from childhood, from New York, from LA, and from the Keys. There was even Julie's high school friend Frank, who was born on the same day in the same hospital as Julie. We all spent the weekend together. We went swimming with the dolphins and had brunch at Bali Hai. For the party, I made a twenty-two-minute video celebrating Julie's wonderful life. I had our art department put Jamie into makeup to look like an old Mike Wallace. Instead of *60 Minutes*, he was hosting *60 Years*. Jamie and Jodie recorded a song in harmony, called "Mama." There was a roomful of people laughing and in tears watching it—Julie most of all. It was like her bat mitzvah video, except that Julie's not Jewish.

We got very involved in the community in the Keys. We hosted fundraisers at our home for the local hospital, Mariners, and for Habitat for Humanity, Swim Across America for cancer research, the Florida Keys Concert Association, congressional campaigns, and more. Each year we gave a scholarship to a graduating student at the local high school who wanted to major in any of the arts, whether it was filmmaking, music, dance, fine art, or something of the like. Each of those students still keeps in touch and lets us know where they are in their careers. It is very gratifying.

Although I was working in LA, Bali Hai came to feel more and more like my true home. Each weekend, I would fly to Miami on the red-eye on Friday night and then fly back to LA early on Monday morning. Julie mostly stayed in the Keys and built a very full life for herself and our family there. The boys would come whenever they could and they, too, liked bringing their friends for long weekends. That was the best thing about Bali Hai—it was a place to bring people together. A place where the pressures and stresses of everyday life would fall away. Where time slowed and no one was in a rush to be anywhere else.

Chapter 9

Alita: Battle Angel, the film we nearly went with instead of *Avatar,* never left Jim's or my mind. We wanted to see the movie get made. We were preparing to embark on the yearslong task of bringing the Avatar sequels to life, so we knew it was time to open the door to producing *Alita* with another director at the helm.

Battle Angel Alita is a Japanese cyberpunk manga series by Yukito Kishiro that had been adapted into an anime film, introduced to Jim by Guillermo del Toro. The story has timeless echoes of a Pinocchio tale—but this one is set in a postapocalyptic world.

Jim usually works from original screenplays with characters and stories that come from his own imagination. *Alita* was a different kind of challenge. Its story unfolds across nine volumes in the manga series.

The director Robert Rodriguez, a longtime friend of Jim's, came to Lightstorm to check out our operation. Best known for the family-friendly movies *Spy Kids* and *Spy Kids 2: Island of Lost Dreams,* he had also found success with a handful of gruesome action flicks—*Desperado, From Dusk till Dawn*, and *Sin City*.

I gave him the usual tour, then brought him in to see Jim. They talked shop for twenty minutes, then shook hands. When he was one step out the door, Robert said, "Hey Jim. Do you have any projects for me?"

A lightbulb lit up over Jim's head—you could see it.

"Wait a second," he said. "Come with me."

He showed Robert the art reel we had done on *Alita*—a rough idea of what the story might look like—then handed him a copy of the script. Robert, excited by the prospect, read the script and offered to give it a rewrite. He worked on it for several months without a deal, or commitment, or compensation. He did it just because he wanted to. He came back with a much, much shorter version of the script. I was nervous when I sat down to read it. Jim is not an easy person to rewrite. But Robert's feel for the story and understanding of the themes were immediately clear. Though he cut many pages, nothing important was missing. We knew then that Robert was the right choice for the project.

This would be our second attempt at producing a film with another director at the helm, and we were determined to apply what we had learned from our experience on *Solaris*. I sat down with Robert to lay out some ground rules. I said, "Robert, we're prepared to go down this path, but we have a few conditions. One, we want you to hire a cinematographer." Robert often shoots his own movies, but we wanted him to focus on directing. "Two, we want to hire the editor." That had been one of the mistakes we learned from *Solaris*. "Three, we want you to work with Wētā on the special effects."

Alita: Battle Angel was similar to *Avatar* in that it depended on performance capture—emotive, authentic performances—and we believed Wētā was the only company that could do that work the right way. We knew our people at Wētā would make sure the CGI was top level. We also wanted to hire the composer. There are times when Robert does his own composing, and this too would have taken his focus away from directing. We wanted his vision as a director to flourish, unencumbered by the responsibilities and time demanded by other roles.

Not only did Robert accept the conditions, but he embraced them. *Alita* was a true partnership. A few months later, I went to visit Robert at his production company, Troublemaker Studios, in Austin, and he had a sign up that read LIGHTSTORM SOUTH. The next time he visited us in LA, we put up a sign that read TROUBLEMAKER WEST. We collaborated on every step in the process. Robert trusted me to have his back, and we trusted him with the film.

While Jim can be blunt and even harsh with studio bosses, cinematographers, composers, costume designers, and such, he's more sensitive with fellow directors. He understands the nature of their struggle, the fragility of any worthwhile project. He wants to help, but not bigfoot. He gives directors the courtesy and respect the job commands. Jim went to Troublemaker to see the artwork Robert had put together for the movie. We were at a point in the project where we would need to present to the studio and ask for the green light. The art reel would be part of the pitch. I had seen it and thought it wasn't up to snuff. I assumed Jim would feel the same. We're usually on the same page. Robert showed Jim the art reel . . . and Jim told Robert he liked it!

Later, when I asked Jim what he really thought, he said, "No way can we go into the studio with this art." This is where I step in. Giving bad news, asking for change, ensuring the vision is realized.

I went back to Robert and said, "I know what Jim said, but we're going to try something new anyway."

I pulled together several members of the *Avatar* art team—Ben Procter, Dylan Cole, Fausto De Martini—to collaborate with Robert, and within a few weeks they'd remade the conceptual design of *Alita*. Jim liked the new take. It let us sell the studio not just on the movie but on our collective vision. And approaching the challenge this way made it clear that I was there to help, to be a partner and a second pair of eyes for Robert all the way through production. I was not there to give input about performance—that's purely for the director—but I could help realize his visual aesthetic from costume to set design.

We ended up doing the *Alita* postproduction in Los Angeles, which allowed me to sit in on the editing and be part of the big decisions. Steve Rivkin, our *Avatar* editor, worked together with Ian Silverstein, an editor who had worked with Robert before.

Each great director is unique. That is precisely what makes them great—they are singular in their perspective, talent, and artistry. As a producer, building trust and understanding with the director is vital to the success of any film. For that matter, those two things are essential to all good relationships—family, friends, and colleagues.

Robert and I established both qualities fairly early on. And, we had fun together. We were working with Wētā as we had on *Avatar*—sending them edited scenes as they were ready. When we both approved a shot, I'd say, "Ship it, Danno," a play on the famous "Book 'em, Danno" catchphrase from *Hawaii Five-0*. The team at Wētā actually made "Ship it, Danno" T-shirts. My experience on *Alita* ended up helping me with our work on *Avatar 2*. Having seen the role I'd taken on with Robert and knowing that I gave Wētā notes on every shot in the film,

Jim recognized that I could play a much more active part in the visual effects on *Way of Water* than I had on the first Avatar.

Alita, which was released February 14, 2019, made close to $500 million at the box office. It has avid fans all over the world. But those two things are not what make me consider it a success. That moment came later, when Jim, having arrived home from a day on the set, turned on his TV just as *Alita* was coming on. He sat and watched the movie through the eyes of a layperson, as if for the first time. When he called that night to say "You know what, Jon? *Alita* is really good," I knew that we'd accomplished something great.

Chapter 10

The idea of turning *Avatar* into an amusement park attraction came slowly, like the dawning of an outrageous idea. Stop and think about this for a second. James Cameron dreams up this wondrous planet Pandora, a world populated by ten-foot-tall blue creatures and humans who move among them in artificial bodies. Not only does this surreal vision end up on the page, but it becomes a ground- and record-breaking movie and then an awe-inspiring attraction at the Walt Disney World Resort. This all started when we realized just how big *Avatar* had become. One billion at the box office? Two billion? Three billion?

Lightstorm controls the intellectual property rights of Avatar— the movies, the characters, the world—and we have our own in-house franchise department. When Walt Disney CEO Bob Iger came to tour our headquarters in Manhattan Beach and I showed him all we were doing to build the Avatar brand and franchise, he said, "Jon, you are quite a storyteller."

Jim overheard this and corrected Bob, saying, "I am the storyteller. Jon is the story *seller*."

Yes, I thought. *True*. I am the story seller. I'm good with that. And good at that.

Jim's plate was more than full with directing the films. My role was—and is—to take as much of the load off his back as possible and not only sell but be a creative driving force behind our forays into comic books, video games, theme parks, and even live performance.

Cirque du Soleil, the French Canadian company, had become a global phenomenon, setting up contemporary, immersive circus spectacles around the world. A Cirque show is like a waking dream in the same way that *Avatar* is. The grounds were ripe for a collaboration. We could give Cirque—and all of our collaborators—Jim's endless trove of notes on Pandora, its history, flora, and fauna. I suggested to them: "We tell the story of our movies. If you're going to play in our sandbox, take everything we give you and then create your own story that can become a part of our canon."

The story they decided to create was that of *Toruk–The First Flight*. In *Avatar*, Jake tames and rides the great leonopteryx, Pandora's largest flying predator, but we had hinted in the movie that there were earlier riders of this "beast of war." The Cirque show takes place several centuries before the events of our films. I made numerous trips to Montreal, through conception, scriptwriting, design, and rehearsals on the show. I brought on Deborah Scott, our costume designer, and her team to help rework their costumes. *Toruk–The First Flight* was one of Cirque du Soleil's most successful touring productions, playing in huge arenas around the world, from Barclays Center in New York and the Staples Center in Los Angeles to their final performances at the O2 Arena in London. Throughout the process, I helped steer them in the right direction—for their work and for the franchise—but thankfully, I did not have the burden of responsibility I feel on the films. To me, this was pure fun.

Since the time I was a little boy, I have always collected sports trading cards and comics, so it was an incredible joy for me to work with trading card companies and McFarlane Toys—for me, Jonny the Jock, to give design notes on the full range of our Avatar collectibles and story suggestions to our graphic novel partners at Dark Horse Comics. And I have always loved games of all sorts. Card games, board games, word games; I even got into computer games very early on. So, I especially looked forward to the several meetings a week I had with our video game partners at Ubisoft. The expansive nature of video games allowed us to broaden our horizons and introduce new clans, creatures, and locations in the game *Avatar: Frontiers of Pandora*. As with all of our franchise partners, I work closely with their designers and programmers to make sure the essence of Avatar remains at the forefront. Everything needs to be in perfect harmony with the movies themselves.

ON MY LIST of top ten wishes when I was a little boy—along with jumping into one of Bert's chalk drawings in *Mary Poppins* and meeting Kareem Abdul-Jabbar—was to "create my own ride at Disney." What kid wouldn't want to do that? We were very lucky to visit Disneyland a few times when we were kids, and there didn't seem to be any place much better to me. The Haunted Mansion, the Matterhorn, Fantasyland, Frontierland—they all thrilled me, swept me up, and carried me away into imagined worlds.

The grown-up me (although some might argue that I have never really grown up) has a top ten list, too. This one, though, is of things I am most proud of, outside of my family. The creation of Pandora— The World of *Avatar* at the Walt Disney World Resort is one of the things at the top of that list.

Jim and I went in together to pitch Disney for a theme park attraction. From the get-go, it was a good meeting. Fox had produced *Avatar*, but they were not in the theme park business. We considered pitching Universal for their park, but we imagined far more than just a ride—we wanted an immersive and expansive experience of Pandora. This was Disney's stock-in-trade, and they understood the big idea right away. It was—and continues to be—a very good partnership. We were never asked to adapt or change the Avatar ethos to fit a certain Disney culture. They assembled their best team, then let us do our thing together.

The Walt Disney World Resort in Orlando is broken into four parks. There is the original theme park, the Magic Kingdom, home of classic rides like Pirates of the Caribbean and the Haunted Mansion. It opened in 1971 as an expansion of the original vision, which Walt Disney realized at Disneyland in Anaheim, California. Then there is Disney's Hollywood Studios, which you enter along a replica of Hollywood Boulevard. Its most popular rides are dedicated to Disney's movie franchises: Star Wars, Toy Story. It might seem like a natural home for Avatar, but we were wary. Setting up at Hollywood Studios would emphasize Avatar as a movie, which is not what we wanted. We wanted the whole world of Avatar. EPCOT, Disney's *E*xperimental *P*rototype *C*ommunity *o*f *T*omorrow, is a tour through the countries and cultures on planet Earth, so our world definitely would not fit in. Then there is Disney's Animal Kingdom, where the theme is the wonder of nature and conservation. There is an animal safari, areas dedicated to a few of the continents, a train ride that takes you through the wilderness, and exhilarating river rapids. It seemed like the perfect home for what we imagined creating for *Avatar*.

We entered the agreement without knowing exactly what we would build. We knew there'd be two attractions dedicated to Pandora. We went back to Disney several months later to share our artwork and ideas. When these were accepted, we began to work with the extraordinary Joe Rohde, who had been at Disney since 1980. He was creative executive and supervising designer for all of Animal Kingdom. Joe became our Chief Imagineer, which is what they call engineers at Disney.

Joe is a guy with twenty-six earrings in one ear, his lobe hanging low. He's quite the character, wonderfully so. Though Jim and I were at first a bit skeptical, Joe turned out to be perfect. It was actually Joe who insisted that we build in Animal Kingdom, which he described as a park dedicated to "adventure through nature." It had the acreage to accommodate the full breadth of what we envisioned, and because it historically had fewer visitors than the other parks, I came to see it as a challenge. We wanted to make it a crown jewel.

We needed a distinct landmark to anchor our part of Animal Kingdom—something to greet visitors and let them know they are entering a new world. The tree at the center of the rainforest in *Avatar*—the Tree of Souls, where the Na'vi connect with Eywa, the guiding force of Pandora—seemed the obvious choice, but Animal Kingdom already had their own Tree of Life. We wanted something identifiably and uniquely ours—something to beckon visitors.

Joe and the other Imagineers explored various ways to mark the threshold—a bridge, arches, etc.—but none seemed unique enough. Then they approached us, giddily, with the idea of building a floating mountain like the floating mountains of Pandora. It would be a massive artificial summit held up by hidden beams. A trick of perspective would make it appear to float. Brilliant.

With the floating mountain as a centerpiece, everything else began to fall into place.

Our two attractions would be Na'vi River Journey, a boat tour of the Pandora forest akin to Pirates of the Caribbean, and *Avatar* Flight of Passage, a 3D simulator of a banshee flight across the planet of Pandora.

I like to think of the land itself as our third and most important attraction. Walking through Pandora—The World of *Avatar*, you come upon giant, alien plant life around every corner. Hidden speakers play the sounds of exotic wildlife. At night, the entire park glows with that iconic bioluminescence.

These attractions took five years to build. While Disney helped us overcome all the physical obstacles, Jim and I were keepers of the *Avatar* flame. We approached it as we had approached the film— questioning, challenging, pushing the boundaries. We did the same with the team of Imagineers. Doing the main attraction as a 3D immersive flight seemed crazy at first. It was just so expensive, not only to create, but to operate. As a movie producer, you budget for production and distribution. You don't have to plan for maintenance, the cost of running and maintaining a ride day after day for years, the inevitability of breakdowns, the practicalities of moving people on and off safely.

All of our key players from Lightstorm came down to Florida to see a prototype of the banshee flight, then still running only in 2D. Our executive producer and brilliant animator, Richie Baneham, and the rest of our team had created content for the ride just like they'd do for a movie. We provided it to the Imagineers, who programmed it into the prototype. Everyone loved it, including Jim. It was so good that he didn't think we needed to take the next step into 3D. That was unexpected, and most definitely not in my plan. Here was the guy who'd reinvented the 3D experience saying we didn't need it!

I was in Europe a week later when I got a call from Bruce Vaughn, the head of Walt Disney Imagineering. He said, "Jon, we've decided to do the ride in 2D."

I said, "No. You can't. Just give me a week."

I got on the phone with our team. "Take what we have, and do it in 3D," I said. "Do it now, so they can see the difference."

That sample footage convinced Jim, Bruce, and the rest of the team.

For me, the 3D experience is what makes that ride so special and immersive. It plunges you right into a full experience of Pandora. You feel the wind and smell the trees. The swooping drop from the clouds on the back of a banshee leaves your stomach behind. We held a soft opening of the park with a limited number of guests invited to try the attractions. I went to Orlando for that. I wanted to observe how people responded and to see what worked and help fix what didn't. To me, it was like the test screening of a movie. I thought I was ready for anything, but the way people reacted—especially to the Flight of Passage ride—astonished me. I was standing beside the floating mountain with Joe Rohde when a woman came over in tears. Joe and I were worried. We asked if she was okay.

"I had to come over because I recognized you," she said. "I had to come over and say thank you. I've been fighting cancer and Flight of Passage gave me more joy than I have had in a long time. I think I even feel a little bit stronger now."

Joe and I looked at each other and I thought, *Well, our work here is done. I mean, how can you change anything in a ride that generated that response?*

Flight of Passage is actually less a ride than an experience. For a lot of people, it's an emotional catharsis. Most theme park attractions are roller coasters or spinning rides designed to elevate your heart rate and flood your body with adrenaline. We tried to establish an emotional connection instead. We flew the *Avatar* cast to Orlando for the grand opening. Sigourney and Zoe came off the ride in tears. People who haven't seen the movie have an equally amazing experience. I stood on a knoll beyond some bushes to watch people and hear their reactions as they came out. I studied their faces. So many were deeply affected, transported to this other land.

I love being a movie producer. In and of itself, it has been a thrilling ride. The ride of a lifetime. But for the little boy with the big dreams who still lives inside of me, bringing Pandora to life for thousands of people every day—and for generations to come—is itself a dream come true.

MARCH 2020: We'd been scheduled to fly back to New Zealand to finish the live-action shoot for *Avatar 2* and *3* in the middle of the month, when covid was just beginning its rampage. I called Alan Bergman at the studio to tell him "I don't think we should go down to New Zealand. I think we have to delay." We were worried about the unknowns of increasing travel restrictions and how they would impact our cast and crew and their families while our team would be working across the Pacific. The studio agreed to extend our timeline. We canceled the flight. That was a fortuitous decision, as New Zealand went into an eight-week, country-wide lockdown precisely at the time we were to have arrived. What we needed was a new plan, and this delay gave us the time to come up with one.

First, we came up with protocols to protect both our LA and New Zealand teams. We set up our LA-based crew with work-from-home capabilities. That comes with a sense of isolation. Times were tense, and people were scared. Covid was spreading, vaccines had not yet been developed, and protests about restrictions within the US were breaking out all over the country. I began to do a series of town hall meetings over Zoom with groups of twenty people at a time until I'd had the chance to speak with every one of the hundreds of people on our Avatar team. I gave them an opportunity to share what they were feeling, so that others could see they were not alone. It was a stressful time, but I look back fondly at the conversations, the feedback, and the sense of connection we forged in those town hall meetings. Throughout those first few months, I leaned in with a sense of humor and a new wardrobe—I traded in my signature Hawaiian shirts for a closet full of crazy T-shirts, all emblazoned with messages that encouraged people to wash their hands and mask up. With each new tee, I would send out videos and photos of myself sporting my latest find.

Because covid protocols for a film set didn't exist, we had to create them. We wanted to be able to bring people back together as soon as possible—we believed strongly that working would help us all through—but we had to make sure that we could keep our staff members and their families safe.

And there was an external pressure—the march of time. We knew we couldn't delay long, because we needed to film the rest of our scenes with Jack Champion, who plays Spider. Jack, a teenager, was growing and changing with every passing day. He was at that age when you'd look at him one day and see a boy, and suddenly the next day, you'd see him becoming a man.

Paul Andreassend, our on-set medic, and Brigitte Yorke, our New Zealand–based coproducer, headed up our medical advisory team, which included infectious disease experts from all over. They undertook intensive research, conducted targeted outreach to the scientific and medical communities, and created protocols that we felt could get us back to work. These included the mandatory use of masks, face shields, and daily on-set testing, among other requirements. The health, safety, and well-being of our teams were the three pillars of the new measures. We still needed the permission of the New Zealand government, too. They finally gave us the okay to bring thirty-three people into the country at the end of May. By then, they'd knocked the international-traveler quarantine down to two weeks.

We would be among the first large-scale productions back in action since covid had broken out.

Locals balked at our being allowed in, when travel restrictions into the country were still in effect and very few entry visas were available. I sympathize, as I know there were New Zealanders who were just trying to get home, but the limited number of available spots in government-approved quarantine facilities caused a long wait list. We did not take anyone's spot on the wait list or in one of the facilities. Key to the plan that the government approved was that we would secure and cover the costs of our own managed isolation facility. The thirty-three of us took over the entire QT Museum Apartment Hotel in Wellington.

We did not have free rein of the hotel during our quarantine. We were each confined to our room. Food was delivered, along with clean sheets and towels, all left outside our doors. Some of us were lucky enough to have a balcony, where we would go and wave to other people on their balconies. Quarantine was unlike anything I had ever experienced before; I am a guy used to being in perpetual motion. On the go. Out and about. A people person. This was a strange and lonely time.

One thing I tell people about our Avatar work down in New Zealand that often surprises them is that we hired over one hundred Kiwis for every crew member we brought in from the US. A film set is like a self-functioning city. While many businesses were still shut down, we were able to employ local electricians, carpenters, construction workers, and caterers. We brought local food trucks to the set to feed our crew, when even the outdoor markets were still shuttered. Long before covid struck, we had made a commitment to be a good partner to the Wellington community. Even as uncertainty swirled all around us, that commitment remained central to all we did.

THAT'S WHERE I was when I received the worst phone call of my life—it was from my sister Kathy, telling me that her twenty-three-year-old son Sacha had been found dead in a hotel room from an accidental drug overdose. My knees buckled. I went down to the floor. The words barely made sense to me. It was only two weeks earlier that Sacha had moved back to Miami, where he'd gone to college—he was just beginning his life. To him, everything seemed possible. From the time he was a little boy, he had been a big dreamer with an abundance of personality and charm. And he had a smile that tore down all resistance to whatever it was he was gaming for. My heart broke immediately and irreparably. All I wanted was to get to Kathy and her family, to be there with and for them. But I couldn't.

It was June of 2020—covid was raging, and our family was spread out across the globe. Jamie and I were each in isolation in Wellington.

Julie in the Keys. Jodie in Sherman Oaks. Edie in LA. Tina in Connecticut. The world was shut down. A private funeral just for the family was held on Zoom. That was its own kind of heartbreak.

We once again gather for birthdays, holidays, premieres, family trips, and the like, but while we have found our way back to happy moments, the hole remains, and none of us will ever be the same.

Chapter 11

What do you want from a sequel? When a movie makes the kind of money *Avatar* made, no one can tell you exactly why. It's a phenomenon, not a formula that can be repeated or reverse engineered. It's a lightning strike. Those who try to replicate the conditions will fail. You have to do something different—connected but new. And you have to push the envelope. That's how we approached *Avatar 2*.

Jim said from the beginning that he would make a sequel or sequels if the first Avatar was a success. His original notes for *Avatar* were over a thousand pages. He had created not just the characters and story, but the world of Pandora, its history, customs, and culture. Jim imagined sequels that would not just expand the original story but bring viewers into new parts of the world, which he'd sketched in great detail.

First, we needed scripts. Jim had two films in mind for the sequels, but by 2013, when Fox gave the go-ahead for the sequels, Jim had already written 1,500 pages of notes for the sequels. We quickly realized there were more than two films in those notes, and the best way forward was to work on several films at once. That way, we could make sure the plots did not conflict, but rather overlapped, wove together, and reinforced one another. We could hopefully also give the studio more bang for its buck by doing them simultaneously. The cost savings would be significant.

It would be an epic undertaking at every point in the process. We decided the best way forward was to set up an Avatar writers' room to break down all the notes into what was at the time three stand-alone films. It's how they do it on a television series, where a single season might consist of eight, ten, or even twenty-two episodes. The writers plot out all those episodes at the same time, breaking the arc of a series into scenes and beats that add up to a whole. That way, you can plant a notion in episode one that doesn't pay off until the finale.

We met with dozens of veteran film and TV writers before narrowing in on Rick Jaffa, Amanda Silver, Josh Friedman, and Shane Salerno. When the writers first came in, they were all bursting with new ideas for the story. We told them we didn't want their new ideas—cue the long faces—not yet, anyway. We wanted them to start by watching or rewatching the first Avatar. I put together a giant notebook of material that had been written about the movie: theories of why it worked, criticisms, critiques. Only if we tried to understand why the first Avatar had worked, we explained, could we hope to succeed with the sequels. Luckily, the answers the writers came up with were all there in Jim's notes: a sense of belonging, a sense of community, a sense of overcoming, a sense of duty, a sense of love. All of those things were there, and they would be amplified by the fact that Jake and Neytiri would now have children, a family of their own.

The writers thought they would spend six or seven weeks together in the room. They ended up working for almost six months. Once we had the overall road map, the writers would be assigned to a specific sequel. But we had much work to do before that would happen. We hired a person to keep track of what we called the Pandorapedia, a catalog of all the facts and details we wanted to keep consistent in every film, as well as all our ancillary opportunities within the greater franchise. It became a sort of Pandora canon. Meanwhile, the art department was working on images as a complement to the work coming out of the writers' room. Those teams worked closely together—it was important that narrative and visual concepts be developed together.

During the early work on the scripts, we purposely did not tell the writers collaborating in the room which sequel they would be working on. We didn't want them to spend more time on or save better ideas for their own installment. In the end, we assigned each writer or writing team to the script that seemed to resonate with their experience. We picked Rick and Amanda for the first sequel. We assigned *Avatar 3* to Shane Salerno and *Avatar 4* to Josh Friedman. Jim, of course, would be a writer on all of them. When Jim realized that *Avatar 2* was turning out to be much longer than we'd expected, he broke it into two scripts— that's how we ended up with four sequels.

As we would be filming the second and third installments— *The Way of Water* and *Fire and Ash*—at the same time, there were many new additions to the cast. The story of the sequels grew from the original *Avatar*, and family would become the overarching theme. This led to our first big challenge, the casting of Jake and Neytiri's kids. The events of the second and third films occur over a period of just a few months. It is not until the fourth film that there is a large time jump. We were casting children and teenagers, so we needed to film all their footage while they were the age their characters are meant to be. That was another factor in deciding to shoot the second and third installments simultaneously. We even shot the beginning section of the fourth Avatar film at the same time.

Margery Simkin, our casting director, did a worldwide search for young actors. Thousands of self-taped auditions were sent in. Margie and her team then narrowed those down to a group who came to Manhattan Beach Studios to try out in person. Jim sets a warm environment in his auditions. He operates the camera himself and encourages creative choices, giving actors notes and multiple chances. Jim might bark at top-level crew on set, but he is a puppy dog with actors. He understands them and their vulnerabilities. I knew he'd treat the kids with an extra layer of kindness.

We cast Britain Dalton as Lo'ak, Jake and Neytiri's rebellious son. Britain has a mischievous nature and could portray heartbreak in his eyes—that made him perfect for the role. Jamie Flatters was our Neteyam, the elder, more responsible son. He took on that role with the rest of the kids on set as well. Trinity Jo-Li Bliss was cast as the youngest, the daughter, Tuk, who just wants to be included in all the fun. Trinity was a wonder at eight years old. There's no telling if she'll end up a concert pianist, astrophysicist, or an Academy Award–winning actress. Maybe all three. Bailey Bass, with eyes wide enough to see her soul, was perfect for Tsireya, the daughter of Ronal and Tonowari, who would teach the Sullys how to navigate the way of water. Filip Geljo was cast as her brother, Aonung, and Duane Evans Jr. was cast as their friend, Rotxo.

The hardest part to cast was that of Spider, a human child left orphaned by the war who is raised around the Sully family. Our plan was to do performance capture at Manhattan Beach Studios in 2017 and 2018 before going to New Zealand and filming the live-action portion in 2019. The kid we cast as Spider would need to be there for all of it—with us across the span of three years and two continents. When we found Jack Champion, our Spider, he was a scrawny twelve-year-old climbing trees in West Virginia. His acting ability, charisma, and vulnerability were all there. During the first two years, we shot Jack with the other actors during the performance capture of their scenes. It was in the third year that we would then shoot his human character—live-action shots that would be integrated with the performance capture scenes at Wētā. It was critical that by the time we got to shooting those scenes in 2019, he could become the buff teenage Tarzan we needed him to be. Jack was an amazing kid, and was exactly the kid we needed throughout every step.

Of course, for our adult cast, Sam Worthington and Zoe Saldaña, the heart and soul of the franchise, were back. Two of our other leads in the first film, Sigourney Weaver and Stephen Lang, had portrayed characters who had died in that film. But there are no limitations within science fiction and fantasy, and Jim had ingenious ideas for the return of both actors. Stephen's Quaritch would come back, in a recombinant body that looks very much like the Na'vi, with one mission: revenge against Jake Sully.

Sigourney's stretch would be even greater—in a new role, she would be Jake and Neytiri's adopted fifteen-year-old daughter, Kiri. Sigourney relished the opportunity to transport herself back in time and embody her awkward teenage self.

With *Avatar: Fire and Ash*, we'd be introducing a new villain, and we knew we'd found her in Oona Chaplin, who I suspect will blow audiences away as Varang, leader of the Mangkwan, the Ash People. Whereas the first two movies mostly focus on the human threat from the RDA, Varang will be an even greater threat and prove that not all Na'vi are good. A good villain cannot be a caricature, and they can never think they are the villain. They have to be the hero of their own story. And Varang, who feels her people were abandoned by Eywa, is on what she considers to be a righteous path. That makes her even more dangerous. Far bigger celebrities auditioned for the part, but Oona was the one who knocked Jim's socks off. Oona is the granddaughter of Charlie Chaplin on one side of her family and Eugene O'Neill on another. But her roots, on her grandmother's side, are of the Mapuche, the Indigenous people of Chile and Argentina. She was able to really bring her ancestral heritage into the role. Oona, who is involved with Indigenous rights, brought a Brazilian shaman in to bless our set and the entire crew.

There are other clans and peoples who enter our story as it unfolds, and getting each role right was critical. There is the sea clan, the Metkayina. Cliff Curtis was cast as Tonowari, the imposing olo'eyktan, chief of the Metkayina clan. The Metkayina are Na'vi, but there is no denying that Jim was influenced by many Polynesian Indigenous cultures in their conception. None more so than the Maori, the original inhabitants of Aotearoa (New Zealand). When we cast Cliff, who is of Maori descent, Jim gave him free rein to bring as much of his culture as possible to the role. Cliff added a regal authenticity to the character. When it came to casting his wife, Ronal, we needed an actress who could be strong and bold, yet subtle in her performance. Ronal is really the one in charge, and she is the tsahík—spiritual leader—of the Metkayina. There was one actress who rose to the top of the list for each of us—Kate Winslet.

Jim reached out to Kate to see whether she would consider playing the part. I was not sure how she would react. She hadn't always said the most glowing things about her experience on *Titanic*. We sent her the script to read, and she fell in love with it. Jim had written Ronal as a heroic role. She is fierce, brave, inspiring—a warrior, a mother, and a leader. And she goes into battle pregnant without as much as a second thought. I can't help but think Kate ate that up. The next thing you knew, we had our Ronal. And we were reunited with Kate, who had been an important part of our life and history. The first day Kate was on set, Jim brought her into his cutting room to show her what we'd been working on. She looked at us and said, "Do you know that you've been a part of my life now for more than half my life?" It was a great reunion.

As Kate does with every part she plays, she threw herself into the deep end. We hear Ronal speak in English with a Na'vi accent, so Kate worked with her long-time dialect coach, Susan Hegarty, and our own Avatar dialect coach, Carla Meyer, to perfect the pronunciation. I think even the returning cast was shocked at how she was able to drop right into it. She also, no pun intended, jumped right into the water with Kirk Krack, our free-dive expert, and John Garvin, our dive master, to train for the part. (Fun fact: Kate smoked the rest of the cast in her free-dive training, even besting Jim, to get a seven-minute-and-fifteen-second breath hold.)

Which brings us to our other big challenge on the sequels. We needed to do performance capture, but this time, underwater. No one had ever done that before. They say necessity is the mother of invention, and we knew what we needed to tell the story, so we invented the tech. A small group headed by our virtual production supervisor, Ryan Champney, did the first successful underwater capture test in the backyard pool of my house in Sherman Oaks, the same one where we had filmed the Heart of the Ocean swirling to the bottom of the sea.

We had thought about taking the easy road. We had done a dry-for-wet test, where our returning stunt coordinator, Garrett Warren, hung performers from wires and gimbals on our capture stage while they pretended to swim. The physicality just felt off. To repeat the success of the first film, we knew we had to do everything as authentically as possible. If a scene required a character to hold their breath and swim, then that's what they'd have to do.

So, we ended up building three massive tanks at our Manhattan Beach Studios, the largest holding nine hundred thousand gallons of water. They had wave machines and current generators to mimic the conditions out at sea.

We decided to do another sense-memory trip to Hawai'i for the new and returning cast—this go-round, adding time in the waters of the Pacific, including night dives with manta rays. Even more informative was our trip to the Bahamas. Jim was introducing a plethora of new aquatic creatures in these films: the dolphin-like ilu, the more aggressive skimwing. We needed to figure out how the characters would ride them. That trip inspired how the characters would tame marine life in the films.

For *Way of Water*, Jim realized that the Metkayina clan would need to communicate underwater. So just as Paul Frommer had created a distinct Na'vi language in *Avatar*, we brought in the extraordinarily talented Deaf actor CJ Jones to create a distinct and unique Na'vi Sign Language (NSL). There are something like three hundred different sign languages in the world right now, but CJ created a new one that was tailored specifically to the Na'vi culture and the Metkayina's connection to the water. At the US premiere of *The Way of Water* in Los Angeles, I loved seeing my niece Twyla, who has studied American Sign Language for years and was a teaching assistant for ASL courses in college, signing with CJ about his work on the movie. It was a meaningful moment for me, watching them connect like that—my work family and my own family coming together.

But well before, with performance capture underway at Manhattan Beach Studios, we were often filming a scene from *Fire and Ash* in the morning and a scene from *Way of Water* in the afternoon. We would sometimes be shooting the two simultaneously. On the first Avatar, we had only one area for performance capture. For the sequels, in addition to the stages that held our three tanks, we had two interconnected stages for dry capture. A few times we would open the elephant door between the two stages and make them one massive area for a large set or for horses to get up to gallop speed. Yes, real horses. Even though their movement would only ever be seen through CGI, authenticity in every moment of the film was essential.

The very nature of the movie business is transient. You typically work on something for a few weeks or months and then, if you are lucky, move on to another production. I have been that lucky, but it is not an easy business, with a tremendous amount of uncertainty built in. There is an old joke in Hollywood—in our business, you don't get depressed between jobs, you get jobs between depressions.

One of the things that I am most proud of is the consistency of work the Avatar films afforded our teams—it is deeply meaningful to see the number of people who have been with us, and who have grown in their responsibilities and roles, from the first Avatar all the way to today. I am equally proud of the way we were able to bring people into the Avatar family from other projects. And not just Kate—I brought Deborah Scott to Jim's attention for costume designer on *Titanic* after first meeting her on *Hoffa* when I was at Fox; she's a permanent fixture of the Avatar family. Josh McLaglen, our first assistant director on *Titanic* and *Avatar*, was brought on because I had been impressed with him on the set of *Alien 3*. Maria Battle-Campbell, who had served as Josh's second AD on *Avatar*, moved to first AD on

The Way of Water and is now a coproducer on the sequels. Simon Franglen, an arranger and music producer for James Horner, stepped up to the role of composer after proving he was the right person for the job with his work on the Disney theme park. Dylan Cole and Ben Procter, both in the art department on the first Avatar, are now our lead production designers. Stunt coordinator Garrett Warren has become our live-action second unit director. Russell Carpenter, director of photography on *True Lies* and *Titanic*, came back to join us for the Avatar sequels. Richie Baneham, Brigitte Yorke, Steve Rivkin, Eric Saindon—the list goes on and on.

There are moments when I am struck by just how big, how beautiful, how close our Avatar family has grown. Through the ups and downs of production and the challenges of doing something unprecedented, yes. But more importantly, by being there for one another day in and day out as a whole lot of life happened along the way.

FOR ALL THE obvious reasons, the Avatar set is closed during production. People working on the project are not even supposed to talk about it. This has been the case from the get-go. When we began to develop the first film, and well into the project, we didn't even refer to it by its title—it was *Project 880*. You know Jim and his code names. To keep things under wraps, our teams are sequestered like a jury, except that they go home each night. But the expectation and responsibility of that kind of secrecy can induce its own kind of stress.

As with every production, it is important to me to put together fun events for the cast and crew. One of my favorites was Family Day. We opened our Manhattan Beach Studio to the families of our cast and crew. We hosted several hundred people and ran tours—some started in the screening room, some in the museum, some on the stages. You could feel their excitement as our teams shared their work with spouses, children, and parents. It was a great morale booster for all. Later in the production, a group of crew members formed a band called the Skxawngs. That word is the Na'vi catchall insult, roughly translating to "moron." They'd play right there on set on Friday nights at wrap, just as if it were a real gig. We brought in drinks and food, and people danced the night away.

MUCH OF OUR live-action shoot in New Zealand focused on Jack Champion playing Spider. He was a human character living in a Na'vi world, and as such, we needed to make advancements to the technology we'd developed on the first Avatar. With these new—and great—advancements, we were able to seamlessly integrate our virtual production process with that of a traditional live-action film shoot. Our Simulcam system on the sequels allowed Jim to look through the lens of a 3D camera and not only see Jack, but see the Na'vi characters and CG backgrounds Spider was interacting with. Jim could move the camera around them as if they were really there.

Being the quintessential prankster, on Halloween I went full Spider. I had our makeup department tan me up and paint blue stripes on me. I was fitted for a wig of faux locs. The costume department made me a loincloth. And when we were set up for our first take of the day, I came running out on the stage right over to Jack as we were rolling. We looked identical. Okay, maybe there was a difference of a few pounds and a couple of decades. Jack, Jim, and most of the crew had no idea I was going to do this, and the belly laughs spiked to the red on our sound recording equipment.

Sometimes, it is laughter that is needed. Other times, it is a friendly ear or a shoulder to cry on. There's a couch in my office, and I often think of it as a therapist's couch, for both the cast and crew—and sometimes for Jim—to come download or off-load. Lots of conversations were held on that sofa. Lots of emotions expressed. Better there than on the set or at home. My door is always open for whomever needs an outlet.

Disney acquired Fox in the middle of our shoot. While we had worked with the Disney theme park teams, the film studio was a whole new set of people, with an entirely different set of circumstances. We suddenly had new bosses and new executives overseeing our finances. There was a learning curve for all of us, but Disney has become an incredible partner.

Our deal with Fox, which transferred with the sale to Disney, ensured that we control the franchise. When the merger first happened, Alan Bergman, cochairman of Disney Entertainment, said, "Well, what does that mean?"

"We decide who we want to be in partnership with," I said.

"Jon, you're telling me that we could have a sixty-five-million-dollar promotion deal with a car company, and you can turn it down for a one-million-dollar deal elsewhere just because you think it's a better fit?"

That's exactly right. We might not want to be in business with some gas-guzzling truck company when there's an electric car over there that will be more in line with the ethos of our universe.

It was during postproduction that I added to my busy schedule by doing my own visual effects reviews with Wētā. I looked at every shot in the movie and gave notes before Jim ever laid eyes on them. Jim and I had worked together closely for more than two decades at that point, so I could foresee the comments he would have. As I've said, Jim trusted me to do this after he recognized the more active and pivotal role I had played on the visual effects portions of *Alita*. In the beginning of the *Way of Water* reviews, I was a bit cautious, but I quickly gained confidence—I had been in enough of these reviews with Jim to start fully trusting my gut. "The corner of her mouth comes to too sharp of a point.... There's not enough deformation on the skin where he's being grabbed.... The reds are too saturated.... Add more atmosphere.... Show me the template, make it look like that." Between my reviews and those that Richie Baneham did, a new acronym was created, FLF. That stands for First Look Final. If Jim would see a render for the first time and have zero notes, in the movie it went—FLF.

As we were heading toward the finish line on *Way of Water*, there was one small, but significant, change I posed to Jim. In one of the final scenes of the film, Jake has just been saved by his son, Lo'ak. In it, Jake said, "You did good, boy." That didn't play well for me. Where did that take us? What significance was there in that line to where we were in our story, in the relationship between father and son?

Right before Jim was about to do a late-in-the-game pickup— a small additional shoot filmed after principal photography has wrapped—with Sam Worthington, I went to Jim and suggested changing the line to "I see you." It is the most meaningful and resonant phrase in *Avatar* and could be the perfect emotional denouement as Jake accepts his son as he is. Jim was quick to dismiss the idea. But then he said he might try it with Sam. He did, but, of course, made it clear that "it only worked because of how Sam performed it." We both smiled. But boy, did it work. That's what's in the movie now, and every time I see that, I take pride in knowing that's one of the little nuggets that I contributed. I hope that many other people on our team see all the nuggets that they contributed throughout the movie.

As had become tradition, we held our world premiere for *Avatar: The Way of Water* in London on December 6, 2022. A blowout screening followed in Paris. If we just did a Los Angeles premiere, we'd be making a statement that this is an American film. Premiering in Europe makes a statement that this is a film for the world. We continued that world tour with premieres in Seoul, South Korea, and Tokyo, Japan, before returning to Los Angeles for the American premiere, an old-fashioned Hollywood event at the Dolby Theatre, where they hold the Academy Awards. By the time of the LA premiere, Jim had come down with covid and was not able to participate in any of the LA events, not even the crew screening. It was, of course, not the same without him, but he was celebrated at every event.

Managing expectations for the studio was possibly my toughest task with *Way of Water*. Everyone, especially the studio, assumed we would at least approach the numbers of the first Avatar, which, being the top-grossing movie of all time, set the bar dangerously high. "Don't expect us to be *Endgame*"—that's what I said at the last meeting with Disney before we went wide. (*Avengers: Endgame*, released in 2019, is, to date, the second-highest-grossing movie ever made. It made $1.2 billion of its nearly $2.8 billion total box office within its first five days in release.) "We're not going to open that way. You're going to have to think about this movie in a more strategic manner."

I think it took the Disney execs a little while to understand what I meant. Our pictures might open strong, but more importantly, they build. They have staying power. See how many people come back to see it a second, third, or fourth time. Keep the meter running.

After the London premiere, Alan asked me, "Are you happy now?"

"Let's wait until *January* 16," I told him. "Then I'll decide if I'm happy."

The big unknown heading into the premiere was covid. People had mostly stopped going out to the movies in 2022, and the industry was suffering. The moviegoing habit had been broken. But *Way of Water*, with its size and scope—best seen in 3D—had to succeed at the Cineplex. Things were beginning to loosen up in the US, so I was less worried about the domestic market than the overseas market. I believed that people would go out to see the right movie, but did we have the right movie? Did we deliver the film we'd promised? Was it a movie that could take viewers out of their everyday lives, away from the pandemic, and give them three-plus hours of escape?

Avatar: The Way of Water grossed $2.3 billion. It is, as of this writing, the third-highest-grossing movie of all time, a spot ahead of *Titanic*, two behind *Avatar*. But the box-office receipts that were the most meaningful came from the most unlikely of places.

I got an email from a sub-distributor in Ukraine that moved me deeply. With his country at war with Russia, he was in the middle of hell in Kyiv but still said *Avatar: The Way of Water* was going to be the number one movie of all time in his country. Whenever there is a moment of quiet, he said, when the air raid sirens stop blaring and the bombs stop falling, Ukrainians run out to see it, because it's about a native population that's been invaded by a larger force with more powerful weapons, and they fight back and win.

Chapter 12

My mother Edie died on December 24, 2022, eight days after *Way of Water* was released in the US. She was ninety-five years old and had outlived my father by almost thirty years. In those intervening years, Edie had found love again. It was with a wonderful man and actor, Martin E. Brooks. I could give you his impressive résumé, but that is not what was most amazing about Marty. It was his kindness and the utter love he felt for Edie. No one could have predicted that Edie would fall in love at seventy. It was a gift to all of us.

I've written much about Ely's accomplishments, but Edie was just as extraordinary—in some ways, more so, as a woman of that generation had to work twice as hard to get half as far, clichéd as that sounds. Her career was groundbreaking. She broke through the glass ceiling and led the way for a generation of women, and not just women who wanted to produce serious pictures focused on social issues. She was a lifelong learner—insatiably curious and deeply committed to the pursuit of knowledge. In her fifties, she went to law school. She passed the bar but never with the intention of practicing—she simply felt that she had been negotiating contracts her entire career and was interested in taking a deeper dive into the legal system. Edie was a corporate executive, a movie producer, a lawyer. And all the while she raised three children and almost never missed a sporting event, dance recital, or school play.

She accomplished much in her life, but whenever she and Ely were asked which of their productions they were most proud of, their answer was always the same: "Our children." Later, that extended to their grandchildren. She relished every moment with her grandkids, as she did with life in general. It was a long, fulfilling, and joyful life—a life not handed to her, but one she built, and then rebuilt when tragedy struck with Ely's stroke. She left nothing on the table, and nothing unsaid. Take that as you will. She was strong, and opinionated, and passionate in her beliefs, her strongest belief being the supreme importance of family. More than anything else, that belief is what she passed on to her three children, and to our children, too.

As she had lived, Edie wanted to go out her own way—in her own home, surrounded by her own things. And that's where she was when she passed away. I think she somehow knew Kathy, Tina, and I were together at Kathy's house in the Berkshires that night.

Edie wrote me a letter when I turned fifty-eight. I read it whenever I need to remember who I am and where I come from, whenever I need to be buoyed up or be reminded that I got the luckiest break of all: I had parents who loved me. I quote it here in full, and without comment, because it says everything.

Jon—

For you, it's your birthday. For me, it's a reminder of your Birth Day. I know that I told you about your birth before, so I won't bore you by repeating it.

I won't tell you that when the doctor came to see me in my hospital room, how I said to him, "When the baby was here with me earlier . . ." and he, in shock, blurted out, "They brought the baby in here?????" as he turned and literally ran out of the room. Whereupon my heart began to pound in my chest as I phoned Ely and cried, "Something's wrong with the baby!!!!!"

But you know all of that, so I won't tell you that Ely and I went home without you, and every day for a month, we came back to the hospital to stand in the hall, peering into the nursery to see you in your cradle as we whispered words of love and encouragement to you. "You can beat this (whatever this is), just keep fighting, you're strong, you can do it, you can conquer it, you can make it." We willed your strength into your body (Ely even went out and bought a pair of gold boxing gloves from Tiffany's), but you were there, so you know it all, so I won't bore you with the details.

I can only say that peering through the window, I could never have dreamed that fifty-eight years later, that little struggling infant would turn out to be the strongest, most loving son, husband and father that God bestowed on any family.

Thank you for being you and allowing us to be a part of your life.

P.S. Happy Birthday!

In January 2023, it was straight back to work on *Avatar: Fire and Ash*. I broke from production only for the most important events, one being the 95th Academy Awards. That fateful night in March when I felt the lump in my throat.

The best thing to happen that night was in the In Memoriam section, in which the Hollywood community pays tribute to its members who have died over the previous year. My father had not been included the year he died. He produced all those great movies, all that important work for social justice, was even nominated for an Oscar, and yet, for whatever reason, he was overlooked. But Edie was there, alongside the other titans who'd passed in 2022—Angela Lansbury, Olivia Newton-John, Bob Rafelson, Jean-Luc Godard. To see Edie on that screen on the same night I was nominated for Best Picture was amazing. I was thrilled. I don't think words can begin to cover it.

One month to the day after the Oscars, I started my first course of radiation and chemotherapy. And thus began my new life—rounds of treatments, hospital stays, advances, setbacks, and surgeries that continue to this day.

I decided to have treatment at Cedars-Sinai in LA, where Ron Sue is affiliated and where we feel very good about the oncology team. It was also important that Julie and I would be near our friends and colleagues in California. I have been incredibly lucky with my friends, among whom I include Ron. He's been a rock star throughout my battle. Day or night, I'd call him. He doesn't text back, he calls back. Every night in the hospital, he would call or visit just to see how I was doing. Remarkable, honest, genuine concern. Sometimes he would use a guiding hand to push the other doctors in a different direction. He let me know I was never alone.

LA has been my home for almost five decades—with Bali Hai and Wellington as wonderful additions to our life. LA is where I want to be to fight this fight, where Julie is surrounded by people who will be there for her. Where I can go to the office and lose myself in work as much as possible. And, it is where I want to be when there are no more battles to fight—now or decades from now.

Julie and I rented an apartment on a high floor with views of downtown, the Hollywood sign, and even a glimpse of the ocean from our bedroom. I did not tell many people about my illness at first. We were reeling. And, I plan to keep working, to take *Fire and Ash* as far as I can, and I do not want pity or people making special allowances. I did tell my family. And I told Jim. I didn't tell Disney until June. I had gone through chemo and radiation by then. I wanted to see how that went before I did anything else. I made a video and sent it to people on the Avatar crew. I said, "Hey, I want to let you know what I've been going through."

The first surgery, which removed my esophagus, was followed by a second the next day. My sisters and their families all flew out to be with Julie, Jamie, Jodie, and me. The doctors removed 115 lymph nodes, which I was told is a record. Not the way in which I'd want to be exceptional. I was in the hospital for eleven days, nine of those in intensive care, but I actually felt pretty good when I came out. I was home just in time for my birthday, but I was very limited in what I could eat at that point, so the family threw me an ice-cream party. Pints and pints of every flavor I was allowed covered the table. I ate little, but we laughed a lot. It was good to be home and in this company. After the weekend, I went into the office to see people.

But the good feeling did not last. I got weaker and weaker, and more and more tired, and the doctors kept saying, "It's natural. You've had two major surgeries." But I knew something else was wrong. Ron had me go back in for tests, and it turns out that I had an internal leak. Six liters of liquid had built up around my lungs. It was depriving me of oxygen. I went for another operation. They took out three giant vials of liquid that could've been mango shakes from Jamba Juice. They never did find the source of the leak, but I was on the table for seven hours. They were doing everything they could to find and fix the source of the problem. But to no avail.

I was hooked up to machines in the hospital for the next twenty-nine days. Every time a doctor or a nurse would come in, I would remind them that I had to be well enough to get on a plane to New York on September 7, because I was going to my niece Emma's wedding, no matter what. It became a running joke—the nurses and doctors all began to enter my room saying "I know, you are getting on a plane on September 7."

I was released from the hospital on September 5, went straight to the tailor to have my suit adjusted, and was on that plane on September 7. Family is everything, and mine is my North Star. Being at that wedding—celebrating, singing, laughing—with the people I love most in the world was the best medicine.

When I came out of the hospital that second time, I couldn't lift my right foot. I could walk, but the foot drooped. And I was in a considerable amount of back pain. I went for an MRI. They discovered a tumor on the bottom of my spine, attached to the tailbone, where the nerves are. That meant more surgery. In doing that, they discovered that several discs in my back had fractured and slipped out of position. So: another surgery. That was supposed to be five hours but turned into ten, followed by five more hours of emergency surgery the next night.

This time, I got out of the hospital with very little back pain, but my drop foot had turned into a drop leg. I could go on like this indefinitely. More operations, more tumors, more radiation, more chemotherapy, and more vague hopes. But I held on to every iota of hope.

Not long after I was diagnosed, I started recording interviews about my life. Telling these stories, it became all the clearer that, though I was having a bit of bad luck, my life had been wonderful. There was so much I might miss out on, but there was so much I had gotten to experience. I was focused on fighting the disease, but I was also being realistic. I knew the odds, but I had beaten them before, and I was still counting on those golden boxing gloves.

I talked to my sister Kathy the night before one of the surgeries.

"Should I come out?" she asked.

I said no. The next day, I'm in bed in the hospital, waking up from the operation, and who walks in but Kathy. "What are you doing here?"

"I know, you told me not to come," she said, "but then I realized that I'm a grown-up, and I don't have to listen to you."

I can't tell you how much that meant to me, and to Julie. That night, Julie and Kathy went to dinner. The next morning, Kathy came to our apartment and had breakfast with Julie. They went to see *Barbie* in the afternoon. Kathy would come work from my hospital room every day, so Julie could have some time for herself.

Kathy gave me some very helpful advice. When I was struggling in rehab with my leg and was feeling very down, she said, "Don't dwell on what you can't do today—remember what you could not do yesterday." And she was right. I could now move my leg, which I couldn't do two days before. I think that's something everyone should keep in mind. Don't focus on the negative. Look at the progress you've already achieved, even if it is infinitesimal.

I was determined to keep working, though my cancer did cause me to question why. What does it mean, why does it matter, how many hours should be spent? Time is limited for all of us, even the healthy and the young. I feel that limitation acutely now—every minute of every day. But . . .

I love what I do. I love the people I get to do it with. We push the boundaries of what is possible. We have developed new technologies, new worlds, new ways of making movies. Movies that provide people with an escape from the everyday stresses and pressures of life. Ones that might inspire the next generation of filmmakers to push the boundaries even further. And all along the way, I get to do it with Julie, Jamie, and Jodie. What a life.

My sisters call every night. *How'd it go today?* Tina, it doesn't matter if she's in rehearsals—she calls. Kathy calls. *How was it today, Jon?* Sometimes I give the honest answer. Sometimes I don't. At one point while I was in the hospital, my brother Les happened to have back surgery at the same hospital, so we took turns visiting each other. Funny in a way, but certainly not fun.

Being sick, in and out of a hospital, leaves you with a lot of time to think and question: What did I do right? What would I have done differently? What mattered and what falls away? What can still be learned from our children? Not only my own children; in the end, we are all one family.

My advice for young filmmakers is go and do. You have the tools to make content, which doesn't have to be movies. There are now so many visual mediums available to a creative person. Use them all. Teach yourself by doing. Learn from others along the way. Go make your art, but remember, you're making it for an audience. Let people see it. Accept their criticism for what it is. A gift. Take and grow from feedback. Don't be arrogant. Don't be narrow-minded, and don't make work for a small niche only. The work we do is meant to be seen. Share what's in your heart in a way people can understand it.

And know this: You don't need to know the answers, just the questions. If you have a choice between answering or asking, ask. And remember you are not alone. It takes a team to realize a vision. And even then, the work may at first seem impossible. But when you start working together, with people you trust and respect, the impossible turns into the probable.

Most importantly, do not become fixated purely on the destination. Take time to enjoy the journey. What happens along the journey might cause you to change your destination. Regrets will not move you forward. Determination will. And moving forward is what matters. Don't lose yourself in your dreams. Find yourself through them. Keep your eyes keenly focused on the future and your feet firmly planted in the present. You know the old saying: When is the best time to plant a tree? Twenty years ago. When is the second-best time to plant it? Today.

If I had the chance to write my own legacy, I hope it would be that I always gave 110 percent. Not only to my family, but to my friends and my work. Although not perfect, I hope people can say that I tried to do right by everybody. What more is there?

Just before *Titanic* hit movie theaters back in 1997—in those stressful and uncertain days when the release could go either way, blockbuster or bust—I told my family that while I might not go down in Hollywood as one of the most successful producers, in the end, I'd like to be remembered as one of the nicest. That is still my hope.

JON LANDAU died July 5, 2024, surrounded by his family. He was sixty-three years old.

AFTERWORD

Kathy Landau

J on was laid to rest at Hillside Memorial Park Cemetery in Los Angeles, where Edie and Ely were both interred, and where we had spread some of my son Sacha's ashes.

His funeral was beautiful—perhaps a strange thing to say about a funeral, but it was. Julie opened the service with a song Jon loved to hear her sing, "A Dream Is a Wish Your Heart Makes." She was brave and strong. Emma Rose and Twyla read one of Edie's favorite poems— one that we had read in that very chapel two years earlier at her funeral. Jamie spoke with humor and heart. Jodie played his harpejji with grace and beauty. Their profound appreciation for Jon—the man, father, husband, and role model—came through in every word and note. Tina spoke, conveying the essence of who Jon was and the loss we all felt. Rae Sanchini gave a eulogy that captured Jon as a friend and colleague, but always friend first. Jim Cameron paid tribute to Jon in a way no one else could.

In the final and darkest hours of my brother's life, Julie and I made him a promise—we would see this book through. The book was important to him. He wanted to share his story—his passions, his joys, his successes, and even his failures—in the hope that people might learn something from his journey, as he had from others'. With thanks to all involved, this book is a promise kept.

At Jon's funeral, I delivered the final eulogy:

With so much already written about Jon in the press and on social media, it made me think about the idea of the public versus private man. So often you hear of an image or persona cultivated for the press.

But, Jon was Jon through and through, and always. He was not enamored with fame, his or anyone else's. The tributes have called him kind, funny, generous, a visionary, tenacious, brilliant, creative, a force of nature, and so much more.

But it is worth noting that he was also grateful—filled with awe, wonder, and amazement at the life he and Julie built.

Jon won awards and accolades and honors. But winning Julie's heart was his greatest joy. He was filled with gratitude for Julie. For Jamie. For Jodie. For this family, which he felt so very lucky to have.

He never took a moment for granted. Even before his diagnosis. Gratitude is what he lived every day, and what he left us with.

And even over the past sixteen months—through which he fought courageously, and with humor, and unbelievable levels of hope and determination—as his body was ravaged and the cancer ate away at him. Surgery after surgery, treatment after treatment, he would emerge and tackle the next challenge with his signature aplomb.

And while the disease attacked so much of his body, it never succeeded in getting to his heart—literally or spiritually. His heart never weakened in these past sixteen months—and his heart was who he was. Jon was all heart—that's who he was as a brother, son, uncle, husband, father, colleague, and friend.

I've said this many times, but it bears repeating. Jon dreamed big. Lived big. Loved big. He loved strong and true and forever. He loved people. He loved dogs. He loved movies. Loved practical jokes. Loved Yodels, and Uncrustables, and Raisinets, and black-and-white cookies, and sushi, and omakase, and matzo brei, and loud shirts, and laughter. And most importantly and deeply, his family. And he loved giving. Giving joy. Giving opportunity. Giving hope. Giving 110 percent.

Jon and I were phone people—and we talked every day. About everything and nothing. So, it's not the big moments I will miss. Not the premieres or birthdays or trips, but the small ones—the everydayness of what we shared.

I've thought a lot about what Jon would want to say to each and every one of you. Without the fanfare or the practical jokes, but rather straight from the heart. His strong and amazing heart. And I realized that he'd want to say "thank you." So simple, but so important.

So, on his behalf, and on behalf of our entire family, thank you from the bottom of our hearts. For being here. For having been on the wild ride that was the life and loves of Jon Landau. You made the adventure all the better for him. And he made the world all the better for all of us.

We found out yesterday that Jon recorded a video message to be played at his memorial. None of us knew he had done it. He entrusted the drive to Geoff Burdick with very specific instructions not to allow the family to see it before the service. So, we will all be seeing the video for the first time together.

And in typical Jon fashion, he also noted to Geoff that "By the way, it will need to be color corrected." So very Jon.

JON'S FINAL MESSAGE TO US ALL

figured if I was putting myself on tape to tell the history of my life, I should also do something and be a part of my own memorial. So here I am.

I want to thank you for being here today. If you're here today, it's because you were a part of my life. And what made my life so special was the people that were part of it. No three people more than Julie, Jamie, and Jodie. I am thankful for every minute I got to spend with them. For every movie we went to, every vacation we went on, every dinner we had, and every Christmas, every holiday.

To the three of you, I am so proud of who you are. And I just want to take this opportunity, to everybody, to say thank you. I will miss the times I never got to experience with you, but I am so thankful for the times that I did get to experience. Go out, live your lives, celebrate the joy of life.

And Jamie, Jodie, and Julie, always be there for each other.

Thank you.